LILLIAN HELLMAN

Playwright

RICHARD MOODY

Pegasus *New York*

A DIVISION OF

The Bobbs-Merrill Company, Inc., Publishers

Lillian Hellman is part of a series, Pegasus American Authors, prepared under the General Editorship of Professor Richard M. Ludwig, Princeton University.

OTHER BOOKS IN THE SERIES

Allen Tate by Radliffe Squires
Clifford Odets by Gerald Weales
Marianne Moore by Donald Hall
Edwin Arlington Robinson by Louis Coxe
Wallace Stevens by Samuel French Morse
George W. Cable by Louis D. Rubin, Jr.
Willa Cather by James Woodress
Robert E. Sherwood by Walter J. Meserve

Printed in the United States of America
Library of Congress Catalogue number 76-175224

FIRST PRINTING

Designed by Tere LoPrete

For three long-time friends and colleagues

HUBERT C. HEFFNER

LEE NORVELLE

WESLEY SWANSON

RICHARD MOODY, Professor of Theatre and Drama and former director of the Theatre at Indiana University, is the author of four other books: *America Takes the Stage; Edwin Forrest, First Star of the American Stage; The Astor Place Riot;* and *Dramas from the American Theatre*, 1762–1909. The first two were chosen for the new White House Library in 1963. He was a student of George P. Baker at Yale, a Guggenheim Fellow, a National Theatre Conference Fellow, and in 1961 he received the Distinguished Alumni Award from Drake University. He has taught and directed plays at Cornell University (where he received his Ph.D.), at the University of Illinois, Northwestern University, and the University of Hawaii.

Contents

Illustrations

Introduction by
HAROLD CLURMAN

There are almost more personal facts about Lillian Hellman in Richard Moody's book than in her memoirs: *An Unfinished Woman.* She does not wish, she has said, to be the bookkeeper of her life. That is why, as Professor Moody points out, there is so little direct use of autobiographical material in her plays. She avows herself "a moral writer." A facet of her morality is evident in her desire to write "beyond" herself, about the world she has observed and thought about. She does not indulge in self-dramatization.

A writer's relation to his work is not a simple matter. The best thing which has been said on the subject was Henry James' dictum that a writer should never put himself into his writing but that he can't possibly keep himself out of it. Lillian Hellman's inner self is in her plays.

I directed what I believe to be her finest play, *The Autumn Garden.* Shortly before rehearsals began, Miss Hellman warned me that I should not take offense if at times she appeared unjust in any critical complaints she might make in the course of our work together. I had occasion to remember this afterwards not because she had been in the least unfair to me but because she could be "difficult," often in a way she herself did not fully understand but which after a while I did. More of this later.

Her warning to me was itself part of her essential sense of justice or *justness.* Her admonition was a kind of self-correction. She disapproved of anything in herself which might hurt another. In rereading some of her plays recently, I have arrived at an insight into her work which had never before struck me with such force: she is a rigorous moralist. This does not connote fanaticism because, to begin with, she is rigorous with herself.

Her excellent dialogue is astringent. In *Toys in the Attic* one of the characters says, "Everybody talks too much, too many words, and gets them out of order." Miss Hellman's avoidance of inflated rhetoric is not stylistic idiosyncracy; it is a form of moral control (almost a repression) which instructs her not to say more than what she thinks is true, precise, just. This characteristic leads to a notable scrupulousness in dramatic diction and meticulous logic of dramatic construction.

What Miss Hellman "represses" is excess of sentiment, a fault which leads to disaster through self-deception as well as to deception of others. The want of justness becomes injustice, hence something which verges on crime. She expresses this in another speech in *Toys in the Attic:* "The pure and innocent sometimes bring harm to themselves and those they love and, when they do, for some reason that I do not know, the injury is very great." One cannot help appreciating the modesty and balance suggested by the phrase, "for some reason that I do not know."

Miss Hellman's suspicion of sentimentality—she often exorcises it by humorous contempt—is at the root of such plays as *The Autumn Garden* and *Toys in the Attic*. In these somewhat acrid comedies (not without their pathos) the characters—by no means evil—fool themselves with dreams they will not fulfill or even attempt to fulfill. Their spiritual prevarication makes them waste their or other people's lives and sometimes both.

Self-delusion is of many kinds. Amorousness, often depicted as a superlative blessing, may become overwhelming and destructive; it often stems from an incapacity to deal with other realities as fateful as love itself. Love doesn't necessarily conquer all! Lily in *Toys in the Attic* spreads havoc through a fierce attachment to her husband. A comfortable, cosy life may have its own sentimentality and is not infrequently the source of social inanition and hence disaster. That is the case in *The Searching Wind.* Mushy sentiment prevents us from recognizing the nature of our own motives; it beclouds reason and is a betrayal of justness. *The Children's Hour,* the dramatization of a personal tragedy, adumbrates the larger calamity of all manner of witchhunting. Here sentimentality takes on the guise of righteous respectability which destroys everyone.

The composition of Miss Hellman's artistic traits lends a certain pristine hardness to her work. This might arouse a suspicion of coldness were it not for her no-nonsense humor and, more especially, for her only half-declared but unmistakable admiration for every kind of excellence: self-discipline, loyalty, the determination never to injure others, and, most important, the unselfish pursuit of humanly valid ideals.

One has only to read her letter to the House UnAmerican Activities Committee, quoted here, a letter which is a model of tempered force and utter probity, to discern how the qualities which I have noted as attributes of her dramaturgy have become integral with her total personality. Many of these same qualities are also evident in the final pages of *An Unfinished Woman.* They reveal her unremitting effort to be objective about herself. She is ever unsure that she knows the truth or even what the truth is. One thing is certain: she has an immense scorn of the phony in life or in art. She is hardheaded but never hardhearted.

Her "toughness" is a quest for the just. Most moralists are inclined to retreat from the consequences of their position. Miss Hellman knows that one must pay the price of one's convictions, which, as Professor Moody's book shows, she has not infrequently been obliged to do. The one positive hero in all her plays is Kurt Müller in *Watch on the Rhine,* who is forced to kill in order to continue his fight against the curse of Nazism. Kurt must also leave his beloved family to fulfill his mission, knowing that he may never be able to return from it. Miss Hellman is in entire accord with the holy injunction to love one's fellow men, but she also understands the severe realism of "an eye for an eye." That is the harshest justice and she is prepared to accept it.

I began this introduction with the hint of some "difficulty" in Miss Hellman's relation to the stage and to her stage colleagues which she herself now acknowledges. I recall a particular episode in the rehearsal period of *The Autumn Garden.* We had both agreed that a certain section of the script required cutting. We arranged to make our suggestions for cuts separately, then to compare them and, depending on her final judgment, to submit them to the cast. Miss Hellman was uncharacteristically late at the rehearsal when the actors were due to make the cuts in their parts. To save time I decided to go ahead and effect the cuts, which I emphasized were the author's. When she arrived and the actors were marking down the cuts, I explained that the cast had several times been told that the cuts were entirely *hers.* She nevertheless felt injured, almost insulted, by what she considered a breach of proper behavior. The play's words belonged to *her* and only she had the right to deal with them. I had preempted her auctorial prerogative.

Miss Hellman has few peers in our country in the mastery of her craft. But her spirit is alien to the theatre. She cannot abide the truth of what Pirandello once set down in a paradoxical apothegm: "In the theatre the work of the author does not exist any longer." The theatre is nothing if it is not the art of collaboration and Miss Hellman has no talent for collaboration. She is a strong individual and a staunch individualist. She is first and foremost a writer, and it has always been a kind of martyrdom to her that after the arduous task of completing a script it must be taken over by those "intrusive strangers"—the actors, the director, the scene designer, and others. One has only to hear her pronounce the words "a good writer" as if she were savoring a choice dish to sense her almost physical appreciation for the art of writing.

Reading Richard Moody's book with its keen devotion to every word and variant in text and thought makes me see her more clearly than ever before as, above all, an admirable citizen in the realm of American letters and, what is perhaps even more rare, a clean and upright person.

I

Discovering the Twenties

Lillian Hellman's love-hate affair with the theatre has endured for more than thirty years, from *The Children's Hour* in 1934 to *My Mother, My Father and Me* in 1963 and the all-star revival of *The Little Foxes* at Lincoln Center in 1967. Most of her dozen plays were hits, or near hits. Only two, *Days to Come* and *My Mother, My Father and Me*, were out-and-out failures. Only these two and *Montserrat* were not included with the ten "Best Plays" of their seasons. Among her contemporaries only Tennessee Williams and Arthur Miller have matched her record; they alone belong in her league.

Her affair has gone smoothly and well. Herman Shumlin and then Kermit Bloomgarden managed her productions, giving them the best actors and designers, lavish scenery and costumes, expert promotion, the best that taste, skill, and money could buy. Her plays may not have required the gilt edging; but they deserved it and profited by it, enlivening the box office with the "long green" that brightens Broadway.

Miss Hellman was rewarded with a fashionable town house on Manhattan's Upper East Side, from which she has just recently moved, a retreat on Martha's Vineyard, and, for several years, a 130-acre farm at Pleasantville, New York. She has delighted in these fruits of her labors, even in the smaller signs of affluence which surround her: an early American highboy, an Empire love seat, Sheraton chairs, a Sheraton bird cage, memory pieces from *The Children's Hour*, *Watch on the Rhine*, *The Searching Wind*, and *The Autumn Garden.* Her paintings would be welcomed in a museum: Rouault, Shahn, Picasso, Toulouse-Lautrec, the latter a gift from Dorothy Parker. She has been able to support her passion for easy living, good food, and extravagant party clothes, though even with the means to support her whims for fancy dresses, she never shook off the hangover from her middle-class background. Anyone visiting the Pleasantville farm in the late forties might have found her in the garden wearing last year's Balenciaga. She could not abandon a gown that had been worn only once or twice.

But if she valued the power of the dollar, she was not a money grubber, a selfish devotee of affluence. When friends needed financial help, their need came before her own. She simply liked to surround herself with those things that money could buy, feel free to move about the world without first balancing the cost against her bank balance, free to share her good fortune with friends, and, above all, free from being obliged to think poor. Because her first strike at the theatre produced a substantial reward and a confidence that withstood the failure of her second effort, she assumed early in her life the luxury of living as she wished, of saying and doing what she pleased. And luckily theatre critics and audiences agreed that what she pleased to write pleased them.

Miss Hellman first sought her own livelihood in the final spirited years of the twenties and during the gloomiest years of the Depression—first as an editorial assistant with Horace Liveright's publishing firm, then as press agent for an arty theatre group, play reader for Anne Nichols, drum beater for a stock company in Rochester, and finally, before she turned playwright, as a script reader for Metro-Goldwyn-Mayer in Hollywood. No irresistible force drew her to the theatre. She was not stage-struck; she had no early visions of her name in lights. She had married Arthur Kober in 1925. He was connected with the theatre and motion pictures, as press agent and script writer. It was easier to find work where his name was known.

In the fall of 1924, when she had passed her nineteenth birthday, finished her junior year at New York University, and resolved to terminate her college career, she was invited to a literary party. The why-and-how circumstances she does not now recall; perhaps the invitation came from one of her friends at Chumley's in the Village, her college hangout. Literary parties were then gay mixtures of the knowns and the unknowns. The knowns thrived on the adulation of the unknowns. Flirtations with attractive young people unencumbered with reputations restored the hungry egos of writers and editors who constantly feared that they were loved only for their literary accomplishments.

On this evening Lillian Hellman met Julian Messner, vice-president of Horace Liveright's. She took his attentions more seriously than he may have intended, and by the end of the evening she was promised a job. She began by writing advertising copy and then moved up to reading manuscripts. For anyone bent toward literature, no publishing enterprise offered a more spectacular opportunity. Liveright had or would soon have all the best writers of the day: Faulkner, Freud, Hemingway, O'Neill, Hart Crane, and Dreiser. He not only provided them with the best in editorial and publishing skill, he showered them with extracurricular attention. He was one of the first to sense that writers needed a publisher's love as much as they needed his money.

The day's work at Liveright's was regularly topped off with an evening party, an "A" or a "B" party. The "A's" were discreet and classy affairs for writers, editors, and critics who had not yet joined the new generation. The "B's" were wild and noisy, supplied with stronger liquor, liberally enriched with "sex stuff," and of longer duration, frequently extending into the next day and even to the next night. This was Lillian Hellman's first first-hand acquaintance with the gay, careless, and adventurous life of the literary world of the twenties. Here was the kind of glamorous living a writer needed and deserved. Living and writing intertwined, making it difficult to discover where one left off and the other began. Publishing books at Liveright's old brownstone on 48th Street was fun, and somehow the more fun, the better the books.

The roar of the twenties was sweet music to the ear of an eager young lady who was just advancing into her own twenties. Bohemian living, the existential mystique that ruled the American writer's world, and the honor and profit that rewarded literary creators intrigued her. If she had nurtured any impulse during her growing-up years, it was to do what she wanted, to find excitement in whatever she did. Long before she was initiated into the easy ways of the twenties, she had discovered the exhilaration of transforming pedestrian routines into exotic adventures. In her living she was a born romantic.

Before she was ten, she had created a magical home for herself in a fig tree around the corner from her aunts' boardinghouse in New Orleans. Here she was deliciously tantalized and sometimes bewildered by the adult adventures she read about in her secret books. Here, in the afternoons, she mooned away her "ill hour," an hour devoted to the special happiness of being melancholy and alone.

When she was twelve, she and a New York school friend formed a superpatriot counterespionage service, seeking to break up the German spy ring they imagined operated along their section of Riverside Drive. They pursued anyone carrying a briefcase or a violin case. One day they trailed two men for ten blocks and became so sure of their prey that they enlisted the assistance of a police sergeant. One spy turned out to be a professor of Greek at Hunter, the other a violinist at the Palace Theatre. But they did not abandon their careers because of a single failure. They shifted their tactics, recruiting a timid blonde friend to eavesdrop on secret conversations and relay them to headquarters. When her reports were not sufficiently lurid, they twisted her arm until she invented more frightening truths.

On two occasions she declared her independence by running away from home. The first time, when she was fourteen, love drove her away. A young man had pledged his devotion with a lock of hair which she wound into the back of her new wrist-watch. When the watch stopped the next day and a jeweler identified the cause, her father demanded the name of her lover. Instead of submitting to this betrayal, she ran away. For the next two days she wandered around the New Orleans French Quarter, along the row of whorehouses on Bourbon Street. She ate her first meal, Tootsie Rolls and a half-loaf of bread, in the St. Louis Cathedral, slept her first night behind a bush in Jackson Square and her second night in a Negro boarding-house. She had bullied her way in by claiming to be part Negro and related to Sophronia Mason, her former nurse. The name got her in; it also got her out. The next morning Sophronia and her father were standing at the foot of the bed. She was ready to return to the comforts of home.

Later in the same year, in New York, parental rigidity again clashed with her rebellious spirit. She had gone to a fencing match and to Reuben's delicatessen at 72nd and Broadway with a nineteen-year-old Columbia student and another couple. When the other girl captured too much attention, bragging about her newly inherited wealth, Lillian invented dark tales about her uncle, the white slaver. Her curfew instructions had specified eleven. When she returned at twelve-thirty, her father's rage was too extravagant. The next day she sacrificed the security of West 95th Street for the excitement of Times Square. She ate candy and talked daringly with strangers. When the Broadway lights came on, she used her last nickel to summon her Columbia friend. He came, but instead of supporting her fugitive adventure, he took her home. When she found her mother in tears, shattered by her escapade, she grasped the dramatic possibilities of the moment. She assumed a painfully pathetic pose and announced that she had heart trouble.

Although this fake heart attack and the earlier arm twisting found their way into *The Children's Hour*, few passages in her plays have been lifted directly from life. Not because of a sparsity of dramatic incidents in her life, but simply because her writer's nature did not tolerate such self-indulgence. When she turned to life, she drew from the family circle of her mother and father. Her uncles and aunts on her mother's side had staged exciting and vigorous family battles that had awed and frightened her. Her father's sisters were warm and affectionate, devoted to him and to her. These childhood memories were stamped so indelibly that when playwriting settled on her as a profession, she found a new usefulness for her family. Certainly *The Little Foxes*, *Another Part of the Forest*, *The Autumn Garden*, and *Toys in the Attic* could not have been written without the backlog of experience her family supplied.

If autobiographical actions photographed from her mature life do not figure prominently in her plays, ideas and actions from the life and times around her do. If her personal adventures have not been admitted, she has not locked the door of her work against the outside world. In all her plays—in some more than in others—one senses the temper of the time and the temper of Miss Hellman. Because she feels strongly about the way the world turns, she has favored characters who share her concern, vigorous characters fired with human passion.

Every writer discovers his own system for transforming life into art, his own ground rules for what is to be admitted, on what terms, and with what special transmutation. The system may change from year to year, from novel to novel, from play to play, but some patterns remain constant, as they have for Miss Hellman. She has chosen to separate her writing and her living. For each she has defined the territory to be exploited and enjoyed, yet the emotional colors on each side of the fence are often remarkably similar. However, the consequences and risks are calculated differently. The scoring is clearer in the plays, and, unlike life, invariably there is more playing for keeps and a final tally.

Although she was pitched into writing somewhat by accident, once the commitment was made, she quickly adopted the stance of a "pro," practicing her profession as one would practice medicine or law. Only after mastering the rules and skills could one safely toy with personal conceits. Self-indulgence, self-glorification, autobiographical rhapsodizing might pass as writing for some; not for the real professional. To be sure, even the pro was bound to the limits of his own mind, his own psyche, but such restrictions were more imagined than real. With the substance of his own life, sensitivity to the riches of the world, a willingness to let the imagination run and then be harnessed with the proper words properly ordered, a professional writer had all he needed.

Miss Hellman has compartmented her living and her writing much more than her contemporaries, Tennessee Williams and Arthur Miller. She may have drawn from her family gallery for *The Little Foxes*, but she could not have indulged in such confessional autobiographies as *The Glass Menagerie* and *After the Fall*. In a way she would regard it as cheating to exhibit events from life so explicitly and so shamelessly. She enjoys the challenge of inventing and disguising. It is part of the game.

Her choice of the cool-headed line of the craftsman would be less remarkable if her own life were devoid of adventure, if psychic poverty and pedestrianism had been her private lot. Quite to the contrary, she could match Williams and Miller experience for experience—if such reckoning is possible. In canvassing her plays and her life, one is struck not only by the sparsity of strictly autobiographical material in her writing but also by the luster of her living. At times it seems as if she regarded her life as an extended chronicle play, each scene to be exploited and enjoyed to its fullest. Her recent memoir,

An Unfinished Woman, supports that view. If she appears to be cool and calculating as a writer and her characters cool and calculating, in her living calculation has been tempered with human compassion and warmth.

She has a gift for seeking adventure, or finding adventure in the events that come her way. The bare facts of existence never remain bare for her. Her imagination enlivens them with wonder and excitement, often making her autobiographical recollections seem more fictional than her plays. But if her vivid responses to her early life in New Orleans, to her initiation into the New York world of publishers and writers, to the expatriates in Paris, and to the gaudy glitter of Hollywood were never exploited in her writing, undoubtedly the emotional pitch at which she lived these and other experiences gave her the power to dramatize scenes and characters that beat and breathe with life. And just as she could not tolerate tame living—whether in New York, on her farm, on her island off the Connecticut shore, in Paris, in Spain, or in Russia—she could never tolerate tame writing. Her plays are strong, vigorous, tense, and commanding. Whatever later retrospective questions may cross a spectator's mind, in the theatre itself he is bound in the grip of a Hellman play.

Like so many American writers, she came to writing and to playwriting more by accident than by design. She was intrigued with words in her early years and with the compelling credibility and vitality of fictional characters. They were more believable and fascinating than their real-life counterparts. And though she found excitement and mystery in her imaginative world, she wrote no early poems or stories, no confessional diary. Nor was she stage-struck, early or late. There were no neighborhood theatricals, no rapturous afternoons in the peanut gallery, no stage heroes or heroines whose lives guided her own.

She had a short career as an actress at Wadleigh High School in New York in 1922. The dramatic coach cast her as the villainess in *Mrs. Gorringe's Necklace*, a mystery thriller by

Hubert Henry Davis that had enjoyed an earlier popularity at Charles Frohman's Empire Theatre early in the century. Although the role had few lines, on the performance night she was given a chance to beef up her part and test her inventive powers. The door stuck when she was taking her third-act exit. She rose to the occasion, inventing a brilliant soliloquy which she was not allowed to complete. The coach got the door unstuck and pulled her off, thus terminating her acting career. Perhaps in this moment of early glory she sensed the fascination of characters with a touch of villainy and sensed her own power and delight in devising lines for an actor to speak. If she ever made any other stage appearances at Wadleigh or elsewhere, they have been forgotten. But Miss Hellman sampled another extracurricular activity at Wadleigh. She conducted a social gossip column in the school paper under the heading "It Seems to Me, Jr." This career was also of brief duration. Not until years later did she return to journalism, first as a book reviewer for the *Herald Tribune* and then with articles in *PM*, *Holiday*, and *Ladies' Home Journal*.

She drifted into writing as she drifted into the offices of Liveright in 1924, and the drift was slow and without a clearly marked course until *The Children's Hour* in 1934. During these ten years, unlike so many of her contemporaries, she was not committed to a monumental work, the great American novel, the great American play. She was not all that sure of what she wanted or intended to do as a writer.

The Liveright year was a coming-of-age year, rich with new experiences, new people, new freedoms in living, new delight in celebrating her independence. When the world opened, Miss Hellman was ready—not because her rebellious spirit was boiling in protest against nineteen years of restraint and repression but because her independent spirit had been well nurtured. In shuttling between New York and New Orleans, between her mother's family and her father's, in testing her special prerogatives as an only child, she had had abundant opportunity to cultivate her free will. She knew and cherished, as she always would, the pleasure of finding her own way.

Even before she was introduced to the bohemianism of Liveright's office and of his parties in the fall of 1924, she was led astray during the summer by a young man who persuaded her that she needed sexual experience and that the latest mores approved such indulgence. She accepted the proposition, but not without later regrets. The bravado of the new generation and the outlawing of sentimentality did not provide sufficient armor for her psyche. A loveless affair left its mark even in the 1920s. In her living and in her writing, affairs of the heart have not obsessed her, and they have frequently been tinged with a touch of cynicism. When men and women in her plays are drawn to each other, their magnetic fields are often charged with perversities, eccentricities, and selfish calculations. The traditional American dream of healthy and irresistible romantic love was not her dream. But the anonymous young man can be allowed too much credit. He simply appeared when she was nineteen, when the moral code prescribed that a young lady should have slept with a man by the time she was twenty. What neither could have known—no one ever does—is the cruel truth: the psyche at that age is dangerously vulnerable.

Late in the spring of her year at Liveright's, she experienced an even more damaging trauma. She became pregnant by the man she was to marry the following winter. Refusing to tell him and with the help of Donald Friede, Liveright's partner, she located an abortionist in Coney Island. Fearful of the consequence if she told her parents that she felt sick, she returned to work as usual the following morning. Although Friede had been pledged to secrecy, everyone in the office knew about her ordeal. Liveright gave her champagne, Messner took her to lunch, T. R. Smith put her to bed on his couch and ordered supper from the speakeasy next door. They admired her courage, her matter-of-factness. Miss Hellman was too weak to protest being treated like a social guinea pig, a specimen of the new generation, and she did appreciate their care. They might see her as the new woman, but at the moment she was a frightened young lady. She could not turn to her family; she refused to share her misery with her husband-to-be. She needed someone, and the Liveright editors were handy and eager. Certainly their solicitude helped to heal over the wound that would stay in her memory.

Even in the 1920s this was not a happy initiation into the life of love for a nineteen-year-old, particularly one who was shy and sensitive. For whatever facade of daring and independence she had shown to the world, her inner being was easily hurt, and these two misfortunes did hurt her. What permanent damage was registered, how they may have shaped her attitudes toward love, toward men, toward marriage in her living and in her writing, can only be guessed. They must be remembered, for she remembers them, though to keep them constantly in mind, to burden them with too much psychological significance, would be wrong. They were tempered and intensified by what went before, by what came after. In the web of human experience who can say which threads are strongest?

For everyone there are turning-point years. Hers were in the mid-twenties. In the spring of 1924 she called quits to her college career at New York University. As a reward, or consolation, her mother took her on a tour of the Midwest and South, returning to New York for her nineteenth birthday on June 20 and, as it turned out, her first date with the young man who introduced her to sex. On New Year's Eve, 1925, she married Arthur Kober—the event was celebrated with a party at her father's club—and began a new life in New York, in Paris, and in Hollywood.

The years between 1925 and 1934 (when *The Children's Hour* appeared) were apprenticeship years, though she had no clear goal for herself as a person or as a writer. The years passed, day-to-day and month-to-month, filled with uncertainty, with doubt, with erratic moments of pleasure, with high living and drab living. At any moment she could not have guessed where the days were leading. There was little substance that could later be worked into her plays. Once she was into the swing of writing for the theatre, she found that it was not these years but the years prior to 1924 that offered material that could be given a new life on the stage.

II

Newhouses and Hellmans: New Orleans and New York

Lillian Hellman was born in New Orleans on June 20, 1906.* Her mother, Julia Newhouse, had spent her first years in Demopolis, Alabama, and then lived in Cincinnati and New Orleans. The Newhouses wanted the best possible showcase for their three pretty, marriageable daughters. Their son could manage anywhere. Max Hellman, her father, and his two sisters were born in New Orleans. Their parents had arrived during the large German immigration in the 1840s.

They were all virile and colorful people, and both families provided vivid domestic scenes to entrance a young girl. The Newhouses outranked the Hellmans in numbers, in financial resources, in strong wills, and in flashy behavior. The excite-

* In *Who's Who* prior to 1967 Miss Hellman's birth date was given as 1905. Beginning with the 1966–67 edition, it has been listed as 1907. According to Miss Hellman, 1906 is the correct date. Because 1905 has been the accepted date for most of her life—probably her father's error—the occasional references to age in this book assume the 1905 date.

ment and turmoil in their household boiled up freely and regularly. With the Hellmans, particularly with her two aunts, distress and tension were kept under control.

The family assemblies that Miss Hellman recalls in greatest detail were in the Newhouse upper-middle-class apartment after they moved to New York. These gatherings were dominated by her grandmother, Sophie Newhouse, an independent power whose severity and assurance commanded respect and obedience. Servants, children, and all relatives except Sophie's brother Jake trembled when she spoke. No one, except Jake, questioned her authority. Miss Hellman was fascinated with her. Again and again grandmother Sophie became the model for a dramatic portrait. The independent, strong-spirited, self-assured elderly lady who speaks her mind with a commanding voice and who smothers the opposition with her sheer power reappears regularly in the plays.

She was also intrigued by the rich furnishings of the Newhouses. The fancy oval rooms were crowded with valuable trappings that never achieved their intended elegance. When Miss Hellman came to furnish her own establishments and her elaborate stage living rooms, she insisted that they be rich, in good taste, and truly stylish.

Many of her impressions reached her in the servants' hall, where she could follow the main show in relative security. There were soirees at which her pretty aunts sparred with their new suitors. More interesting were the following days' post mortems. Invariably the suitors were declared inadequate and unworthy. The big Sunday dinners, augmented with extra great-uncles and -aunts, were noisier and more fascinating. The decorum of the suitor parties was abandoned. These were often bitter stockholders' meetings with grandmother Sophie as vice-chairman and her brother Jake as chairman. Ill will filled the atmosphere and most of the talk was about money and possessions: who had how much and what, and did he deserve what he had. The Newhouses reached the stage as the greedy and scheming Hubbards in *The Little Foxes* and *Another Part of the Forest.*

As a child Miss Hellman tried to fathom the relationship between her grandmother and Jake. Why should Sophie relinquish her leadership to him, when everyone else accepted her authority? Was it because he was wealthier, because he looked after her business affairs? Apparently it was more than that. Jake Newhouse—known to us later as Ben Hubbard—had shared his sister Sophie's genetic inheritance. Like her he was endowed with an independent and aggressive personality. He delighted in subduing the weaklings of the world for the sheer pleasure of seeing them squirm. According to Miss Hellman, he was "witty and rather worldly, seeing his own financial machinations as natural not only to his but to the country's benefit, and seeing that as comic." Her childhood acquaintance with Jake was limited to what she saw from the hallway. Only once, and years later, did she dare to speak to him. When she graduated from high school, he gave her a ring. She wanted books more than a ring, and a pawn shop gave her twenty-five dollars. For some reason she felt obliged to tell Jake. At first he appeared shocked at her daring and disrespect; this gave way to a hearty laugh when he replied, "So you've got spirit after all. Most of the rest of them are made of sugar water." His words were heard again in *The Little Foxes,* though there they were given to Regina rather than to Ben.

The Newhouses were rich. Max Hellman was poor, and she and her mother were not allowed to forget it when they visited the Newhouses. As a child she was either angry and resentful or envious and tortured with self-hatred because of her envy. Not until she released her torment in the two Hubbard plays was she freed from the Newhouses. Even then she did not escape from the attitude toward money they had instilled in her—wild extravagance mixed with respect. The Newhouses were strong and aggressive; they gloried in their independence and had little tolerance for those not similarly endowed. Miss Hellman's vigorous and independent spirit owes a genetic debt to the Newhouses.

If her mother's family provoked terror and anger, her childhood years with her mother and father and with his sisters were filled with joy and love, though there were marital complexities that could not be understood by a child. Her mother was a sweet and gentle eccentric whose deep love for Max Hellman had conquered her fear of her mother, a notable achievement. A Canal Street shoe merchant, however prosperous, was not a proper catch for a rich and delicate Newhouse. Her mother's sisters, with more acceptable prospects, never married, and her brother did not risk matrimony until after Sophie Newhouse's death.

Love and Julia's dreamy nature sustained the Hellman marriage. When Max Hellman turned his eye to other women, when his partner absconded with their capital in 1911 and they moved to New York, whenever their union was threatened, Julia retreated to her own world of wish and fancy. She loved to pass the time of day with simple people, to talk with God in a Baptist church, a Catholic cathedral, or a synagogue, to fill her house and share her dinner with pathetic woebegone ladies whom she had met on the street and whose stories touched her. She was fascinated by misfits, by those whom the world had treated shabbily.

Lillian was puzzled by the relationship between her mother and father and often annoyed at the power her mother seemed to wield. She might wander in a world of fancy, offer only token resistance to Max's diversions, but finally she determined their style of living. Miss Hellman now recalls that it was not until five years after her mother's death in 1935 that she realized how much she had loved her. Certainly she loved her when she became the model for Birdie in *The Little Foxes* and *Another Part of the Forest.*

Being an only child added another complexity to her years of growing up and probably to her later years as well. Her mother had had such a traumatic experience at her birth that she never risked another pregnancy. Her memory of the event was so strong that when Lillian was married and expecting, she was embarrassingly delighted when Lillian had a miscarriage.

Lillian sensed her special powers as an only child, her extraordinary importance to these two people whose lives revolved around her; and though she may never have set one against the other in a major battle, she did engineer minor skirmishes. And Max Hellman treasured her allegiance when he teased his wife about her family. They were money mad; Sophie was a tyrant who had ruined her children's lives; the Newhouses treated him and his daughter like worthless vagabonds. His attacks never became vicious. He maintained his gaiety and his wit, yet there was truth in what he said and Lillian was drawn to him.

She was also drawn to his two sisters. After the Hellmans had moved to New York when she was six and she began dividing her year between New York and New Orleans, half in each place, the New Orleans half was spent with her Hellman aunts, Jenny and Hannah. Their boardinghouse was a gay and happy place. Unlike the Newhouses, the Hellmans specialized in light, good-humored banter, and the delights they provided were augmented by the fascinations of their boarders: the handsome Mr. Stillman who flirted with her mother and who sang, but should not have; Collie, gaunt, unhappy, and filled with liquor every night after his dreary day at the bank; two silly sisters named Fizzy and Sarah. Though their beauty was fading, they still possessed remnants of their female powers. Once her mother accused her father of showing too much attention to Sarah. As it turned out it was Fizzy who had caught his eye, and when Lillian once saw them get into a taxi together, she was filled with rage. This memory stayed with her for years, probably because she could not comprehend her reaction. She pitied her mother, yet she blamed her for tolerating Max's adventures. She wanted to follow the lovers and kill them. She settled for jumping from her fig tree and breaking her nose. As usual it was to Sophronia she ran for help. Sophronia bandaged her face, gave her a pill, watched while she slept off the initial pain, walked her back to her aunts' house, and warned her not to speak of Fizzy and her father: "Don't go through life making trouble for people." It was good advice and she remembered it.

Her aunts were devoted to her, as they were to her mother and father. They were strong and industrious ladies who uncomplainingly accepted the necessity of earning their own way and who maintained their dignity and their genteel manners as they catered to their eccentric boarders. Lillian loved her aunts, loved the six months of the year she lived with them, loved the real and imagined adventures available in their household and in New Orleans. Being with them also gave her a chance to be with Sophronia, "the first and most certain love of my life."

When they had moved to New York, the Hellmans could not afford to take Sophronia with them, and she was obliged to hire out to another family. Still she was ready whenever Lillian needed her. Most Southern children may forget their Negro nurses when their protection is no longer needed, but not Lillian. Even after Sophronia's death in 1930, she tried to maintain contact with her family. In 1964 when she covered the march on Washington for the *Ladies' Home Journal*, she entitled her piece "Sophronia's Grandson Goes to Washington." Her roots were deep in the South, the South that she loved and often hated. She could never forget, as she once said, "how so much of me had been molded by a Negro woman, and molded to last for good."

Sophronia was not a weepy sentimentalist. She was often impatient with her own people, with the uppity Negro butler who worked for one of their neighbors, with their "bootlicking" cook. The Hellmans were devoted to her and she to them, but Max Hellman could not conceal his jealousy of Sophronia's influence on his daughter. An anecdote illustrates his feelings.

When the family journeyed from New York to New Orleans, her father invariably chose an itinerary that would take them to out-of-the-way places where he could spend a few hours with business friends. Her father had given up shoes and was now a traveling salesman for a New York clothing firm. Late one night when they waited on a lonely station platform in Attalla, Alabama, they watched two white men pursuing a Negro girl. As the train pulled in, the men grabbed her. Her father beat off the girl's attackers and pushed her onto the train while her mother picked up the girl's belongings. When Lillian told her father that Sophronia would be proud of him, he shouted, "To hell with Sophronia. I don't want to hear about her anymore." When Lillian reported her father's heroism to Sophronia, she simply replied, "Your father's all right, as white men come. Things not going to get themselves fixed by one white man being nice to one nigger girl."

Sophronia struggled to teach Lillian to ignore the color line, to respect their affection for each other without battling the system. The big lesson came when Lillian was thirteen, a year after the Attalla incident. One day when she and Sophronia were returning from a movie on the streetcar, she insisted that they sit in the seat behind the driver. He ordered them to the back of the car. She held Sophronia in place, refusing to move. The car stopped. The driver opened the door; the passengers were on their feet; one old lady came toward them. As Sophronia moved to the door, Lillian shouted, "Come back, Sophronia, don't you dare move. You're better than anybody." Finally, after the old lady slapped her and she swung at the conductor with her book bag, Sophronia pulled her off. As they walked toward her aunts' boardinghouse, she insisted she wanted to go away with Sophronia, she didn't want to live with white people any longer. If she thought this was happy news, she was wrong. Sophronia dropped her hand in anger: "There are too many niggers who like white people. Then there are too many white people think they like niggers. You just be careful." Lillian had to walk the rest of the way alone. Sophronia had crossed the street and turned the other direction.

Two days later Lillian found Sophronia in Audubon Park.

They sat for several minutes without speaking. Finally Lillian blurted out, "Aren't you going to see me anymore?" Sophronia knew the time had come. "Time's approachin' to straighten things out. Straighten things out in your own head. Then maybe you goin' to be some good and pleasure me." For a thirteen-year-old the meaning may not have been clear; the contempt in Sophronia's voice was. If Sophronia didn't want to see her, she would not hang around and be a bother. Sophronia drew her close and kissed her, probably for the first time since she was three or four, and said, "You all I got, baby, all I'm goin' to have." It was a happy moment.

Her affection for Sophronia and her race has been evident constantly in her living and in her plays. In a letter to the *Atlantic Monthly* in July, 1969, praising Miss Hellman's *An Unfinished Woman*, Jeanne Noble of the National Council of Negro Women praised her remarkable empathic understanding. She said it was "inspiring to sense that Miss Hellman understood so well the inner world of black domestics. She could love them, and still see the frailty of their argument about civil rights, or the defenses they used to protect themselves from an overload of hurt."

For anyone the years from six to sixteen are well-remembered. Any man is lucky if fate gives him happy scenes during those early years. Miss Hellman was at least half-lucky, with her half-years with Aunt Hannah and Aunt Jenny. Although they were spinsters, somehow they escaped the rigidity and intolerance of the committed virgin. They were lively and gay, with healthy attitudes toward married people, toward children, and toward sex. During the first years of her visits, her grandmother, Babette Kochland Hellman, was still living. She was a tall, handsome woman with a severe face but a kind and gentle manner. Lillian learned about her grandfather, Bernard Hellman, from her aunts. The elder Hellmans were reputable, if unconventional, middle-class citizens, apparently unconcerned about money and position; going one's own way, finding happiness where it could be found, was more important. Like their children, they tolerated eccentrics and eccentric fancies. Aunt Hannah reported that as a child she had eaten her meals on the front steps for two years, her mother delivering the tray. When she decided to return to the family table, no one commented on her absence.

Lillian learned many things in her aunts' boardinghouse: to knit, to embroider, to sew, and to cook. She became expert at cleaning crayfish and preparing the bisque, at making turtle soup, at cleaning chickens and ducks. She quickly understood that the unfortunates who begged at the kitchen door and feasted on the leftovers were to be treated with dignity. Hellmans did not boast of their good deeds.

Many attitudes that were to retain their force evolved during the New Orleans years. She discovered her sensitivity to the sights and sounds around her, her fascination with what people said and did, her power to spark adventures with her imagination. On the many days she skipped school and retreated to her fig tree or wandered around the French Quarter, she savored the pleasure of being alone and feeding on her own fancies. Throughout her life she has stubbornly tried to maintain her only-child privilege: to be alone when she wanted to be alone, to have people around when she wanted them.

Her aunts also introduced her to the delights of a sense of humor. When a young neighbor girl about to be married came to Jenny for last-minute sex instruction, Jenny told her that if she drank a glass of ice water right before the sacred act and three sips during, pregnancy would be avoided. Later Jenny explained that in this instance the advice was correct. The boy was marrying her for her money and would desert her as soon as he had it. "This way at least maybe she'll have a few babies for herself." Four years later when Lillian wrote to her aunts announcing that she was about to be married, they telegraphed, "FORGET ABOUT THE GLASS OF ICE WATER TIMES HAVE CHANGED."

Much of the colorful and happy life with her aunts has stayed with her, in her memory and in her way of living. Their boardinghouse and their eccentric guests provided the models for *The Autumn Garden.* The portraits of Carrie and Anna in *Toys in the Attic,* probably the most affectionate and true-to-life she ever drew, were modeled on Hannah and Jenny. And though the circumstances are altered, the lovable and roguish Julian, the spinsters' younger brother, is created in the likeness of her father. Their extraordinary devotion to him echoes the affection her aunts felt for their brother.

The regular visits to New Orleans had ceased long before she began her three-year term at the Washington Square branch of New York University. Her mother had gone to Sophie Newcomb College and had always expected her to do the same. Lillian held out for Smith, where most of her friends were going. Her family proposed Goucher as a compromise; Baltimore was closer to New York. The question was settled when her mother became ill, and she agreed to stay at home.

Lillian was not a conscientious student. She cut classes, before copping-out had become fashionable. She walked out on lectures, particularly those of Alexander Woollcott. She was annoyed with his know-it-all glibness, with his cuteness. Woollcott was intrigued by her exits, sought her out, and frequently offered her a ride uptown. She sometimes accepted, grudgingly. Only her introduction to Kant and Hegel and a casual acquaintance with Marx and Engels aroused any wonder and excitement. She really preferred the school hours she spent reading and talking in Greenwich Village restaurants.

With her lack of enthusiasm for college, it is surprising that she stayed for three years and even more surprising that before and after she married Arthur Kober, she took classes at Columbia in the Russian and English novel and in Dante. While at Columbia she developed a passion for Dostoevski, thought of trying to write a book on Lewis Carroll and a biography of Melville. Her courses at Columbia never qualified her for a degree. Her degrees came later—an honorary M.A. from Tufts in 1941, a Litt.D. from Wheaton College in 1961, and another Litt.D. from Douglass College (the women's division of Rutgers) in 1963.

III

Marriage, Hollywood, and Hammett

When she married Arthur Kober, her life style changed radically. She moved away from her parents for the first time, left Liveright, filled her days with reading, bridge, and New Orleans cooking, stole secret hours for working on short stories, and experimented with various press-agenting, book-reviewing, and play-reading jobs.

She beat the drum for a musical revue, *The Bunk of 1926*, sketches, lyrics, and book by Gene Lockhart, which opened in February, 1926. On her first time out as a publicity agent she got the break all publicists dream of. The district attorney declared the show was smutty and ordered it closed. The producers went to court and got a restraining injunction, but despite all the easy sensational copy, she could not keep it running.

She broke into print for the first time with a by-line—Lillian F. Hellman—on November 28, 1926, with a book review of *Our Doctors* by Maurice Duplay in the New York *Herald*

Tribune Books. The middle initial stood for Florence, a name she disliked and never used except here. With her ninth and last review, June 2, 1929, the "F." was dropped. She treated all the now-forgotten novels kindly, even those she disliked. It might be "plain trash," but it was "excellent of its kind . . . interesting and even exciting." She was generous, even lavish, in her praise of clear, precise, and direct writing, critical, though never brutal, when she encountered pretentious postures and fancy phrases. A few passages give a foretaste of Miss Hellman's power and delight in turning a sharp, neat sentence: "If Mr. Strachey has done wonders for the semicolon, it is more than possible that Miss Solano will start a new vogue for old commas." "The plot resembles too closely the invention of an intelligent child writing a story with too much material and too little restraint to tell the story properly." "You may not be able to believe that a book chiefly concerned with the activities of a Parisian brothel may well claim first place for the most moral performance of the year." Book reviewing for the *Tribune* was not a profitable profession. At $4.70 per column, she was overjoyed when the editor allowed her two columns.

During these early years of marriage she also read play scripts for Harry Moses and Leo Bulgakov and for Anne Nichols, who wished to turn producer with something that would match the success of her own *Abie's Irish Rose*. Mrs. Kober never uncovered a hit for Miss Nichols, but for Moses and Bulgakov she spotted W. A. Drake's adaptation of Vicki Baum's *Grand Hotel*. The original had been produced by Max Reinhardt at his *Deutsches Theater* in Berlin. Moses was an "underwear magnate" from Cleveland and Chicago who had bought a place for his wife in Bulgakov's acting company. Moses acquired the rights but, unable to swing a production, transferred his interest to Herman Shumlin, a young man from Colorado who had come East to seek his fortune. Shumlin had in turn been a factory worker, a salesman, and a reporter before turning theatrical producer with sudden success. His first venture, *The Last Mile* with Spencer Tracy, had been highly acclaimed at its opening on February 13, 1930, and had run for 140 performances. He struck gold again as producer and director of *Grand Hotel*, the sensation of the 1930-31 season with 257 performances.

No great passion for the theatre drove Miss Hellman toward Broadway. She simply dogged her husband's path. Kober had been a press agent for the Shuberts and for Edgar Selwyn and was now with Jed Harris. A month before their marriage he had taken a fling at producing with a melodrama called *Me* by Henry Myers. It closed a week before they were married. Later, of course, Kober made his name with some thirty motion pictures, his *New Yorker* pieces, and with his stage successes, *Having Wonderful Time* (1937) and *Wish You Were Here* (1952).

Although the Kobers were near enough to the center of the Broadway scene to savor the glamour and excitement, she found most of it dreary and shoddy, the moments of excitement rare, and her part of the work tedious. Her days, whether around Times Square or in their decaying old house at Douglaston, Long Island, were filled either with bored acceptance of her lot or with impatience and restlessness. At times she was convinced that she was destined to be a writer and turned to her short stories. These were "very lady-writer" stories, as she recalls, "the kind where the man puts his fork down and the woman knows it's all over." These writing periods were brief and unrewarding. She was drifting. Somehow she knew she was not living the way she wanted to live, yet she had no clear notion of how she wanted to live. She held no obsessive dreams of position, of wealth, of success. She had a reasonable respect for money and its power, yet she was not painfully enough deprived to be driven to alter her situation. At least, not at first.

Before they moved to Hollywood, she found some independent moments that invigorated her ego. When they spent four months living in a small hotel on the Rue Jacob in Paris,

Arthur worked for the *Paris Comet*, a weekly imitation of *The New Yorker* fashioned for Americans suffering from nostalgia, and she wandered about making her acquaintance with the American expatriates and getting her first story published in the *Paris Comet*, a short sketch about an American girl in Italy. Every now and again she tested her Puritan conscience with some hasty flirtations. These were unrewarding; her conscience could not tolerate the strain.

Back in New York they returned to their old routines until the spring of 1929, when she took a four-month publicity job with the Cukor-Kondolph stock company in Rochester, New York. (George Cukor later became a leading Hollywood director.) A few hours per day took care of her drum-beating. The rest of the time she read, drank, and explored life in Rochester, some seamy, some fashionable. She gambled, learned about the upstate underworld from the local gangster leader, and won enough money at bridge from Rochester's society folks to finance a trip to Europe the following summer.

The Kobers were moving apart, though both regarded their separations as accidental and inconsequential. Arthur never questioned her need for independence. On this second European excursion she traveled around Germany, finally settling in Bonn, intending to enter the university. While she waited for school to open and lived in a student boardinghouse, she made some new discoveries. The first seeds for *Watch on the Rhine* and *The Searching Wind* were planted that summer of 1929. Most of her classmates-to-be were strong, blond, Nordic types devoted to physical culture, to fresh air, and to social reform. They were vigorous companions and she enjoyed their company until the day they invited her to join their youth group and gave her a pamphlet expounding the glories of National Socialism. Any foreign student, uncontaminated with Jewish blood, was eligible and would be enrolled without dues. They had not spotted Hellman as a Jewish name and apparently missed her point when she explained that she had a cousin by marriage who operated a non-Jewish whorehouse in Mobile. She had never encountered such raw and brutal antisemitism. She departed for home immediately.

The following year the Kobers deserted New York for Hollywood. Paramount had offered Arthur a job as a script writer, and as soon as he had launched the initial publicity for *Green Pastures* in the spring of 1930, he departed for the West. She stayed behind to close up the house at Douglaston.

When she joined him in the fall, she discovered little Hollywood glamour in their one-room, Murphy-bed apartment on Sunset Boulevard. Arthur could have afforded better quarters on his incredible $450 per week, but he feared his weeks might be numbered. Even after they moved to the Garden of Allah and then to a large, dark house in the hills above Hollywood Boulevard, she could not arouse any enthusiasm for her new life. During the day she settled into a leather chair and read. The evenings she devoted to therapeutic drinking, preparation for the night and the next day.

When the routine became unbearable and frightening, she persuaded Arthur to help her get a job. He did, and she went to work as a manuscript reader for Metro-Goldwyn-Mayer. At eight-thirty every morning she drove off to Culver City to join her fellow readers, a strange and pitiful collection of literary has-beens, former novelists, short-story writers, and editors, daily struggling to arouse some enthusiasm for the two manuscripts allotted to them. If she found the work tedious, she dreaded even more the drive home at the end of the day. Often she lingered after closing hours, faking a sudden passion for a new manuscript. At times she drove at a snail's pace, as if hypnotized by the dull landscape, occasionally pulling to the side of the road to clear her head. Irrational fear had not been a part of her nature. She was shocked and annoyed to find that she could not suppress it. She simply had to battle her way through and hope that it might not surface the next day. It always did.

Though the print of these unpleasant memories now seems to blot out all others, there were gay days and nights: when her mother and father visited and her father chastised their ex-actress cook for serving grapefruit for dinner and salad before soup; when they joined S. J. Perelman, his wife Laura and Laura's brother, Nathanael West, their closest friends, to laugh at the crazy and grubby life of Hollywood and at the faded refugees from the real world who thrived on drink, dope, and unconventional sex and who lived in gaudy and garish houses.

More than anyone else, Dashiell Hammett helped her to tolerate Hollywood. When they first met in a restaurant, he was recovering from a five-day drunk. His face was drawn and haggard, his tall figure drooped and swayed, his clothes had been lived in too long. Yet Hammett at his poorest was the equal of most men at their best, or so it seemed to his new admirer. In fact, it seemed so to almost everyone who ever met him. His charm was irresistible and it had little to do with who he was or what he had done. When he served in the Aleutians during World War II, editing a camp newspaper, all the soldiers in his outfit turned to him for advice and help. He was known as Pop to some, Grandpop to others. Richard Wilbur once said that "as you came toward Hammett to shake his hand in the first meeting, you wanted him to approve of you." Howard Bay calls him simply a "great guy."

They met casually and in public places at first. Then more often, privately, and as drinking companions. In the beginning his age advantage of thirteen years appeared excessive, as it would to any girl in her mid-twenties. She was awed by his adventurous former life as a Pinkerton private eye, by his best-seller success as a detective-story writer, by his top rank as a motion-picture scenarist. She was intrigued and disturbed by his phenomenal power over women. More than his Christian name had given him the nickname of "Dash."

Neither could have guessed that their friendship would endure until Hammett's death in 1961, that in their early years together she found him exactly the cool-headed tutor and affectionate critic she needed, that in the later years he found in her the Samaritan he required to ease the burden of his last days, when he was dying of lung cancer. Without his needling, his persistence, his comfort on the bad days, she might never have written *The Children's Hour*. Without his encouragement after the failure of *Days to Come*, she might have abandoned playwriting.

Gradually during that first Hollywood winter she began spending more and more time with Hammett, less and less at home with Kober. When she took a leave of absence from her job at Metro and returned to New York for a visit with her family and to meditate on her shifting allegiance, Hammett's letters revealed his growing love and dependence on her. The night she departed, March 4, 1931, he wrote, "Darling, It's ten o'clock and you haven't come back, so maybe you didn't miss the train after all. . . . My headache is gone, my respiration seems normal, and if I had a thermometer I'd give you a report on my temperature. I think I've been to the toilet twice since you left: I'll try to keep more complete records hereafter. . . . Don't forget to write me your impressions of the Aquarium, the Chrysler Building, traffic, the Great White Way, Wall Street, the Subway, greed for gold, Central Park, and Anna Held. . . . The emptiness I thought was hunger for chow mein turned out to be for you. . . . Love in quantities that permit you to pass some on to Laura [Perelman]."

The next night he wrote, "Sweet, Jones rescued the pajamas from the cleaners this evening. I'll dispatch them to you presently. Arthur [Kober] was in for a couple of hours, left just a few minutes ago for an early bed so he could rise early. If I can make it we'll probably do the fights tomorrow night. . . . I've been to the toilet approximately eight times today, with hopes of running it up to a round ten before bedtime, and I've shut the door each time, and locked it once. . . . I daresay my absence from the Brown Derby, coinciding with your departure, has started a crop of fresh and juicy rumors. I'll see they don't die from want of feeding. . . . Beginning a thousand-stanza narrative verse: In San Francisco, Elfinstone/ Fell in with a red-haired slut/ Whose eyes were bright as the devil's own/ With green-eyed greed, whose jaw was cut/ Wolfishly. Her body was lean and tough as a whip,/ With little of breast and little of hip,/ And her voice was thin and hard as her lip,/ And her lip was hard as bone. Lecherously, Dash."

At the end of April he wrote, "Darling, I ran into Arthur, Sid, and Laura in the Brern Doiby. I tried to pump Laura about your conduct in New York. . . . Suspected you of the loosest sort of conduct. Just a she-Hammett. . . . Alfred [Knopf] wired me. *Glass Key* off to a swell start. Made him come across with a thousand dollars. I won't have to eat Jones until perhaps the latter part of next week. . . . My ambition now is to collect enough money to be able to take a couple of months to finish *The Thin Man,* which, God willing, will be my last detective novel. This is my seventh day on the wagon. When are you coming home? Love, Dash."

The following year, after her return to Hollywood, she and Kober were divorced. The legal necessities were managed discreetly and amicably. Kober's lawyer represented her, and a partner in the firm spoke for him. When the charge of cruelty against Kober was read in court, Miss Hellman could hardly suppress her laughter. There was no bitterness. Kober and Hammett remained friends. She and Kober have maintained a warm relationship over the years, depending on each other for advice and encouragement. Whenever Kober rented a new apartment in New York, she conducted the final inspection before the lease was signed. When he planned to remarry in 1941, his fiancée, Margaret Frohnknecht, had to have Lillian's approval; at the wedding, Lillian acted as matron of honor. That was her final participation in such a ceremony. She and Dashiell Hammett never married.

After the divorce she and Hammett moved to New York. Although he had been one of the highest-paid writers, had turned out four of his five best-selling detective novels, and was still regarded as a "hot property" in the writing game, he had run through his ready cash. He solicited another advance from Knopf to pay their rent for the Diplomat's Suite in the Sutton Hotel. Fortunately the hotel was managed by their friend Nathanael West, who allowed them to charge their meals. The quarters were dingy, the food unpalatable—unfit for the most underprivileged diplomat—but they thrived on the excitement of being together, and Hammett began a regimen which fascinated and impressed her. No more drinking, no more partying. He was locked in with his typewriter and *The Thin Man.* Nothing else mattered. When he allowed her to read the manuscript and explained that she would see her reflection in Nora, she was ecstatic. He had a masterful way with women, in life and in fiction. When Gertrude Stein visited Hollywood, he was the only writer she wanted to meet because he was the only American who wrote well about women, and the witty, charming, and adventurous Nora was certainly one his finest portraits.

Not only did she learn about the loneliness and one-track concentration demanded of a writer; Hammett talked to her about her writing. His criticism was unyielding, yet tempered with encouragement. A writer must learn to write by practice. Read, think, and study, and then write some more. The world would not be much poorer if she didn't write a line, and if she wasn't going to be a good writer, she would be happier if she didn't write a line. Each session followed the same pattern and invariably ended with, "Go back now and try again." She did.

Two of her short-short stories got into print in *The American Spectator*, the "literary newspaper" which George Jean Nathan, Ernest Boyd, Theodore Dreiser, James Branch Cabell, and Eugene O'Neill edited from November, 1932, until its demise in March, 1935. "I Call Her Mama Now" by Lillian Hellman Kober appeared in September, 1933, and "Perberty in Los Angeles," in January, 1934. Both stories are told by a ten-year-old girl whose life has been disrupted by her parents' divorce. In the first she runs away when her mother constantly reads aloud from Spengler and writes strange poetry

—"Chaos in Taos" was her latest. The girl is also annoyed with her Aunt Minnie's silly talk about sexual freedom; she says she likes "to pick up her sex in the gutter." After the girl moves to Tacoma to be near her father, she hears about her mother's new diversions. "This year she's taken up dogs and Jews and has them in on Sundays" and now believes that "the future of the country is in Union Square." In Tacoma the girl finds happiness in her new life style: "Now I go to a very strict convent school and I'm translating the sixth book of Virgil into Hebrew. I think I'm going to marry a man called Morton. Morton used to be a waiter in Bullock's Los Angeles roof-garden restaurant. He likes good, plain food and he's ashamed of sex, which is swell."

In the second story the girl recounts her visit to Los Angeles to join Mama, Aunt Minnie, and Uncle Wallace, who have come West to help her through "perberty." She resents leaving her convent school, where she is translating Xenophon's *Memorabilia.* When she arrives at their rented house on Cedar Drive, they are sitting at the bottom of the swimming pool. The reunion upsets them; they cannot fathom her lack of curiosity about herself. Mama cannot believe that she has "no stirrings." They abandon their lost cause and go off to a party for a prizefighter, and the girl happily returns to Tacoma to see an outdoor production of *Il Penseroso.*

These first excursions into fiction are primitive, bare, and awkward, revealing little of her later skill. Her satirical bent is evident, as is her preoccupation with eccentric and perverse characters; sex is on her mind, as it will be in *The Children's Hour*. However, the strong absurdist quality, her fascination with the outrageous and outlandish, does not appear in her playwriting until her last play, *My Mother, My Father and Me* (1963).

On her return to New York she had renewed her acquaintance with some of her publishing friends, particularly with Louis Kronenberger, who had come to Liveright just before she departed. Together they began dreaming up a play about an eighteenth-century queen who became so bored with her royal routine that she determined to become a commoner. The eighteenth century was Kronenberger's specialty, and they delighted in the collaboration. Hammett insisted the play was no good: Kronenberger laughed only at his lines, Lillian at hers; an audience would laugh at neither.

Set in a mythical middle-European kingdom, *The Dear Queen* recounts the disillusioning adventures of Sophia, the Dowager Queen, who becomes wearied by the madcap inanities of her family—her son Charles, the King, who thinks of nothing but bridge, his stamp collection, and relearning his annual Accession Day speech, her grandson who is constantly searching for a tune on his accordion, her granddaughter who pedals her spinning wheel, and her other son who perpetually badgers her for money to support the illegitimate children he imagines he's fathered. Sophia wants to live in a house. She's "tired of being in the Almanach de Gotha. I want to be in the telephone book." By chance she meets Alfred Jenkins Fortescue, a rope-manufacturing commoner who shares her dislike of music and her ideas about cancer, and persuades him to marry her. After a fake ceremony performed by one of the Prime Minister's flunkeys, she moves with Fortescue to Mrs. Mommett's boardinghouse in the Roselawn Subdivision. One evening with her rope manufacturer and his fellow boarders cures her. If they live free, freedom is not for her. Coffee must not be served in the dining room, the kitchen is closed at seven, they cherish virginity, will not tolerate cheating at cards, and go to bed on schedule. Middle-class morality has made them "snooping, mean, dirty-minded fatheads." She reveals her identity, they drop to their knees, and she escapes to the palace. In her absence King Charles and her granddaughter Elizabeth have also tried unsuccessfully to defect. Charles returns because he has to go to the bathroom. Elizabeth has not succeeded in picking up a sailor as she had hoped, though she's found a new dream. "It's not the bourgeoisie who are free and fine. It is the peasantry. The house of thatch, the tilled field. It is toward that I stretch out my arms and toward that I will be journeying tomorrow." Sophia ridicules her new nonsense, and they all return to their comfortable royal madness.

The play was entered for copyright on December 30, 1932, got into most theatre managers' offices, and stayed there. Finally it appeared headed for production. On May 27, 1934, the *Herald Tribune* announced that the newest producing firm in town would do "*The Dear Queen* by Lillian Kober [the *Times* identified her as Lillian Hellman Kober] and Louis Kronenberger. George Kaufman will stage the farce. . . . As to the new managerial partners, Mr. Stein is a brother of the Ben Stein who is sponsoring *Invitation to a Murder*, while Mr. LaMarr is a casting agent." If George Kaufman had really agreed to stage it, it must have shown some promise, but anyone wise to Broadway would not hold much hope for a play produced by a management so new to the game that their identities had to be explained. *The Dear Queen* never reached the stage and was never published, and Miss Hellman and Mr. Kronenberger would gladly forget their first and final collaboration.

After Hammett delivered *The Thin Man* manuscript to Knopf, they had gay days and nights of drinking and partying, of intense talk about books and writers. For several weeks running they met almost nightly with William Faulkner to drink and argue. Years later Faulkner spoke of what a good time they had together. These sessions often ran until morning, when the two men rejuvenated themselves with breakfast or another bottle. Miss Hellman had gone to sleep hours earlier. Although they ranged widely over the literary scene, one argument recurred: Faulkner insisted that he had written *Sanctuary* as a potboiler. Hammett refused to believe that any writer wrote deliberately for money.

On other evenings they swung through parties with artists, musicians, theatre personalities, and literary luminaries. "With all its foolishness," she later recalled, "the thirties were a good time and I often have regrets for it." At a cocktail gathering given by William Rose Benét, she first met Dorothy Parker. This was not a case of affection at first sight. Dorothy Parker greatly admired Hammett's work, particularly *The Maltese Falcon* and *Red Harvest*. She dropped to her knees, smothering his hand with kisses. Hammett and Miss Hellman were embarrassed by the exhibition. In 1935, when the two ladies met again in Hollywood, the first encounter was forgotten and they became life-long friends. Hammett held to his initial reaction. He never liked Dorothy Parker, and in later years when she came to visit, he invariably disappeared until she was gone.

At a party given by Ira Gershwin in the fall of 1933, she renewed her acquaintance with Herman Shumlin. Shumlin was now a successful producer, with *Grand Hotel* and *The Last Mile* to his credit. She took advantage of the occasion to recite the story-line of a play on which she was working. He listened, advised her to abandon playwriting and instead come to work for him as a play reader at $15.00 per week. She amazed herself and him by accepting the offer.

The previous spring she and Hammett had been away from New York, drinking and fishing in the Florida Keys, with occasional hours at the typewriter. Hammett had not encouraged her playwriting; he disliked the theatre and wanted her to try a novel, but when she persisted, he introduced her to William Roughead's *Bad Companions*. One chapter, "Closed Doors; or, The Great Drumsheugh Case," could form the basis for a play. She followed his suggestion and now thought that if she planted herself in the middle of the theatrical scene in Shumlin's office and learned the ropes, she might have a better chance than she'd had with *The Dear Queen*.

V

The Children's Hour

Nineteen thirty-four was a big year for Hellman and Hammett. In January, *The Thin Man,* dedicated "To Lillian," was published by Knopf. It not only created a sensation among detective-story enthusiasts, it attracted a host of new fans. In November, Hammett wrote from Hollywood, "I'm still surprised at the fuss *The Thin Man* made out here. People bring the Joan Crawfords and Gables over to meet me instead of the usual vice versa! Hot-cha!" Later the circle of Hammett devotees expanded with the series of "Thin Man" movies, and a whole generation of cinema addicts knew Myrna Loy and William Powell as Nora and Nick.

Miss Hellman's success year began in May when *The Children's Hour* was accepted for production, and culminated with the opening night on Broadway, November 20, and publication, also by Knopf, on November 21. Her dedication read, "For D. Hammett with thanks." It was the beginning of a career that would mark her as a major dramatist. For him it was the climax of a career. This was his last novel.

Hammett had held the limelight since the publication of *Red Harvest* in 1929. After their meeting in Hollywood, she had shared the mixed pleasures of public adulation. Now the focus was shifting. He was to delight in her success, and she well knew that the rewards that were hers belonged also to him. He taught her to persist, to learn her craft, to scrap whatever did not qualify, to sharpen, to mold, to rework, to temper until they both approved. He started her on her way as a playwright and from then until his death in 1961, every play had to have his critical stamp before being released to the producers. At least once, for *The Autumn Garden*, he supplied a major speech. At the same time, she recalled long after his death, we "thought differently and were totally different writers. He frequently objected to my use of violence. He felt that I was far too held up by how to do things, by the technique."

When *The Children's Hour* was ready in May, 1934, she placed it on Shumlin's desk, insisting that he read it at once. Unaccustomed as he was to taking orders from playwrights, least of all young-lady, would-be playwrights, he obeyed. She had planted herself in the corner with a magazine and appeared permanently settled. He began reading. After the first act, he glanced up and said, "Swell." After the second, "I hope it keeps up." And after the third, "I'll produce it." This was more than she had bargained for. She could only mutter, "You really mean it? You'll lose your shirt!" She would have been satisfied with a promise to read it again, with suggestions for improvement, simply with words of encouragement. She had not really thought that there might be gold in what she'd written, for herself and for others, or that Shumlin would respond so quickly. Twenty-five years later she told a reporter, "I don't think success or failure meant much to me then, and when success came, I gave it four days of fun and then ran away fast, frightened that it would become a way of life. Writers are wacks, aren't they?"

When Shumlin took the play, she had $55 in the bank.

The Children's Hour was eventually to add more than $125,000 to her account. In its initial New York engagement it ran for eighty-six weeks (691 performances), took to the road for a year, and was produced in London and Paris. It was more than a success; it was a sensation, particularly for audiences and censors who were shocked by the subject matter. It was banned in London, Boston, and Chicago. The Lord Chamberlain automatically disqualified any play dealing with Lesbianism. When it was performed privately in London's Gate Theatre Studio in November, 1936, the critics complained vigorously. Why should a play dealing with Sapphism—their word—be forbidden when the London stage was filled with bawdy bedroom farces, crude and vulgar jokes, and half-nude girls? When Shumlin announced his plans for a Boston showing in January, 1936, Mayor Frederick Mansfield insisted that it violated the regulation against the portrayal of perverts. Shumlin volunteered to bring the entire production to Boston at his expense for a private showing for the Mayor and his board of censors. When that was refused, he filed a suit in Federal Court for $250,000 damages. He lost.

If sensationalism kept the play away from London, Boston, and Chicago, it helped to keep it going in New York and on the road. And though audiences may have focused on the evil machinations of the child as they watched the story unfold, it was the advance gossip about unnatural love that drew them in. Even before rehearsals began, word about its Lesbian theme had circulated around Times Square, and at least eight actresses refused to accept parts. They recalled Broadway's venture into Lesbianism eight years earlier. The cast of *The Captive* had been arrested and the play closed.

Miss Hellman did not set out to write a shocker; this was simply a fortunate accident. All the sensational facts were detailed in "Closed Doors; or, The Great Drumsheugh Case," one of the eight crime stories in William Roughead's *Bad Companions*. Roughead reported that in 1810, "there stood somewhere about the northeast corner of Drumsheugh Gardens in the West End of Edinburgh, a certain genteel establishment for the board and education of young ladies. . . . The priestesses of this scholastic temple, twin tenders of the virgin flame of which it was the shrine, were two gentlewomen [Marianne Woods and Jane Pirie] of high endowments and fair repute." Miss Woods' aunt, a former actress, lived with them and earned her keep by looking after the girls' wardrobes.

Among the pupils, all from Edinburgh's first families, was the black granddaughter of Lady Cumming Gordon. Lady Gordon's son had died in India, "bequeathing to his aristocratic parent a bastard, borne to him by a black woman." Although the fourteen-year-old girl "with the courtesy title of Miss Jane Cumming" was "wanting in the advantage of legitimacy and of a European complexion," they were obliged to accept her. Lady Gordon had been one of the staunchest supporters of the school.

Jane Cumming was a troublesome scholar, repeatedly punished for her misdeeds, and when she discovered that she could not curry favor by fawning on her teachers, she became bitter and determined to escape. On November 14, 1810, when she was granted a day's absence to visit her grandmamma in Charlotte Square, she whispered the evil gossip which persuaded her grandmother to write to the parents of all the other pupils urging them to remove their children from the school. For days after the mass exodus, Misses Woods and Pirie could not discover why their charges had departed. Finally, the horrible story reached them. The black child had accused them of conceiving "for one another an inordinate affection, which they did not scruple wantonly to display in the very presence of their pupils."

The teachers consulted their law agent who advised them "to raise an action against the dowager for defamation of character" and to ask damages of £10,000. The case was brought to court on December 8, 1810, and was not concluded until the following June. One bit of evidence that weighed strongly against the teachers was supplied by Charlotte Whiffin, a maid at the school. She swore that "looking through the keyhole of the drawing-room door, [she] beheld her mistresses in a compromising situation on the sofa." The judges, disturbed by this charge, went to Drumsheugh to investigate and found that there was no keyhole in the drawing-room door. Jane Munro, a pupil who had apparently been coached by Jane Cumming, insisted that Miss Woods had repeatedly come to Miss Pirie's bed, and "though she admitted that she could not distinguish the respective voices in their whispered conversations, she was able to report divers improprieties uttered."

The verdict was rendered on June 25, 1811. Three of the seven judges favored the teachers; four found for Lady Cumming Gordon. The following October the decision was appealed to the House of Lords. Ten years later, according to the last records Roughead could find, the case still had not been settled. The school had not reopened and Misses Woods and Pirie, sad and embittered, were forced to depend for their livelihood on the kindness and sympathy of friends.

These were the facts and the dramatis personae supplied by Roughead. Miss Hellman used most of them. She changed the skin color of the evil child, added a doctor to render professional service and to supply love interest, and invented the incidents to transform the story into a play. She also drew on her own memories of childish brutality, of arms twisted, of dreadful secret vows, on her own experience with a faked heart attack, but this was the limit of her autobiographical contributions. As she once remarked, she had not even been to a boarding school.

When the curtain rises on the common room of a girls' boarding school, the converted living room of an old New England farmhouse, eight awkward girls are busily engaged in tasks beyond their grasp: sewing, Latin verbs, trimming hair, and reciting Shakespeare. No garment will evolve from their haphazard cutting and basting; the *ferebas*, *ferebat*, *fere-*

bamus chant sounds foreign to their tongues; the barbering produces a new style, hair with holes; and Peggy's Portia strains Shakespeare's mercy and ours. If the moppets are painfully inept, their tutor, Mrs. Mortar, appears ridiculously miscast in her role as cultivator of the social and domestic graces. She is forty-five, plump, florid, overdressed, and over-coiffed. Her fake elegance and fancy talk arouse our curiosity; clearly this is not her native habitat.

Miss Hellman holds our attention with the rich Breughel-like comic detail, the true-to-life bumbling of these awkward-age young ladies. Already at the beginning of her first play to reach the stage, she seems wise to the drama's demand for clarity and economy, for the proper mixture of words and deeds, neither carrying the full burden, for incidents that command a life of their own as they also reveal character and unfold the story. Some of this she may have learned from Hammett, but her own natural inclination also supported these demands. She abhorred excess, obscurity, and extravagance.

As the sewing circus continues to the tunes of Latin and Shakespeare, Mrs. Mortar focuses on Portia. Feeding the soul is more important than sewing and Latin. She recalls that Sir Henry told her that "pity makes the actress." We are not surprised when she takes over the Portia recitation, with ringing tones and flashy gestures. Miss Hellman has set a pattern she will frequently employ: arousing our curiosity and then satisfying it. When she leads us on, we know we will not be cheated or frustrated.

If Mrs. Mortar did not appear so pompous riding under full sail and the whole panorama so ridiculous, we might weep instead of laugh. The girls do not respect her histrionics. When she hits the climactic "and earthly power doth then show likest God's/ When mercy seasons justice," Lois, the Latinist, sings out, "*Utor*, *fruor*, *fungor*, *potior*, and *vescor* take the dative," and Peggy announces that Mrs. Mortar has skipped three lines.

While Shakespeare, Latin, and sewing hold the stage, we have caught sight of Mary Tilford squeezing into the room "clutching a slightly faded bunch of wild flowers." By the sullen expression on her face, by her tardy arrival, we know that this fourteen-year-old deserves special attention. Our hunch is supported by Mrs. Mortar, who covers her mnemonic humiliation by chastising Mary. Courtesy, if nothing else, should bring Mary on time to her sewing class. "Courtesy is breeding. Breeding is an excellent thing." Mary is not intimidated. She's been picking flowers for Mrs. Mortar. If we are tempted to allow her the benefit of the doubt, that temptation is quickly dispelled for us, if not for Mrs. Mortar. As Mary exits to get a vase, she sticks her tongue out at Helen.

As the girls return to their tasks, the background scene seems to be fading, and Karen Wright enters. She's near thirty, attractive, pleasant, warm, and dignified. The girls snap to attention, without resentment. Clearly they like and respect her. As Karen goes to her desk, she corrects Lois's Latin pronunciation, observes the damage to Rosalie's hair, asks if Helen has found her bracelet. If Rosalie will come up to her room later, she'll see if she can repair her hair. Did Karen stumble just a bit over the "Come up"? There appears to be a bit of mystery about the lost bracelet. And Mary returns with her vase of flowers just after the bracelet talk. Is the juxtaposition sheer accident? All this passes quickly, casually, naturally, yet we have stored the hints for future reference. We already sense that we'll be told only what we need to know.

Our attention is now on Karen and Mary. Karen is staring at the flowers. Mary has lost her earlier cockiness; she ventures a timid "Good afternoon." Karen wonders if the wild flowers she's picked for Mrs. Mortar are really the first of the season, really from near Conway's cornfield. She saw a similar bunch in the garbage can. Mary is saved by the bell or, for a moment, seems to be. She is not. When the others depart for their classes, Karen orders Mary to remain.

Miss Hellman has registered another trademark of her dramaturgy. She welcomes awkward, embarrassing, and unyielding confrontations. She walks her characters into battle, not away. Truth must out, but only if characters stand toe to toe, eyeball to eyeball. No critic could ever accuse Miss Hellman of avoiding obligatory scenes.

Karen is reasonable and understanding, yet firm. Why was everything at the school going smoothly and happily until a year ago when Mary arrived? Why does she find it necessary to lie so often, why lie about the flowers? Mary is unmoved; she sticks to her story. Karen's patience is slipping; she knows the flowers came from the garbage can. Mary shifts to whimpering. Everyone picks on her; everything she does is wrong. For a moment her problem-child technique works. If Mary feels that she must take a walk instead of coming to class, they'll try to excuse her. Mary grasps her advantage. She did pick the flowers near Conway's cornfield.

Karen's patience has broken. Mary will have no recreation, no horseback riding, no hockey, and will not leave the grounds, not even for the Saturday boat races! Mary meets the challenge; she'll tell her grandmother. When Karen ignores that threat, Mary plays her trump. She doubles up in pain: "It's my heart! It's stopping or something. I can't breathe." The trick works. As Karen carries Mary into the next room, Mrs. Mortar is sent to ask Martha to telephone Joe Cardin, the local doctor. We have had our first frightening encounter with the little monster.

Martha Dobie has now come in after calling Joe, and Karen returns to report on Mary's latest maneuver. They're both concerned about Mary's grandmother. She's been nice to them; they know she'll believe whatever Mary tells her. They've both tried to deal with Mary in the past, tried to understand her; neither has "the faintest idea what goes on inside her head." Perhaps Joe can help them. While they're waiting for him, they shift to their other "pet nuisance," Martha's aunt, Mrs. Mortar. Apparently we have not seen her at her worst.

She's been jabbering to the girls about losing her trunks in Butte, about her magnificent performance of Rosalind during a hurricane. Miss Hellman enjoys the portrait of this decaying second-rate actress. She abhors the incessant high-flying talk of actors, bragging about their past histrionic exploits and dreaming out loud about tomorrow's glories. Rarely does Miss Hellman use her plays to register personal annoyances; here she does, in good fun and without disservice to the play.

Karen and Martha decide that they must scrape together enough money to send Mrs. Mortar packing, and with that settled Martha pats Karen's head "affectionately." Is this the first unnatural act? It appears innocent enough, since the two girls have been college friends and Karen is about to marry Joe. But is it as innocent as it seems? Karen supports our suspicion. When Martha protests too strongly about the imminent marriage, about Karen deserting her, about their not vacationing together, Karen shouts, "For God's sake, do you expect me to give up my marriage?" Martha has gone too far and knows it, but she has no opportunity to explain. Dr. Joseph Cardin enters. Another Hellman trademark has been registered. Scenes are interrupted before they have run their course; unfinished business is left on our minds, to be resumed at a later moment.

Dr. Cardin is a "pleasant-looking, carelessly dressed man of about thirty-five," with a sense of humor. He relieves the tension immediately. On his way he's seen a beautiful little black bull. He's sure there's "going to be plenty of good breeding done in these hills." He does not know, of course, that his marriage has been the most recent topic of conversation. He'll give Mary his best attention. "Heart attacks are nothing to play with," and he's "never played with one in [his] life." Miss Hellman enjoys puncturing solemnity and high seriousness with a sharp quip, and in most of her plays she finds a character who shares her delight. One suspects that some of these smart cracks with a satirical bite may have been devised for the benefit of Hammett and Dorothy Parker; this was their game.

While Doctor Cardin and Karen are attending their heart patient, Martha briefs her aunt on their plans. They'll pay her passage to London and give her enough money to live on. Mrs. Mortar refuses. She won't go to London; she won't take their charity; she'll write her agent and return to the stage. The pitch is rising. Mrs. Mortar knows she should stay out of Martha's way when "*he's* in the house." Martha can't stand "the idea of them being together," she's "jealous of him." More than that, Martha's fondness for Karen is unnatural, "just as unnatural as it can be." She's gone too far. Martha orders her to leave, but as she does we detect a sound outside the center doors. Again the scene has been interrupted at the boil. Martha opens the doors, revealing Evelyn and Peggy. They didn't mean to listen. Martha, not yet prepared to know how much they heard, sends them upstairs.

As Cardin returns from his patient, Mrs. Mortar sweeps out with majestic indignation, "just keeping her hand in, in case Sir Henry's watching her from above," according to Martha. Joe has found nothing wrong with Mary, "just a little something she thought up." His Aunt Amelia may also be Mary's grandmother, but Mary belongs to another side of the family and he does not propose to advise his aunt about Mary even after he's married to Karen. As Martha tries to escape, he catches her. Why should marriage make a difference? "What is it?" Martha cannot control herself. She pushes him away and shouts, "God damn you." The shock reverberates, while Cardin lights a cigarette and before Martha apologizes. In the thirties young ladies did not shout "God damn." The future for this trio does not appear promising as Karen returns and the school bell summons Martha to class.

The focus shifts back to Mary. She has recovered momentarily, though still insisting that her heart hurts and that she wants to see her grandmother; and when Karen, having learned about the eavesdropping and summoned the culprits, orders a new arrangement of roommates, Mary engineers another tantrum. Cardin immediately carries her to the couch, instructing Karen to ignore any future faintings. He must now return to his normal duties, and Karen goes with him to his car.

Freed from her tormentors, Mary's fury explodes. She throws a cushion at the door and kicks the table, shattering a vase, a gift from Dr. Cardin. Peggy and Evelyn are trembling, but not Mary; she knows she can "get out of it." She is more confident of her power than we had imagined. When Rosalie arrives to remind them about moving their things, Mary commands her to do the job for her. She possesses some secret hold over Rosalie. Miss Hellman knows the games that girls play. With Rosalie dispatched to her slave duties, Mary must now hear all the lurid details they overheard in the hallway. Peggy willingly obliges. Mortar was very angry and said that Dobie was like that even when she was a little girl: "She'd better get herself a beau of her own because it was unnatural, and that she never wanted anybody to like Miss Wright, and that was unnatural." The girls may not fully grasp the meaning of "unnatural," but it has an intriguingly evil sound, matching the fascination of *Mademoiselle de Maupin*, the secret book they have been sharing. Sex is on the minds of these young girls who are struggling with their own physiology.

Mary will report everything to Grandma. She is not afraid to run away and Evelyn and Peggy must help her. When Peggy refuses to turn over the $2.25 she's saved from her allowance, Mary twists her arm until she cringes, and when Evelyn screams and tries to help Peggy, Mary slaps her face. They are forced to submit, and Mary rewards them with a sinister smile as the curtain falls. The prospects ahead are frightening. Authority and maturity seem useless weapons against Mary.

Miss Hellman knows the power of physical action. Pussyfooting on the fringes of confrontation, sparring, pretending are not her way. She wants to make the adrenalin flow, the nerve ends tingle, the muscles tighten. This is the stuff of which her drama is made.

Another quality of her playwriting is also apparent: her sparing use of biographical detail. Mary knows that Grandma is fond of her "on account my father was her favorite son." That is all we ever learn about Mary's heritage. About the others we know only that Grandma is Cardin's aunt; Mrs. Mortar is Martha's aunt; Karen and Martha have been at college together. Miss Hellman focuses on their present life, without distracting speculations about their pasts.

In the second act Miss Hellman introduces her favorite stage setting: an elegant room, warm, spacious, and filled with expensive furniture, everything in good taste and suggesting upper-crust affluence. Variations of this room appear in most of the later plays. Agatha, the well-weathered maid, seems to understand Mary. She's sure she's come home because she's "been up to something again," not because she's ill. While Agatha goes for Mrs. Tilford (Grandma), Mary experiments with faces in front of the mirror, searching for her most sick and haggard look. The more we see of her, the more frightening and abhorrent she becomes.

Mrs. Tilford is a "dignified woman in her sixties, with a pleasant, strong face," a favorite Hellman character. Many of the later plays feature ladies who speak with assurance and authority, who are comfortable with their wealth, who recognize and trade on their superiority, yet without arrogance. Most of them are less gullible than Grandma Tilford. Mary immediately runs to her, burying her head in her ample bosom. She's weeping because she's so happy to see her. We could gladly wring her neck. Another Hellman trademark. She devises these moments when our righteous indignation becomes so intense that we are tempted to defy convention and mount the stage to set things right.

Grandma is touched by Mary's homesickness, yet John must drive her back to school. Only hysterics will save her. Mary pulls the stops and sobs, "I can't go back! I can't! They'll kill me! They will, Grandma! They'll kill me!" She tells about her fainting, the heart trouble, of how she's punished for everything, then stops a moment to test her success. She misses her Grandma so much; can't she stay at home? When Grandma refuses, she tries a higher card. "You don't love me. You don't care whether they kill me or not." Grandma's protests spur her on. Peggy and Evelyn heard awful things, heard Mrs. Mortar say, "it was unnatural for a girl to feel that way." Mary is watching her victim. "Unnatural" reached the mark. She's heard other things, "bad things." Sometimes "Miss Dobie cries and Miss Wright gets mad, and then they make up again, and there are funny noises and we get scared." And she's seen strange things. These must be whispered in Grandma's ear. Grandma stares at her in amazement: "*Are you telling me the truth?*" Mary knows she's won. We cringe as Mary hugs her Grandma: "You're the nicest, loveliest grandma in all the world."

As Mary runs out victoriously to wash for dinner, Mrs. Tilford telephones the school but hangs up, calls Dr. Cardin, asks him to come immediately, and then begins telephoning the children's parents. She's reached the first one as the curtain comes down. Castastrophe is in the making.

Only a few hours have passed when the curtain rises on the second scene of Act II. Rosalie has moved in. Mrs. Tilford had called her mother in New York—"three dollars and eighty-five cents and families starving," according to Agatha. Miss Hellman's servants are invariably stand-up comics. Mary insists that Rosalie share the responsibility for the havoc at the school. If not, she'll tell about Rosalie stealing Helen Burton's bracelet; the police will be called and she'll spend her life in a solitary prison, and when she gets out her father and mother will be dead and she'll be forced to beg. If she wants to escape this fate, she must swear, "From now on, I, Rosalie Wells, am the vassal of Mary Tilford and will do and say whatever she tells me under the solemn oath of a knight." Rosalie submits, awed by the mystery and solemnity of the pledge.

Mrs. Tilford is expecting Dr. Cardin and hustles the girls to bed. When he arrives, she begins with questions about the hospital—he's been busy "getting the results from the mating-season"—about the fainting, about his fondness for Karen, about the expulsion of Mrs. Mortar. Finally she's ready for the critical stroke. He must not marry Karen: "there's something wrong with Karen—something horrible." Before she can continue, we hear Karen's voice off-stage. Mrs. Tilford refuses to see her but has no choice. Karen rushes in, followed by Martha.

The school has become an "insane asylum," with parents rushing in and out, with children being hustled into cars. From one of the mothers Karen has finally heard the horrible truth. Mrs. Tilford has told them that "Martha and I have been—have been lovers." The accusation sounds even nastier from her lips. This is confrontation with a vengeance. Mrs. Tilford admits that she's spread the word; Martha and Karen were playing with children's lives and she had to stop them. Karen is incredulous that Mrs. Tilford really believes what she's said. Martha is furious. Can't she understand that she's not playing with "paper dolls" but with the lives of human beings?

The scene is carefully orchestrated. After the initial outbursts, the intensity is maintained, though the volume is reduced, as they survey the damage and contemplate the future. Finally their anguish again demands full voice. Karen damns Mrs. Tilford for making them defend themselves against a "great, awful lie." Cardin pounds the table and shouts, "What the hell did you do it for?" And Martha discovers the path to revenge. They'll not let her whisper the lie: "We'll *make* you shriek it—and we'll make you do it in a court room. Tomorrow, Mrs. Tilford, you will have a libel suit on your hands." We share their frustrations; we cheer Martha's cry for justice; yet we are painfully aware that Mrs. Tilford may be right when she says, "That can bring you nothing but pain."

Over Mrs. Tilford's protests, Cardin insists that Mary be brought in to confront her victims. He assumes the role of gentle prosecutor as he begins the inquisition. (The scene could have been lifted from a Hammett novel.) Everyone lies sometimes; he's giving her a second chance to substitute the truth. Mary refuses the bait. She now speaks out what she had whispered: "I looked through the keyhole and they were kissing and saying things." Her shamelessness is incredible. She stands up to every question, savors every reply. When Karen insists that Mary repeat how she saw them, Karen punctures her story: "*There's no keyhole on my door.*" Our momentary hope that truth has a chance is quickly shattered. Mary shifts her story: she heard them in Miss Dobie's room. When Martha reminds her that would be impossible—she lives at the other end of the house with her aunt—Mary recovers her command with hysterics. Everybody is yelling at her and mixing her up. It was really Rosalie who saw them; Rosalie must be brought in. We have not forgotten that she's Mary's vassal; we heard the vow.

Rosalie, frightened by her inquisitors, admits that certain things at school puzzle her, history, for example. A reminder of how far we have strayed from normal school-girl worries! Karen does not spare her or herself. Did Rosalie see them "kissing each other in a way that—women don't kiss one another?" Rosalie is weeping; she never saw such a thing, never thought it. Mary is ready for her denial. It happened the same day Helen's bracelet was stolen. Twice before we've heard about the bracelet; we now know why. When Mary threatens to tell Grandma about the bracelet, Rosalie's resistance is broken. She cries shrilly, "What Mary said was right. I said it, I said it—" As the curtain is coming down, Rosalie is weeping hysterically, Martha is leaning against the door, the others are staring at Rosalie. Mary is in command. The adults are helpless against the machinations of this hateful child. Perhaps Cardin can save them, but during these final moments he has not spoken.

Critics and audience knew that they had been hearing a new, strong voice in the American theatre. Here was a dramatist who could make the stage blaze, who was not afraid of fire, and she laid the coals carefully, warm and dry, ready to ignite as soon as the sparks reached them.

When the curtain rises on the final act, we have jumped

The Children's Hour

NEW YORK PUBLIC LIBRARY

from April to November. The common room that was alive with high-pitched chatter is now dark, dreary, and uncared for, the windows shut, the curtains drawn. In the first half-dozen lines we know that Karen and Martha have been shattered:

MARTHA. It's cold in here.
KAREN. Yes.
MARTHA. What time is it?
KAREN. I don't know. What's the difference?
MARTHA. None. I was hoping it was time for my bath.
KAREN. Take it early today.

They are foundering helplessly at the bottom of the world. Martha's bath is her "last touch with the full life," and "at five o'clock I'll comb my hair." In this morguelike atmosphere they fall into a long silence. The telephone rings. They ignore it. Finally Karen takes it off the hook and returns to her chair. Quickly, clearly, with chilling tell-tale signs, Miss Hellman commands our sympathy for the pathetic pair.

For eight days they have languished in their present state. "It never seemed real until the last day." In court? Cardin has come every day, urging them to go out, not to cower like frightened animals; but they know the local ladies have spread the word. They cling desperately to their sense of humor, dark as it has now become. When a giggling grocery boy appears and stares at them in wonder, Martha waves her hand in his face: "I've got eight fingers, see? I'm a freak."

Someone else is in the hall. It should be Cardin. Instead it's Mrs. Mortar with a suitcase. The irony of Martha's greeting reaches us, if not Mrs. Mortar. She's just in time for tea and wouldn't she like some small sandwiches and a little brandy? The game is brief. Mrs. Mortar didn't answer their telegrams because she was on tour, and she's discovered many things about the state of the new theatre: the Lyceum in Rochester now has a toilet backstage. (That convenience was probably not there when Miss Hellman worked in Rochester!)

Martha is revolted by her ridiculous theatre chatter, her absurd sense of moral obligation. She must know what happened when she refused to return: "Karen Wright and Martha Dobie brought a libel suit against a woman called Tilford. . . . A great part of the defense's case was based on remarks made by Lily Mortar, actress in the toilets of Rochester, against her niece, Martha . . . on the telling fact that Mrs. Mortar would not appear in court to deny or explain those remarks. As you probably read in the papers, we lost the case." Mrs. Mortar's reappearance has given the playwright a chance to confirm our worst fears.

Mrs. Mortar refuses to leave. She'll wait in her old room for their apology. As she is going, Dr. Cardin arrives. He has new plans; he's sold his office; they're all going to Vienna together. Martha protests, then agrees, and taking the groceries to the kitchen, leaves Cardin to persuade Karen. She cannot allow him to leave his practice. The signs of strain are painfully clear. When she leans down to kiss him, he pulls back "almost imperceptibly." When he agrees to accept that what she's done, she's done, Karen demands to know what he means by "what you've done." When she asks if they can have a baby right away, he seems to have lost his former enthusiasm. She finally prods him to ask the hateful question; she had seen the shame on his face in court. The question is barely formed, "Is it—was it ever—" when she puts her hand over his mouth: "No. Martha and I have never touched each other." The record is straight; Karen and Martha have not been lovers. Yet Karen knows that the question will hound Joe and her. Neither will ever really know what the other believes. He must go away for two days, a day at least, think everything over and then decide if they can pick up the pieces. He assures her that he'll be coming back. Karen is wiser. After he's gone, she says to herself, "No, you won't. Never, darling."

Karen is right, yet we wonder if they fought hard enough. Weren't Karen's arguments a bit thin, fevered rationalizations about the shadow that hung over them? What happened to the no-nonsense Cardin who first exposed Mary's trickery? Was he in court? On the stand?

But in the theatre there is no time for questions. Martha has returned to learn that Joe has gone, will not be coming back, and that he thought they had been lovers. Martha searches for the truth. They have been close; she has loved Karen like a friend, "the way thousands of women feel about other women." She probes deeper; finally she cannot suppress her inner torment. She does love Karen, has loved her "the way they said." She's never loved a man; she's resented the marriage. She knows Karen does not share her feelings; she's ruined their lives. Her hysterical confession has drained the last ounce of emotional reserve. Karen is weeping as Martha, slowly surveying the room, goes out, shutting the door behind her.

Karen is alone, tortured with Cardin's departure and now with Martha's confession. Suddenly a shot is heard. Miss Hellman anticipates the melodramatic hazard: "The sound of the shot should not be too loud or too strong; the act has not been sensational." Her warning may be futile. Karen is stunned for a moment, then races out the door. When she returns, Mrs. Mortar is in the room. Karen's expression conveys the terrible message. Before they have recovered enough to telephone for help, Agatha appears, announcing that Mrs. Tilford is outside. If they won't talk with her, "it's going to kill her." Mrs. Mortar is unwilling, but Karen finally relents.

When Mrs. Tilford now admits that the accusation was untrue and offers to apologize publicly and pay the damages that were denied in court, Karen summons her strength for one final bitter explosion. An apology and money paid may let Mrs. Tilford sleep again, "But what of me? It's a whole life for me. A whole God-damned life. And what of her?" She's pointing toward Martha's door. Still, she's unable to fight a battle that is already lost. After the funeral she may go away; she'll even accept Mrs. Tilford's help if it makes her feel better. Karen is at the window talking about the weather as Mrs. Tilford departs and the curtain comes down. Their "goodbyes" are hardly audible.

The playwright is not at her best in this final scene or in the final act, as Miss Hellman acknowledged some seven years later. In the introduction to *Four Plays*, she wrote, "The play probably should have been ended with Martha's suicide; the last scene is tense and over-burdened. I knew this at the time, but I could not help myself. I am a moral writer, often too moral a writer, and I cannot avoid, it seems, that last summing-up. I think that is only a mistake when it fails to achieve its purpose, and I would rather make the attempt, and fail, than fail to make the attempt."

The third act is less intriguing for other reasons. Mary has disappeared from the scene. Abhorrent as she is, she is the most compelling character in the play, and we miss her. There are other difficulties. Until the last act we believe everything that has transpired. Now too many troublesome questions go unanswered. Why didn't Cardin shake the truth out of Mary, out of Rosalie? Why didn't he testify at the trial? And for two acts our sympathies are invested with two heterosexual teachers, falsely accused of Lesbianism, who are being punished by a society that can be perverted by lies and can tolerate the punishment of the innocent. In the third act the ground has shifted. Another play is beginning about Lesbians who live in a society that punishes Lesbians. It is too late to begin again.

Most critics deplored the inadequacies of the third act. Brooks Atkinson pleaded, "Please Miss Hellman, conclude the play before the pistol shot and before the long arm of coincidence starts wobbling in its socket. Leave them the dignity of their hatred and despair." Joseph Wood Krutch found it improbable and boring. He was amazed that "anything so inept was ever allowed to reach production." Yet, even with its faults, the critics recognized the play's power: "a terrifying and ennobling experience"; "it shines with integrity"; "the work of a courageous dramatist"; "a stinging tragedy, written with hard, clean economy." Miss Hellman's name was mentioned infrequently; she was not yet a name to be reckoned with. And in most of the review columns, *The Children's Hour* shared space and surrendered top billing to such now-forgotten attractions as *Gold Eagle Guy*, *The Jayhawker*, *Dark Victory*, *Page Miss Glory*, and *Say When* (with Bob Hope). After the play caught on, it appeared to be a strong contender for the Pulitzer Prize, but William Lyon Phelps, who dominated the committee, was revolted by the advance reports and refused to see it. Now, when the motion pictures are exploring the clinical and how-to-do-it aspects of this once-forbidden subject, it is difficult to comprehend the shock waves that emanated from the stage of the Maxine Elliott Theatre in the mid-thirties.

The heart of the play, black heart that it is, rests in the poisonous young viper Mary Tilford. And in the theatre Florence McGee, a twenty-four-year-old actress, captured Mary's fiendish disposition so completely that one could not escape the conviction, as one critic remarked, that "capital punishment for children was an urgent social necessity." If Miss Hellman did not at first recognize this peculiar power of the theatre, she did later. When *The Children's Hour* was being revived, she wrote in the Sunday New York *Times* (December 14, 1952), "On the stage a person is twice as villainous as say in a novel. When I read that story I thought of the child as neurotic, sly, but not the utterly malignant creature which playgoers see in her. I never see characters as monstrously as the audiences do."

Neither the program, the advance notices, nor the published text, which appeared the day after the opening, indicated that the story was not original. John Mason Brown, in his New York *Post* review (November 21, 1934), was the first to refer to the source. A letter to the *Saturday Review* (March

16, 1935) reported that after the opening Miss Hellman said that the satanic "imp came out of my own head. She should have said that the imp came out of my own Roughead. But perhaps Miss Hellman doesn't like wise cracks."

Shumlin had carefully guided the play through rehearsals, and when it opened on November 20, 1934, all its fierce intensity had been transferred to the stage. He and the playwright had no strong differences about the staging, though he recalls that peace and calm did not always prevail. He feared the title was "poor box office," but he respected her wish to keep it. Then and later, he insisted that "her plays are her plays and no one else's"; he merely helped; he could not claim a share in their creation.

Neither Kober nor Hammett were on hand during the rehearsals, nor at the opening. They were both in Hollywood. "I miss you awfully, honey," Hammett wrote in late October. "It would be so thoroughly nice being back if you were only along." He was "tickled to death that your cast still looks good! . . . I hope the rehearsals are going smoothly and I hope you are being a good girl." Shortly before the opening, he and Kober met for lunch and "got pretty tight together," drinking to her success. Even now, Kober recalls her thoughtfulness in sending tickets to his family.

The opening night was glorious, even without Hammett. George Jean Nathan stayed until the final curtain and even applauded. Backstage, friends and strangers surrounded her, wildly announcing that she was the "second Ibsen," "the new O'Neill," "the American Strindberg," "the 1934 Chekhov." Only her mother kept her head. Through the din she repeated, in her well-bred Southern voice, "Honey, don't forget you have your new hat on." The final irrevocable verdict would, of course, be rendered at the box office. The first week's take, $8,611, was promising; the second hit capacity, $12,683. Throughout its run of twenty-one months, the longest for any of her plays, hardly a week missed capacity.

Audiences were undisturbed by the weaknesses in the play:

Cardin's silence, Mary's absence from the final act, the anti-climactic closing scene. They did not sense that Miss Hellman had become inordinately fascinated with Mary, allowing the tool to become the machine. They were absorbed in the detectivelike pace of a strange and chilling story. Here was a courageous playwright, unintimidated by social taboos, who thrived on evil, shame, and catastrophe, who encouraged and respected their emotional investments, who had something to say and said it well. It was a remarkable beginning for a new playwright.

In the *Four Plays* volume, Miss Hellman recalled that she had had "problems in writing the play. . . . It took a year-and-a-half of stumbling stubbornness. I remember how many times I tore it up, how many characters I took out and put back and took out again; how I reached back into my childhood and found the day I finished *Mlle. de Maupin;* the day I faked a heart attack; the day I saw an arm get twisted."

Part of the record of her problems and stumbling can be found in the collection of Lillian Hellman manuscripts at the University of Texas. Her first notes and early drafts reveal her workmanlike approach in transforming the story into dramatic terms, substituting indirect suggestion for direct exposition and continually tightening and compressing. Unfortunately, if she ever had an annotated copy of the Drumsheugh case, it no longer exists. Her earliest notes and first drafts of Act II, Scene 2, and Act III outline all the characters and complications that are finally employed plus some that are eliminated.

The first Act II, Scene 2, is dropped completely. It contains a long 1930s smart-talk love scene between Karen and Cardin: Karen saddened because they won't be "living in sin much longer" and Cardin comforting her with the assurance that once a year they "can go to a nasty hotel and pretend." Their passionate embrace is interrupted by Martha, who deplores their "lust," and Mrs. Mortar, who is searching for a copy of *'Tis Pity She's a Whore* to read to her charges. Their banter is interrupted by a chauffeur who has come for two of the girls and by Mrs. Wells, who has come for Rosalie. She has read about "women like that . . . I think it's called Lesbianism —I really don't know." She looks at their frozen faces and runs from the room as the curtain comes down.

The original third act approximates the final version, though the depressing opening scene is yet to be written. Cardin believes that "a little something must have existed," but he's willing to forgive and forget. Martha's hysterical confession is not yet developed, though she admits, "I did love you. I do love you." She recalls her fascination in watching Karen undress when they were in college. After the suicide Mrs. Tilford arrives with her friend Judge Amory Potter to apologize and make a settlement. Karen refuses with a harsh and vindictive final speech: "Go home to your Mary, your viper, and watch her grow. . . . She's yours and you'll be reminded of it all the time. It will be years of darkness, years of hell. . . . Go home and send the people for Martha. I'm very tired."

In the first complete draft, the first act is divided into two scenes: the first in the parlor–common room, the second on the playground after the heart attack. The vase breaking, the arm twisting, Mary's plans for escape, the forbidden book are all here, though the secret volume is more sensational: *Women Without Men* rather than *Mademoiselle de Maupin*. The scene concludes with an inexplicable stage direction: "The three enter a little room."

In this draft, the second act, also in two scenes, has almost reached its final form. The third act differs from the earlier and final versions in several respects. Martha's confession is more fully, though not finally, developed. The Judge has been eliminated. The suicide comes while Mrs. Tilford is trying to persuade Karen to accept her apology. Martha is typing off-stage; the typing stops and we hear the shot. Mrs. Tilford has the final speech: "Mrs. Mortar, you are not innocent. We are both guilty, as guilty as if we had pulled the trigger ourselves. And so is the judge and jury . . . the newspapers, and yes, the church too. . . . Why—why—were we so willing—even anxious to believe the lie. Oh, Karen, do pray for me. Do pray for me." Miss Hellman is intrigued with the idea that guilt cannot be assigned or borne by one person; every man must share the burden.

In the next draft, labeled "first full early version of 'The Children's Hour' by Lillian Hellman Kober," the play has almost reached its final form, though she continued to tinker with some passages. Even after the play was mimeographed for the actors, and on the printer's galleys, she changed the time of the opening from December to April, gave Evelyn a lisp, and rewrote the Cardin and Karen farewell scene.

Miss Hellman worked over a play again and again until the characters were sharp and sound, the actions in their most telling order, and all ambiguities and superfluities eliminated. The clarity, precision, and dramatic impact in all her plays result from her power to perceive the error of her ways in the early drafts and to correct them before the director and actors take over. *The Children's Hour* is no exception.

V

Days to Come

With the success of *The Children's Hour*, the motion-picture scouts quickly trailed her. She had no great urge to leave New York, except to be with Hammett, but she was flattered to return to Hollywood as a full-fledged screenwriter, to work in the famous Samuel Goldwyn shop and at $2500 a week. She took a house in the Pacific Palisades and, as she recalls, spent "a lot of time making ice-cream sodas at the improbable soda bar in the basement."

Her life changed in many ways during this Hollywood year of 1935. Hearing her name on the lips of strangers and eager new friends was not always pleasant. "I was new enough to fame," she once said, "to think that the great fuss made over me meant that people were interested in me." She began a period of rambunctious drinking with old friends and new; somehow liquor seemed to make life easier. It made it easier when her mother died and for the first time she realized how deeply she had loved her, how much she would be missed.

She met Dorothy Parker again and began a friendship that was to endure until Miss Parker's death in 1967. It was she who introduced Miss Hellman to political activism, when they campaigned together for the passage of the Wagner Act and the revival of the Screen Writers' Guild. Together the pair attacked the citadel of Hollywood power, Sam Goldwyn. In characteristic Goldwyn fashion, he missed—or pretended to miss—the point of the companion arguments for their two causes. He insisted that he could not possibly support the Guild, but as a special favor to them, he would speak against the Wagner Act. Confronted with the Goldwyn logic for the first time, Miss Hellman's screams echoed through the Hollywood hills.

Unlike most of his employees, she was never terrified by Goldwyn. As Hammett once explained, "When Sam doesn't look at you, you cease to exist. Lillian solves that by just not looking at him." Apparently Goldwyn never noticed that though he always called her Lillian, she addressed him as Mr. Goldwyn. He was pleased with her work and by the end of the year had raised her salary to $3,500, for as many weeks as she wanted to work. His generosity along with her share of *The Children's Hour* profits and the then less greedy tax collectors brought a new way of life. She could support the comfortable living she enjoyed, move about as she chose, and buy what struck her fancy.

Dark Angel, her first film, adapted from Guy Bolton's play, was released in September, 1935. Starring Merle Oberon and Frederic March, it was described as "one of those agony films that may kill you, but it's going to get you sobbing first." A London reviewer reported that "it lasts three good, small handkerchiefs." In characteristic Hollywood fashion, Mordaunt Shairp, who had jolted New York in 1933 with his male homosexuals in *The Green Bay Tree*, was chosen as her collaborator.

Her second venture, *These Three*, was an adaptation of *The Children's Hour*. When Goldwyn acquired the script for \$50,000, the Hays Office would not allow him to use the title nor even announce that he had bought the play. In refurbishing it "for the great, right-thinking public of the screen," she substituted a love triangle for the Lesbianism. Mary, at the keyhole, catches Martha and Cardin in an embrace. She spreads the word; Karen's jealousy is aroused; a slander suit is brought to court and dismissed; Cardin loses his hospital post and Martha confesses to Karen that she had loved Cardin. Finally peace and understanding are restored, and Karen and Cardin are happily reunited in Vienna. If Miss Hellman had not developed a protective cynicism about Hollywood, she probably would not have tolerated these changes. When the picture was released in March, 1936, Joel McCrea, Merle Oberon, and Miriam Hopkins were praised for their "impressively restrained" performances and Bonita Granville, as Mary, for her "antidote to Shirley Temple." One critic called the "literary carpentry little short of brilliant."

Miss Hellman had begun a new play while she was still in Hollywood, and when she returned to New York in the spring of 1936, she took a month's layover in an Ohio town near Cleveland, studying the locale and absorbing atmospheric details for the new play. She stopped in New York only long enough to take an apartment at 14 East 75th Street before going to Cuba, where, in Hammett fashion, she could block out the world and write.

On June 15, a newspaper story datelined Havana announced that Miss Hellman was finishing a new play and that when she returned Dashiell Hammett might help in "doctoring" it. (Hammett as doctor was the reporter's invention.) She returned at the end of June on the Grace liner *Elena*, looked in on *The Children's Hour* which was now in its last weeks, then went to Connecticut with Hammett where they took a cottage on Tavern Island, off the coast at South Norwalk. It was a happy summer of work and play.

When *Days to Come* went into rehearsal in early November, the cards seemed stacked in her favor. Shumlin was in control. Florence Eldridge and William Harrigan had been engaged for the principal parts. The critics waited eagerly for the second play from a promising new dramatist, and the advance word hinted that she had written a strong social document to rival what Clifford Odets and the Group Theatre were doing. Only one quirk of opening-night scheduling raised some doubts: Kaufman and Hart's zany *You Can't Take It With You* was to open on December 14, 1936, and *Days to Come* on the 15th.

Doom pervaded the atmosphere almost as soon as the first-night curtain was up at the Vanderbilt Theatre. William Randolph Hearst and his party of ten filed out during the first act. Miss Hellman sought a half-escape by sending the doorman out for a bottle of brandy. With this rejuvenating elixir her spirits improved momentarily, then she was suddenly doubled over with pain that could not be attributed to the play. When the cramps subsided and she unclinched her fist, she discovered she had $9.06 change from her ten dollars. She was suffering from ninety-four cent brandy.

The long and painful evening in the theatre was not relieved by the gloom of Ralph Ingersoll's opening-night party. (Ingersoll was later to become the editor of *PM*, a New York newspaper to which Miss Hellman contributed the name as well as financial support.) Even Hammett thought the play was terrible. When she subdued her drunken tears to remind him that earlier he had said it was a good play, he mumbled that he had changed his mind and left the party.

The critics struggled to praise her dramatic powers, her compassion, her sensitivity to the battle between capital and labor, the "burning intensity of her utterance," yet they could not strike a balance in her favor. Too many awkward questions had to be raised: What was the play really about? Were our sympathies pulled in too many directions? Audiences were equally troubled. The play survived for seven performances.

Days to Come was a failure, but not because its essential

dramaturgy was different from *The Children's Hour* or different from the later plays. It was simply managed less expertly. The hints and signs were revealed in Ibsen-like fashion, a bit at a time, no more than needed, no more than easily grasped. Yet the manipulative hand of the playwright came into view too frequently. The characters, though vigorously committeed to their beliefs, seemed bound by the playwright's harness rather than their own. The crucial confrontations, though never sidestepped, often became strident, embarrassingly simplified, and too dependent on knives and guns. The audience was asked to invest with the good guys and decry the bad, yet too often they were confused and uncertain about where to stake their allegiance. This frustration might have been more tolerable with a dramatist less occupied with good and evil.

The story of *Days to Come* centers on strikers and strikebreakers at the Rodman brush factory in Callom, Ohio, a small town two hundred miles from Cleveland. Arthur Rodman and his sister Cora have inherited the business from their father and for years have lived as one happy family with their workers. Now the brush business has deteriorated. Rodman has been forced to cut wages. A unionist, Leo Whalen, has organized the workers and persuaded them to strike. Henry Ellicott, Rodman's lawyer, has imported a trainload of strikebreakers, led by Sam Wilkie.

Whalen knows the hazards of allowing the workers to be tempted into violence by the strikebreakers. He cannot, however, control all the participants. Wilkie has stationed two thugs, Easter and Mossie, in the Rodman house to protect the family. They are more grotesquely vulgar than necessary. Mossie constantly cracks his knuckles; Easter plays with knives. They are constitutionally incapable of following Wilkie's admonition to act "as if you've been in a house with a bathroom before." They burn the furniture with their cigarettes and sprinkle the floor with their ashes. We are well prepared for their violence at the end of the first scene of the second act. Easter accuses Mossie of cheating at cards. Mossie cracks his knuckles and challenges Easter to come over and get the dough. Easter pulls his knife and throws it at Mossie. The stage direction could have been lifted from a Hammett detective story: "Mossie screams softly, pushes with his feet from the ground as he topples from the chair. For a second Easter stands watching him, listening to the two soft groans. The groans cease and Easter suddenly begins to move. He turns out the lamp nearest him, shuts the library door, and moves to center doors. As he starts to turn the key, the door is violently pushed open by Wilkie. Easter steps back, frightened." Wilkie knows what to do. And he speaks like a Hammett character: "Take that knife out of him. Take him out and dump him. Dump him in the right place—with no fancy work. . . . If it goes wrong, you slob, it goes wrong for you. I'll turn you in myself if I have to—and with plenty of story to keep me in the clear. Do you understand me?" Easter understands and the curtain comes down.

The right place for the body is in the alley outside Whalen's temporary union headquarters. The right time, though not by calculation, is when Julie Rodman, Arthur's wife, is visiting Whalen. Early in the play we have learned that Julie Rodman is an emancipated woman intent on breaking out of the cocoon of conventionality. She has now fallen in love with Leo Whalen and has come to his office. Earlier, too, we have learned that Wilkie is having her trailed. With Mossie's body planted outside Whalen's office with Julie Rodman inside, a showdown is inevitable. Whalen knows he will be incriminated and sent to jail. He saves Mrs. Rodman by pushing her out the rear entrance. She races home, but when she arrives, in the next scene, she announces to Ellicott and Wilkie that she was with Whalen. Wilkie knows that he holds the winning cards. Her story won't stand up. Everyone will believe that Mossie found them together and that Whalen killed him. And with Whalen in jail, no one can restrain the strikers; we hear their guns as the second-act curtain comes down.

The next morning the consequences are quickly revealed. Firth's daughter has been killed. Firth, the only employee we ever meet, has been devoted to the family; he made brushes for Rodman's father. His tragedy is further compounded. Unable to have a child of his own, he had adopted the girl who is now dead. Rodman, convinced that he, not the strikebreakers, is the real murderer, orders Wilkie and his thugs to depart. He finds little comfort in knowing that the strike has been broken, that the workers, desperate for food, must return to the factory.

Rodman's torment is not concluded. Julie confesses her visit to Whalen. She has never loved Rodman. Over the years she has tried to escape, with an affair with Ellicott, with her trips abroad. Still a kind of respect and dependence has developed which now binds her to him. She has not known, but learns now, that they are both trapped by Ellicott. Rodman has had to borrow from him to support her trips and to keep the factory going. Ellicott persuaded him to call the strikebreakers. Cora, Rodman's sister, has also disturbed the domestic scene. She owns half the factory and has insisted on staying on in the family home in spite of the mutual hate between her and Julie. In the days to come, peace cannot prevail in the Rodman household, even with the workers back on the job.

Miss Hellman must have perceived that she had the makings of a strong play with the substance of the third act. Family loves, hates, and suspicions mixed with a bit of American business greed and an outside catalyst could make a powerful drama. Some of the seeds of *The Little Foxes*, her next play, were planted in the third act of *Days to Come*.

Her remarks on *Days to Come* in the Introduction to *Four Plays* are helpful in understanding the play and why it failed. She spoiled what could have been a good play because she returned to the "amateur's mistake: everything you think and feel must be written *this* time, because you may never have another chance to write it." Her personal feelings were too strongly involved: "I knew a woman like Cora and I hated her, and *that* hate had to go in the play; I knew a woman like Julie, I pitied her, and *that* pity had to go in the play; I had been raised with the Ellicotts of the world, and what I felt about them had to go in the play, too; I knew Leo Whalen and I wanted to say how much I respected men who work for other men. I wanted to say too much." Faults in the production also contributed to its failure. "The confusion in the script confused the best director [Shumlin] in the theatre, who, in turn, managed to confuse one of its most inadequate casts. (There were exceptions, of course.) . . . I do not believe actors break plays, or make them, either. And nothing would have affected the play if I had done what the writer must do: kick and fight his way through until the whole is good."

Certainly Miss Hellman did try to say too much, crowded in too many melodramatic episodes, labored the explanations in the third act, and struggled for hyperbolic characterizations. Rodman need not have been so helplessly ineffective in managing his business and his household, his wife Julie so blindly seeking her own romantic fortune, his sister Cora so hateful, selfish, and insensitive, Firth so pitiful and so humbly loyal to Rodman, Whalen so righteous and noble, Ellicott so ruthless, and Wilkie and his thugs so monstrous.

Almost everything appears a bit overdone, too explicit, and exposed too blatantly. We are not permitted to contribute our share in detecting the evidence and building the story. Miss Hellman does all the work. The basic facts about the household and about the strike are revealed in an old-fashioned expository scene between Hannah, the housekeeper, and Lucy, a servant; then the dramatis personae are introduced in order, almost as if we were checking off the program.

Miss Hellman may have intended, as she once said, that the strike was to be only a background, that the play was to be a "study of innocent people on both sides who are drawn into conflicts and events far beyond their comprehension." It never achieves that goal, though it certainly is more than a melodrama of the class struggle. She is too fascinated with the humanity of her characters to cast them simply as symbols for capital and labor. Each has his own compulsions. Mrs. Rodman must seek her fulfillment as a woman regardless of the consequences. Whatever his ineptitude, Rodman always means well. Whalen is the practical labor leader, yet always the idealist. Cora is born to be an acidulous old maid.

However confused and diffuse the total effect, *Days to Come* has many qualities of her first and of her later plays. Shifting tensions permeate the atmosphere. We sense the unresolved discords, the sultry hates and murderous impulses that lie below the surface. The utterances may often be quiet and decorous, yet there's a burning intensity behind them. As Joseph Wood Krutch commented, "Miss Hellman is not a specialist in abnormal psychology or in Marxian interpretation of society. She is a specialist in hate and frustration, a student of helpless rage, an articulator of inarticulate loathings."

Had she been more deeply involved with the class struggle, she might have sought a Group Theatre production for her play. They would have sharpened her message. She had seen *Awake and Sing* and *Waiting for Lefty* and admired Odets, but she was temperamentally indisposed to join any group obsessed with a cause. Then and later she placed her plays, however political, with conventional commercial managements. Someone else could buck the Broadway system.

The short life of *Days to Come* did not enliven the 1936 Christmas season. Only snatches from the critics could be read with pleasure: praise for her fearless intensity, for her Ibsen-like unfolding of the story, and, particularly flattering, the suggestion that Andrew Rodman and Julie Rodman seemed Chekhovian. Unfortunately, the more abundant comments centered on the lack of a central idea, on her concessions to melodramatic sensation, on her inability "to make a spiritual tragedy out of a labor impasse." Even the left-wing press complained. The *New Masses* (December 29, 1936) noted the duality of focus in her attempt "to give dramatic life to the twin phenomena of capitalist society, the outbreak of class strife and the decay of human relations in the bourgeois stratum." The *Daily Worker* (December 18, 1936) deplored her treatment of the struggle from the point of view of rotting capitalists. Even a sympathetic audience could not enjoy "the pallid and vexatious mutterings of these disgusting people." She could have made a great play with a chorus of workers who reminded the audience that workers must sacrifice everything to attain victory.

The notes and early drafts for *Days to Come* are not extensive. Perhaps its failure can be attributed partly to her incomplete background preparation and settling on a final version too hastily. Thirteen pages of loose notes contain possible character names: "Rodman or Blagden or Merrill." Possible titles: *House Upon a Rock*, *This Was My Home*, *Shadow of a Cloud*, and *Days to Come*. (From Ecclesiastes, II, 16: "For there is no remembrance of the wise more than of the fool forever; seeing that which now is in the days to come shall all be forgotten. And how dieth the wise man? as the fool.") Short character sketches: "Hannah—Went to school with Cora. Cora—Was a disagreeable, neurotic, complaining child. Papa didn't like her." Notes on the factory and the workers, some of which must have come from her on-the-spot observations: "Factory was nice, old-fashioned red brick and clean inside. Brushes sell 5c to $40. Hair comes from Chinese and Russian boars. 1851—grandfather established the factory. All American workmen. Nicely dressed people; really less yokel than Cleveland. Skilled worker $24 a week." On one page, she drew a ground-plan sketch of the Rodman living room.

In a small school notebook she listed other character and town names, possible speeches, and comments on what would appear to have been a first draft of the play, now lost. Somewhere Cora might say, "Nymphomania is on the increase." And Wilkie, about the strikebreakers, "I admit they don't look like anything Oscar Wilde would want." Wilkie's line is used, Cora's not. Her notes suggest that she was troubled about the intricacies of the characters, the ordering of events, about centering attention properly. For example: "The whole Whalen-Julie business should not be played up too much or it will have a false importance since it comes to nothing in the end." She was more uncertain than she was about *The Children's Hour* and the later plays.

The two early drafts now extant are remarkably close to the final version though she did cut and tighten, particularly Julie's final confession and Wilkie's concluding speeches. Perhaps if she had given *Days to Come* the attention she lavished on the later plays, it would have commanded a place among her major works.

Harsh as the critics were, none suggested that *The Children's Hour* was beginner's luck and that she should abandon playwriting, and with her Goldwyn contract still in force, she limited her dejection to the holiday season. As always, Hammett's friendship and good humor helped. On December 30, 1936, he wrote from Princeton, "Dear Lilushka—Wolcott Gibbs sent me a dollar check for the Raised Eyebrow Department [in the *New Yorker*] Colony Club contribution, so I'm going into the New Year well-heeled financially as well as with the knowledge that I can still sell stuff."

In February she returned to Hollywood, assigned to do the screen version of Sidney Kingsley's *Dead End*. If her own social document had failed, she had another chance with Kingsley's. With the original Dead End Kids, a Hollywood reconstruction of Norman Bel Geddes' waterfront scene, and with selected fresh garbage floated on Goldwyn's East River each morning, it seemed certain to be one of the major motion pictures of the year. Only one difficulty was encountered in the filming and this was William Wyler's worry rather than hers: the kids had difficulty remembering her "cleansed" lines and frequently reverted to the original. The writing and shooting went quickly. She returned to New York on July 30, went to the *Dead End* opening at the Rivoli on August 24, and the next day sailed on the *Normandie*.

VI

War in Spain

The newspapers announced that she planned to be away for two to five months, visiting Russia, Spain, and Paris. She wanted to see the results of the Russian experiment at first-hand, and she had been invited to a Moscow theatre festival. She also wanted to visit the battlefields in Spain, to experience for herself the horrors of the Fascist menace, and to give what advice she could on the filming of a documentary on the war. She had joined Archibald MacLeish and John Dos Passos in a film company called Contemporary Historians, Inc. Their first film was to be directed by Joris Ivens, the Dutch photographer, Hemingway was to write and speak the narration, and Virgil Thompson and Marc Blitzstein were to provide the musical score.

She had urged Hammett to go abroad with her, but he refused. Not only did he not share her passion for local color, he was skeptical of her missions. He had met MacLeish at Princeton during the spring and had written to her, "your friend MacLeish is a stuffed shirt if I ever saw one." He was sure she had no uncontrollable desire to see the Russian theatre. She just couldn't refuse when they invited her at their expense. "You'll see three plays and I'll bet you'll leave all of them by intermission," he wrote to her in Paris. "Someone will give a party and the cultivated guests will besiege you with questions about your work methods, about your theatre experiences. You'll say you never have had any, and you'll believe what you're saying. The truth is you don't like the theatre except the times when you're in a room by yourself putting the play on paper."

In 1937, Hammett sensed better than she her love-hate complex about the theatre. In 1969, she wrote in *An Unfinished Woman:*

> I know as little [now] as I knew then about the conflict that would keep me hard at work in a world that is not my world, although it has been my life. I have had great benefits from the theatre, but I have wandered through it as if I were a kind of stranger. Except when I was writing, or the plays were in rehearsal: then all the natural instincts are at work the way some people play a musical instrument without a lesson and others, even as children, understand an engine. Maybe it happened because I started out wanting to write novels and didn't have much interest in the theatre or movies: maybe my own nature does not fit the rushing strong tones of the theatre, although certainly my own tones are often shrill; maybe because I am not good at collaboration, the essence of the theatre; maybe because I like fame, but don't like, and am no good at, its requirements; or maybe vanity of any kind other than my own seems to me at first funny and at last boring. But most of all, the theatre is not a natural world for those who question whatever is meant by glamour.

Fortunately her revulsion at the marquee glitter did not keep her from playwriting, from honoring the collaborative demands. She could tolerate, if not join, the hyperbolic, heart-on-the-sleeve camaraderie of the theatre crowd.

For the crossing and the first days in Paris, she enjoyed the companionship of Dorothy Parker and her husband Alan Campbell. Dorothy Parker introduced her to Hemingway, to the most fashionable and sophisticated expatriates, Sara and Gerald Murphy, and through them she met the leading writers and artists. With Hemingway and Dorothy Parker she spent many evenings in the Left Bank bistros. Her encounters with Hemingway never ran smoothly. One night when he wanted her to read the proofs of *To Have and Have Not,* she made the mistake of saying some pages seemed to be missing. He had botched the job of cutting, but he didn't want to be told. As Dorothy Parker explained, "You're not allowed to think a comma could be in the wrong place." Later at a dinner in Spain she offended him again by refusing to go out on the balcony to see the beautiful sight, Franco's forces bombarding the telephone building. And the following year, when she and Hammett were with him in the Stork Club, Hemingway became enraged when Hammett refused to play his game of bending a spoon between the muscles of his upper and lower arm, presumably to illustrate his power as a writer.

In spite of the sparks that often flew when she met Hemingway, *The Spanish Earth* documentary turned out well. When she first attended a private showing at Frederic March's in March, 1938—it had been released the previous August—she recognized that it was Hemingway's narration added to the gruesome unposed shots of the fighting in the suburbs of Madrid that gave the film its special power. The critics had been right in calling it "the most powerful and moving documentary film ever screened."

The train journey from Paris to Moscow was not uneventful. Somewhere between Berlin and Warsaw her trunk disappeared and when it finally arrived, all her bottles had been emptied and her books mutilated. Moscow did not provide any compensatory delights. She tried to like the theatre, if for no other reason than to prove Hammett wrong. She did not succeed. Only one production—*Hamlet* with a fat, lethargic Prince—offered anything unusual. None of her letters of introduction had been answered, and her American friends either didn't know or were unwilling to tell her what was going on in the country. Not until later did she learn that she had arrived during one of the ugliest purges. She returned to Paris, by way of Prague, to prepare for her adventure into Spain. She was delighted to find a letter from Hammett waiting for her in Paris, reporting that *Dead End* was doing terrific business with lots of nice things being said about her contribution, that he had been divorced in Mexico, and that Al Lichtman's chemin-de-fer had been doing poorly since she left Hollywood. How remote and inconsequential all of this seemed as she departed for the front.

She arrived in Valencia in early October, 1937, and just three days later she was caught in an air raid. When everyone began running, she ran too, until a policeman pushed her under a bench. No bombs dropped near her, but she learned later that in the port area sixty-three people had been killed by the Italian bombers.

For two weeks she wandered around Valencia among the shattered buildings, trying to understand, trying to give what comfort she could. Everywhere lonely figures sat in the sun, aimlessly staring into the distance. In the evening they tramped off in search of a shelter for the long night hours. Ghost figures in a ghost town. With Gustav Regler, a German army officer turned novelist who had fled Germany and was now in the International Brigade, she visited the recovery hospital at Benicasim. Here she saw the damage to human lives. When the patients learned she was a visiting American, they pleaded with her to tell Roosevelt the story. If he knew they were fighting for freedom, trying to stop Fascism in its tracks, he would send guns and planes. She felt pitifully helpless, when she had to tell them she had no influence with Roosevelt.

On October 22, an official guide drove her to Madrid. The combination of precipitous mountain roads and Luis' foolhardy courage in passing everything in sight unnerved her. Several times she tried to take the wheel, but Luis insisted that she was too old and unacquainted with the advances in automotive engineering. When they reached Madrid after dark, a note from Hemingway asked her to join him for dinner. She chose bed instead. The next night she did join him, at the apartment of an English journalist where they feasted on a tough piece of beef Hemingway's bullfighting friends had given him. This was the night she refused to view the bombardment, yet risked her neck to make a broadcast.

She had planned to go to the front, at the urging of the Press Office, but Otto Simon, a journalist who had fled Germany after he wrote *The Brown Book of the Hitler Terror*, persuaded her that nothing was to be gained from such an adventure. For two weeks she explored the plaguelike destruction of Madrid, wept over the rubble of University City, lent her voice and presence, feeble as it might be, to the cause. She spoke to the International Brigade people, made recordings, visited nurseries and hospitals, and promised to carry the message back to America. On November 5, she returned to Valencia. She was glad to be back. The air raids were less frightening than the nightly bombardments in Madrid.

A week later she began her homeward journey via Barcelona, Toulouse, Paris, and London. Fresh from the war zone, she found British smugness intolerable. At one party of smart, well-heeled Englishmen, she became so infuriated at the talk of "not being able to fathom the issues" that when one man asked her what side she had visited, she turned over her chair as she rushed from the table. Back in her hotel, racing for her bed, she fell and broke her ankle. Now she remembers those days when her ankle was mending as the "root-time of my turn toward the radical movements of the late thirties. (I was late: by that period many intellectuals had made the turn. So many, in fact, that some were even turning another way.) It saddens me now to admit that my political convictions were never very radical, in the true, best, serious sense."

If she was distressed by the lack of concern and understanding in Britain, she found little more sympathy at home. When Walter Winchell asked her to contribute a piece on Spain for his column, Hearst refused to permit his King Features to syndicate it. (It finally appeared as "Day in Spain" in the *New Republic*, April 13, 1938.) She wrote an unpublished story, "Richard Harding Davis, 1938" about a New York *Times* correspondent who was covering the Spanish War. On the manuscript she noted that the view from her window on Tavern Island off the coast of South Norwalk looked like the port of Valencia. Before settling down to serious work, she also took a momentary whirl at theatre reviewing for *Time*. Her first piece (December 13, 1937) on Thomas Job's adaptation of *Barchester Towers* was her last. Perhaps she was too harsh, even for *Time*, when she wrote, "Ina Claire's fashionable audience gave up giggling during the second act and sat back to chat in peace."

Hammett's Christmas letter reminded her that she should not waste her efforts on minor literary endeavors. He was on the wagon and working industriously at his "new fable of how Nick loved Nora and Nora loved Nick." Maybe there were better writers in the world, but "nobody ever invented a more insufferably smug pair of characters. They can't take that away from me, even for $40,000." She should follow his example and get to work.

VII

The Little Foxes

Although not fired with any burning ambition, as she once confessed, and still sore from the sting of the *Days to Come* failure, she might have preferred to desert the theatre, but she couldn't. "I guess I must want to write plays, I am always fascinated by what can be done in a little space," she told an interviewer. "You always do the things you want to do." Whatever line the play might take, she knew it must carry some social significance, even if unrelated to the sights and sounds of Spain that still tortured her. Every man must bear his share of the world's guilt. She had begun to speculate on *The Little Foxes* on her journey out of Spain and her forced detention in London. She dug among the skeletons in her family closet, into the American past in the South that she had known as a child. Here was greed and evil and hate to be exposed. For too long the old South had gloried in the sweet smell of Confederate magnolia blossoms.

If she needed a text for the play, other than what was imbedded in her childhood memories, it could have been taken from Hammett's *The Thin Man*. He wrote about his Jorgensen family, "There doesn't seem to be a single one in the family—now that Mimi's turned against her Chris—who has even the slightest reasonably friendly feeling for any of the others, and yet there's something very alike in all of them." Her debt to Dorothy Parker is more explicit. Miss Parker suggested the Biblical text from which the title derived: "Take us the foxes, the little foxes, that spoil the vines, for our vines have tender grapes." (Song of Solomon, II, 15. Five years later John Van Druten found his title, *The Voice of the Turtle*, in the twelfth verse.)

She did not begin writing immediately. While the characters and actions were forming in her mind, she became an avid researcher, studying all the books, magazines, and newspapers of 1900 that the New York libraries could supply. She could have written a comprehensive social history of the period from the 108 single-spaced pages of notes that filled her looseleaf ledger. There were sections on The Negro, Cotton, Industrial South, Agricultural South, Historical Backgrounds, and Bibliography. Among the items of incidental intelligence: The first automobile ad appeared in a national magazine in 1900; Christian Science had 80,000 followers; John D. Rockefeller succeeded Charles Evans Hughes as leader of the Men's Bible Class at the Fifth Avenue Baptist Church; Andrew Carnegie's business motto, "Put all your eggs in one basket and then watch the basket"; there were 800,000 telephones in the U.S.; Oscar Wilde's name was mentioned in at least 900 known sermons, 1895–1900; Olga Nethersole and her manager were arrested following a performance of *Sappho*. There were notes on hotels and hotel prices, on cotton prices and cotton mills, on domestic interiors, and there were pages of common names. Although few of the items were used in the play, they gave her the solid background she needed to write with authority. And because her research was so thorough, social historians have praised the play as a remarkable documentary of a Southern town at the turn of the century.

Another small spiral notebook contains other items: "Maybe the problem is to find one large deal which will clean out the town and at the same time connect with, and lead them to, a place like Chicago." This idea is modified, and part of it abandoned. There is a section on land schemes and building schemes and a note on cotton: "Speculation from 1885–92; collapse came in '92; low price of cotton from 1891–1900; 1896 started to rise." Also some items that appear in the first draft of the play: "syphilis in the girl; a shooting brother; free water power and electricity; to attic and slave quarters."

Before beginning to write she took a quick trip to Hollywood in February, stopping in New Orleans to visit her aunts. Hammett was so impatient for their reunion that he wired her in New Orleans, "It is raining here but only on the streets where they don't know you are coming. Dotty expects you for dinner and I love you." They had a sweet month together, and when she returned to New York, she was ready to give herself completely to the new play.

By early summer she had completed a first draft of two acts, although at one moment she had thought of putting the play aside to follow another scenario that intrigued her, the first sketchy notions of what was to become *Watch on the Rhine*. The play was to be set in a Midwestern town. What would happen, she wondered, if a titled European couple, on their way to the West coast, were thrown into the home of a wealthy American and forced to adapt their meticulous and elegant routine of living to the wild rushing about of the Americans. Unable to get beyond this one idea, she returned to her avaricious Southerners. Hammett had come to Tavern Island late in the spring, and Herman Shumlin was visiting the weekend she wrote curtain to the second act. Confident that she had two splendid acts, she gave them each a copy to read.

When she awoke the next morning, there were two notes under her door. Shumlin had been called back to the city. He might or might not return; he had taken his dog with him.

Hammett wrote, "It's too hot to return to the city. Me, now, I go to bed. Me say nothing velly wrong with play if only Miss Lillian would write 'em and not be so busy with blackamoor chitchat. Missy better stop writing blackamoor chitchat." She went for a swim and thought of drowning herself.

For a week she fussed at everything except the play, but try as she would, the Hubbard family, as if coached by Pirandello, pursued her. Finally she submitted to their demands, tore up the manuscript and began again, resolved to concentrate on the Hubbards and avoid the chitchat.

When Shumlin read the completed new *Foxes* in early November, he immediately put his production machinery in motion, aiming at an opening in early 1939. With so little lead time, it was sheer luck that he could assemble such strong box-office names as Tallulah Bankhead, Patricia Collinge, and Frank Conroy to head the company. Rehearsals began on January 9, and by the end of the month they were ready to move to Baltimore for a tryout. No delays were required for rewriting. When Miss Hellman released a script to Shumlin or later to Kermit Bloomgarden, most of her work was finished. She had to write in private, not in the frantic and public atmosphere of a rehearsal hall or in sleepless hours between rehearsals. As both Shumlin and Bloomgarden have testified, she spared the nerves and purses of a producer by providing a finished script at the beginning.

She did not, however, abandon her play when it took to the stage. She followed the rehearsals intently, ready to protect her text from actors wishing to be authors. It was a stormy period, as she remembers; "Almost everybody fought with somebody." Actors believed in the "civil rights of something called temperament," but she could match them. She had been a strong-minded child, and in 1939 had grown into a strong-minded woman. She complained and fussed and drank as much as Miss Bankhead, if with somewhat different results. "While a mint julep made Tallulah's temper flashing and often attractive, it often fixed me in a kind of gloom whose quiet was broken by sudden swings of anger, more unpleasant, I guess, because they were preceded by soft politeness."

Of the opening-night performance at Ford's Theatre in Baltimore on February 2, 1939, she remembered little; of the party that followed she had vivid memories. Among the guests were Tallulah's father, Speaker of the House, her uncle, the Senator from Alabama, Dorothy Parker and her husband, Hammett, the Gerald Murphys, her father, and several unidentified hangers-on and strays. Tallulah's father and uncle livened the party with their songs, partly to escape Max Hellman, who repeatedly tried to explain that Lillian's mother had come from the town next to theirs in Alabama. Dorothy Parker was trapped in a corner by someone, her "round eyes trying to stay open in what people always took to be sympathetic interest." When Miss Hellman refused to rescue her, she grabbed her arm: "OK, but promise me something for the future. Promise that you will have engraved on my funeral stone these words: 'If you can read this, you've come too close.'" Hammett, heavy with alcohol, was giving a literary lecture to a stranger from across the hall. Among the unidentified ladies who wandered in, one kept explaining that heroin could not be habit-forming because she had been taking it for years.

Miss Bankhead's recollections did not coincide with Miss Hellman's: "No one fought with anyone. It was the most pleasant experience I ever had in the theatre." And about the party, she insisted that "Daddy never sang in this life," the unidentified guests were figments of Miss Hellman's imagination, in fact there had been little celebrating because they were still busy trying to cut fifteen minutes from the last act. Miss Bankhead's memory appears faulty. The prerehearsal text is almost identical with the final script.

The next day's reviews took the line common to critics viewing a tryout. They perceived the strengths, as they also discovered the weaknesses that needed to be remedied before the play reached New York. In spite of expert and dynamic writing, the central theme needed to be clarified. In spite of "clean-cut impersonations and dialogue" that at times had both "bark and bite," it seemed like a "lot of pother over things remote and inconsequential." Although Bankhead was often most eloquent and persuasive, she encouraged the suspicion that "she is confusing Regina with Shakespeare's Lady Macbeth."

While the company rehearsed the next day and ran their second performance, Miss Hellman stayed in the hotel dining room with Dorothy Parker and the Murphys. It was a mad day of zany jokes, liquor, and weird culinary concoctions. She remembers that "a whiskey sour and a dry martini stirred into baked Maryland crabmeat seemed a great creation." When the troupe moved to Pittsburgh, she trailed them a few days late. Kermit Bloomgarden, then Shumlin's assistant, recalls that during those stormy days Miss Hellman was never to be found. Even when the play opened in New York on February 15, 1939, and was clearly destined for a long run, she avoided the theatre. "Most certainly I wanted success," she recalls, "but most certainly I snarled at it. It took me years to find that I was frightened of what it did to people, and instinctively, I did not trust myself to handle it."

Again, as with *The Children's Hour*, an engrossing play was supported by striking performances. Atkinson said that it would be "hard to find another cast so perfectly chosen and so thoroughly trained." Most reviewers centered on Bankhead's Regina. She finally had a part worthy of her remarkable talents, "the finest thing she's done in this country." Others thought that Patricia Collinge's brilliant portrayal of Birdie ran Bankhead a close second. Howard Bay's setting conveyed "the dark stealthiness of the story." There was one dissenting voice. Otis Ferguson (*New Republic*, April 12, 1939) found only "bombast and embarrassment" in all the actors and Bankhead laboring under the "conviction that acting is great according to how low a girl can go in the baritone register." Too often she sounded like a "Wagner trombone section."

The public ignored the minority opinion and kept the play running for 410 performances. Not only did Bankhead possess the aggressive bitchiness needed for Regina, her flamboyant personality attracted audiences. She once called herself "the champion of excess," and according to Richard Maney, interviewing her was "like taking your finger out of a dike." Throughout the run of the play her extravagant behavior was widely and regularly reported. No actress in recent years has matched her in providing publicists with flashy copy.

Miss Bankhead was not the first choice for the role. According to Shumlin, Miss Hellman had approached Ina Claire, but she was bound by a Hollywood contract. He then sent the script to Judith Anderson; she hated it. When he next tried Bankhead, she needed no persuasion. She loved the part and immediately canceled the remainder of the pre-Broadway tour of a play called *I Am Different*. According to Shumlin, no actress ever attacked a role with such fervor and such total commitment, and, remarkable for Bankhead, her enthusiasm did not diminish until a few weeks after the Broadway opening.

No bond developed between Hellman and Bankhead. Their common heritage in the South and their professional respect for each other promoted no more than a cool and polite tolerance. Even that was strained when Miss Hellman asked the cast to do a benefit for the Spanish Loyalists and Miss Bankhead refused. After the play closed in New York on February 3, 1940, and Bankhead proposed a benefit for Finnish Relief in Washington, Miss Hellman, supported by Shumlin, refused. She insisted that charity for that "lovable little pro-Nazi Republic" would give a "dangerous impetus to the war spirit in this country."

During the run of *The Little Foxes* Miss Hellman was saddled with two irritating labels: "woman playwright" and "fellow traveler." One was simply a discriminatory annoyance; the other carried damaging consequences, as she was to learn later. Dorothy Thompson's Valentine Day's column in 1940 identified her with the left-wingers: "To the Communist

Party of America—'The Little Foxes.'" When Joe McCarthy later took over the battle, Miss Thompson's comment would seem remarkably tame.

She resented being called a "woman playwright," even if George Jean Nathan (*Newsweek*, February 27, 1939) found her dramaturgy infinitely superior to that of Susan Glaspell, her grip on character more firm than that of Lulu Vollmer, and Rachel Crothers' plays "water-colored parlor tracts" by comparison. There are none among the "whole kit and caboodle, whose work shows so courageous and unflinching adherence to higher and better standards of drama." *Time* extended the comparison to Zona Gale, Zoë Akins, and Clare Boothe; Miss Hellman was the only woman now writing powerful dramas. One now forgets that the thirties was a lush period for female playwrights. At the prize-giving time at the end of the season, with such stiff competition as Barry's *The Philadelphia Story*, Anderson's *Knickerbocker Holiday*, Behrman's *No Time for Comedy*, Odets' *Rocket to the Moon*, Saroyan's *My Heart's in the Highlands*, and Sherwood's *Abe Lincoln in Illinois*, she held her own against the men. Sherwood's play won the Pulitzer Prize, but she was in the running; and though she did not win the Critics' Circle Award, she got six votes against five for *Abe Lincoln*. Three-fourths of the votes were required to win. Later the Circle changed the rules, providing for a simple majority if after five ballots no play had received three-fourths. Perhaps if she had belonged to the dominant sex, they would have changed the rules that year.

She won with the public and with the critics and not because of Bankhead and the other players, though they helped. She won with a taut and biting drama of greed and avarice, with a scornful parable of the ruthless rise of the Industrial South, with an indictment of rugged individualism, with a vibrant exercise in malice, an adult horror play, and above all, as Joseph Wood Krutch remarked, because she possessed the Ancient Mariner's gift, "one stays in one's seat because one cannot choose but hear."

The spacious and elegant Hubbard living room with its

expensive furniture and decorations, everything the best, and with two Negro servants tidying up and setting the after-dinner port, informs us immediately that we will follow the fortunes of affluent Southerners. Whatever drives and frustrations might propel the inhabitants of this establishment, they do not evolve from economic deprivation. Miss Hellman's human and political sympathies may be aligned with the oppressed, with the pathetic poor, but she does not write their lives into her plays. She chooses instead the lives of the favored few who accept their status as their due and who are oblivious of social guilt.

From Addie and Cal we learn that a family dinner for an honored guest is concluding, that Miss Regina commands the household, that her daughter, Miss Zan, is their favorite. Miss Birdie slips in from the dining room, leading the parade of the dramatis personae. Gay and excited from the party, she whirls wildly and aimlessly from one subject to another. Their guest, the cultured Mr. Marshall, has reminded her of her aristocratic girlhood, when her mother and father went to Europe just to listen to music. Cal must race to her house for her music album, so she can play for Mr. Marshall and show him the autographed picture of Wagner.

Her wild chatter is interrupted by Oscar, her husband. He countermands her request for the music. She has been boring Mr. Marshall with her magpie chatter. She must get herself in hand and sit down. Leo appears, announcing too loudly, "Mama! Papa! They are coming in now." Already we have invested our sympathies with Birdie, deplore Oscar's brutality and sense that their son is a bit of an oaf.

The dining-room doors are pushed back, and we meet the other Hubbards: Regina Giddens, a handsome beauty of forty; her daughter Alexandra, a delicate-looking seventeen-year-old; Benjamin Hubbard, a large man of fifty-five with a jovial face; and their guest, William Marshall from Chicago, a pleasant self-possessed business man of forty-five. With the exception of Alexandra, they are all strong figures. Miss Hellman does not waste her time with weaklings. She has invariably favored the aggressive, the self-assured. That the abused and helpless Birdie was singled out as a moving portrait proved an embarrassment. She had thought Birdie simply silly and pathetic.

Regina has ordered their best port, and even Alexandra is to have a glass, her first, in honor of the occasion. Marshall is impressed by their Southern hospitality. They eat better and drink better than people in Chicago. He wonders how they manage to find time for business; perhaps they all live together. Regina is amused by the suggestion. Ben lives next door, Oscar and Birdie in the next square; her husband is a banker, now ill and at Johns Hopkins but expected home; Leo works for him. At the mention of his name, Leo feels obligated to speak. He's proud to keep his "eye on things" while his uncle is away. Leo invariably says the wrong thing. Marshall has not forgotten Birdie. He's ready to hear her play. Still frightened, she begs off; she's developed a headache. Regina relieves the awkwardness by offering her daughter as a substitute. Alexandra is willing, but only if Birdie will join her in a duet. Oscar realizes he must shift his ground. Birdie shouldn't be so stubborn; can't she see that Mr. Marshall wants her to play?

Birdie obeys and as they go to the piano, Marshall again expresses his admiration for the Southern aristocrats who have kept together and kept what belonged to them. If he intended a touch of irony, Ben missed it. He must tell him truthfully that they have not kept together and have not kept what belonged to them. Birdie is the only aristocrat among them. Her family owned Lionnet, a great plantation with the best cotton land in the South; but her brothers, like all Southern aristocrats, were too high-toned to adapt to the postwar economy. Twenty years ago the Hubbards took over their land, their cotton, and their daughter. Ben has aroused memories in the others. Leo remembers that his grandfather was once governor of the state, and Birdie dreamily recalls her childhood.

Her family were good people. Her father was killed in the war, "a fine soldier, Mr. Marshall. A fine man." Birdie has been at the mercy of the Hubbards too long; only in her reveries can she find peace.

Regina deplores these "ancient family tales." Ben must stop boring Mr. Marshall. She's too harsh; he simply wants their future business partner to be informed about them. Now we know why they've broken out the best port, and Marshall prefers to stick with the port and their fine company until train time. Their business was settled in the afternoon. Ben bows to his wishes; even he recognizes that "money isn't all. Not by three shots," and he invokes an old Southern custom, the last drink as a toast, to show that you're still on your feet. Their "Southern cotton mills *will be* the Rembrandts of investment. So I give you the firm of Hubbard Sons and Marshall, Cotton Mills, and to it a long and prosperous life." Marshall joins in the toast, though his smile suggests that he is not taken in by the palaver. When Leo and Alexandra depart to drive him to the depot and the men to see him to the carriage, Regina and Birdie are left alone.

With Ibsen-like precision, Miss Hellman has dispensed the details naturally, gradually, sparingly, moment by moment, always whetting our appetite for the next morsel and filling in the portraits as the action unfolds. We are comfortable with Miss Hellman in the theatre. She keeps our curiosity alive without straining credibility.

Regina throws up her arms and laughs happily: "And there, Birdie, goes the man who has opened the door to our future." She's bubbling with the prospect of Chicago, where the ladies will envy her manners and the gentlemen admire her looks, and she'll have money to indulge her fancies. She's always said, "You should either be a nigger or a millionaire." When Birdie reminds her of her husband, her enthusiasm is not dampened. There'll be plenty of time to worry about Horace when he comes home, if he ever decides to come home. The life force runs strong in Regina. She is self-centered, aggressive, and

The Little Foxes

NEW YORK PUBLIC LIBRARY

unencumbered by petty human sympathies. She will dominate the play, as she clearly dominates the Hubbards.

With Oscar and Ben back, we are eager to see the Hubbards without their party manners, but they're too intoxicated with their success to come down to earth. Regina has never seen Ben looking so much "like a cat who's been licking the cream." Oscar is at the window admiring the handsome young couple driving off with Marshall. The observation does not delight Regina, but she restrains herself. Another complication is in the wind. Ben is proud of his last-drink toast, an old Southern custom invented for the occasion. It's sharing time for their avaricious dreams. Ben will buy a stable in Savannah. Oscar dreams of seeing the bricks grow on the mill, and perhaps they'll take a few trips. In his euphoria, he even consults Birdie. She'll restore Lionnet to its old glory, where Papa "never let anybody be nasty-spoken or mean." When Regina has met the right people in Chicago and learned the right things to buy, she'll move to Paris. She'll live up to her name and leave the brick-counting to Ben and Oscar.

We suspect they're reckoning their profits too quickly. No deal is that good; there'll be rough weather ahead. It moves in gradually. Birdie's mind wanders from Lionnet to Oscar; she wants him to stop shooting. She doesn't like to see animals and birds killed. Regina speculates that she'll need substantial funds to support her plans. Oscar is trying to quiet Birdie's chatter. Everyone is talking at once, when Ben announces that "he's estimated the profits very high—for myself." Regina did not hear him; we're not sure that we did. When the other conversations subside, he repeats himself: "I said that I had, and I do, estimate the profits very high—for myself, and Oscar, of course."

The celebration is over. For the $225,000 the Hubbards are to invest, they're to hold 51 percent of the new company, Marshall 49. Horace has been in Baltimore for five months; they've all written to him. But he has ignored Regina's request to come home, and the money for his third share has not been forthcoming. They now need the cash. Ben says he wants to keep control in the family. Regina knows that he's only afraid that an outsider would demand more than a third interest. In fact, Horace may be keeping silent because he doesn't think he is getting enough for his money. Oscar misses the point, but not Ben. He wonders if it's Horace who is holding out for a larger share. More likely it's Regina, particularly when she protests her ignorance of business matters, yet says, "I should think that if you knew your money was very badly needed, well, you just might say, I want more, I want a bigger share. You boys have done that. I've heard you say so." Brotherly love does not inhibit the Hubbards. This is a power struggle, and in their world power is all that counts.

Oscar, as expected, cannot understand where the larger percentage would come from. Regina does. It would be taken from his portion. Ben shares Regina's sadistic delight in watching Oscar squirm. Oscar has got the short end of the stick before. For thirty-five years he's worked his hands to the bone for Ben. Ben assures him that allowing Horace 40 percent is not all that bad. Oscar will still be a very rich man, and everything will stay in the family. Ben's not intending to marry, so his money will go to Alexandra and Leo: "They may even marry some day." That would satisfy Oscar if Regina would endorse the arrangement. She hedges. Leo and Alexandra are first cousins. Oscar reminds her that their grandmother and grandfather were first cousins. Regina, and Miss Hellman, cannot resist the opportunity to say, "And look at us." Regina has other reservations about Leo. There were those times when he took a little money from the bank. (The information will be handy later.) Ben pulls her away from this track; all she needs to do is assure Oscar that she'll think about it seriously. That much she'll agree to.

Alexandra and Leo are now back from the depot. As we see them again, the prospect of Alexandra being trapped by Leo seems more distasteful. Leo is blubbering about Marshall's expensive clothes, and when Ben asks him if he was careful with the horses, we know from Alexandra's angry look that he was not.

The action pushes ahead. Regina has a plan. In the morning Alexandra will go to Baltimore to bring her father home. Alexandra is delighted: "Think of it, he'll be back home again." At least there's one spark of love in the family. Regina's instructions are precise. She will "tell Papa how much you missed him, and he must come home now—for your sake." He must not stay in Baltimore listening to "those alarmist doctors." With that settled, Regina dismisses the family and goes upstairs to help Addie with Alexandra's things. Ben will buy the ticket, and Oscar must quit looking as if he had "chronic indigestion." Family meanness surfaces easily for the Hubbards.

With the others gone, we get a quick glimpse of the warm intimacy between Alexandra and Birdie. The contrast sets the Hubbards in a darker light. Alexandra must tell someone that Leo did beat the horses. Birdie is not worrying about the horses. She's worried about Leo and Alexandra; even if he is her son, he's no good for Alexandra, and she knows what Regina and the others can do once they've set their minds. Oscar has slipped back in to get Birdie and has overheard her subversive talk. As Alexandra goes upstairs and Birdie goes toward the door, Oscar slaps her hard across the face. Alexandra, hearing her whimper, comes back. Birdie assures her it was nothing; she only twisted her ankle.

As the curtain comes down, the battle lines are drawn. Alexandra and Birdie are no match for Oscar, Ben, and Regina. Oscar is no match for his brother and sister. Only Ben and Regina are fighting in the same class. Human compassion will never impede them; each is out to win, whatever the consequences. In our right minds we might turn our backs on these hateful Southerners. In the theatre we are fascinated by their evil ways.

As the second act begins, new trouble is in the air. Alexandra, expected with Horace the night before, has not arrived.

Addie has been up all night waiting. Oscar has sacrificed his usual early-morning shooting to seek the latest news. Regina, looking down from the landing, is undisturbed; she's sure they've simply missed connections somewhere. Leo rushes in to report that nothing's been heard at the bank. As usual, Leo has done the wrong thing. Oscar had ordered him to stay at the bank if there was no news. He must settle down to his work, now that he's going to be married, and what's more, give up the woman in Mobile. Outside women are all right in their place, but "*now* isn't their place." There's too much at stake. Leo agrees; he's his father's son.

That settled, they revive the serious business. What if they have to get the $75,000 from an outsider? Oscar is not worried. Might serve Ben right to have to give up part of his share. Oscar is willing to wait until after he dies to get even, when Leo would have his share and probably Alexandra's. He could die happy, if he knew he had won. Leo must learn his father's motto: "It's every man's duty to think of himself." Leo has. Uncle Horace has $88,000 in Union Pacific bonds in his safe-deposit box. More than that—Leo is carried away—the box also contains Zan's baby shoe, an old cameo, and a piece of a violin. At first he insists that he peeked in the box when one of the boys at the bank opened it. Finally, under Oscar's prodding, he admits that he opened it himself. Shamelessly father and son drool over the prospect: "A man can't be shot for wanting to see his son get on in the world, can he, boy?" It'll be four months before Horace looks in the box again. Certainly Horace could lend Leo the bonds for four months. Their melodramatic scheme is interrupted by Ben and Regina.

For a moment it appears that we're retreating into the theatre of nineteenth-century villainy, of stolen stocks and widow's mortgages, yet we've seen enough of Oscar and Leo to believe they'll stop at nothing. Ben and Regina are not worried about Horace's tardiness. Regina is sure they'll arrive later in the day; he probably stopped off in Savannah to see his favorite cousin. When Ben reminds her that his cousin is dead, that the train doesn't go through Savannah, she ignores his facts. She is going to eat her breakfast in peace and read her newspaper. The others follow. Apparently it is not uncommon for the family to get its sustenance at Regina's table. Before the doors are closed, we hear Regina sending the grits back and Cal announcing to the kitchen, "Grits didn't hold the heat. Grits didn't hold the heat." Parsimonious as she is with the chit-chat, Miss Hellman gives it a sharp comic edge.

With the principals offstage, and with Addie gathering up the coffee cups, the stage is cleared for Horace and Alexandra. Addie hears them in the hall and helps Horace into the room. He's been a handsome man, though now he looks tired and ill. Alexandra's explanation of their delay is simple. Horace wasn't feeling well; they stopped for the night in Mobile; there was no way to send a message. Horace stops her, when she moves toward the dining room. He's not ready to be announced, and at Addie's urging, Alexandra goes upstairs to wash off the train dirt. Horace wants some good Southern coffee; he wants to know why Zan came to fetch him. Addie only knows that big things are going on: "Everybody going to be high-tone rich. Big rich. You too. All because smoke's going to start out of a building that ain't even up yet." More than that, there's talk of a wedding.

With Addie's briefing, his arrival can be announced. Regina greets him warmly, if perfunctorily, with a kiss. The others assure him that he looks fine. Oscar overdoes it. Leo, in character, is still munching on a biscuit. Horace is not overjoyed to be surrounded by Hubbards; it's just as if he'd never been away. Only Birdie welcomes him with honest affection. She has run in, dressed in a flannel kimono. She sees that he doesn't look well and tells him so, the only truthful one in the lot. The happy reunion quickly runs its course. The Hubbards return to normal. Oscar pushes Leo back to the dining room with his biscuit and chastises Birdie for cutting across the square in her robe. She tries to escape upstairs to Zan; Oscar sends her home to change; he's sure she's gone crazy. Horace wearily recognizes that "it's just like old times," and Regina clears the room, sending her brothers back to their breakfasts. Miss Hellman skillfully makes her character's wishes coincide with ours. We want to see Regina and Horace alone.

During his five-month absence, Regina has wanted to come to the hospital, but she was obliged to stay with Alexandra. Horace has not had too bad a time, after his first shock at the doctor's report. He's testing Regina, and she doesn't pass. She's sure he liked it so well he didn't want to come home. Horace gives her another chance. He had simply resigned himself to the inevitable and cherished the moments to think about himself and about them. She can't understand why he couldn't do his thinking at home. Horace shifts to the attack. Why did she send Zan to Baltimore? What about the crazy talk of Zan marrying Leo? That, she insists, was simply done to keep Oscar quiet. Whatever the reason, he wants no such talk. They must try to get along better, yet he wonders why she has not inquired about his health. No doubt the hospital reported that he could not live very long. He is not asking for sympathy, and Regina obliges. What did the doctors think caused his heart attack? "They didn't think it possible, did they, that your fancy women have—"

With this familiar cliché of the old South, our sympathies may shift slightly, though not seriously. Horace's sense of humor helps. He doesn't think that's "the best scientific theory. You don't catch heart trouble in bed." His flip reply angers Regina: "I only thought you might catch a bad conscience—in bed, as you say." Horace can no longer hold back; his five months of thinking have given him new courage: "I didn't tell them about my bad conscience. Or about my fancy women. Nor did I tell them that my wife has not wanted me in bed with her for—how long is it, Regina? Ten years? Did you bring me home for this, to make me feel guilty again? That means you want something. But you'll not make me feel guilty any more." Freud and Strindberg have collaborated on this scene. Miss Hellman accepts their guidance infrequently; she is not fascinated by the ravages of sex. Even here, sex is not at the root of Regina's evil. She is concerned with more important matters and refuses to fight on these terms.

She has not inquired about his health because she did not want to remind him of his illness, and she takes no stock in alarmist doctors. They must not continue this stupid bickering. Horace accepts the truce, knowing that it will not endure. He's right. When he starts for the stairs, she insists that he stay and talk about business. She ignores his protests and calls Ben from the dining room, announcing that Horace would like to talk to him, now. Ben is not sure this is the time, but Regina will not tolerate any delay.

Ben's story is simple. Why should they continue to slave over their cotton plantation and send their harvest to the mills in the North? Why not bring the mills to the cotton? He's swung a deal with Marshall in Chicago, and with Horace's cooperation they can complete the transaction. Regina fills in what Ben omits. She's persuaded Ben to give Horace a larger share. Horace is amazed at this uncommon generosity: "Who's getting less?" Oscar angrily supplies the answer, but he'll get his reward in the end. Horace sees the cards falling into place. But Ben must have had to offer Marshall more than money. He has. The state has guaranteed free water power, and Ben has promised cheap wages, less than half the scale in Massachusetts. Horace knows the Hubbards. Ben will set the "mountain whites" against the "town niggers" to keep the wages down.

Horace moves quietly toward the stairs. His answer is not encouraging. He's willing to sit by and "watch the boys grow rich." As he passes Leo and inquires about the bank and about the ladies in Mobile, he cannot suppress his anger: "Whatever made you think I'd let Zan marry—" Regina will not be put off. Oscar must be in Chicago with the money by the end of the week; they've been waiting for him "like children." She storms after him, ignoring Ben's reminder that "softness and a smile" can work wonders with the heart of a man. Regina is in no mood for such nonsense.

As the Hubbards contemplate their next move, we hear Regina's voice from upstairs, hard and hateful: "I won't let you pass up this chance. . . . All my life I've had to force you to make something of yourself. . . . Did you think I wanted you home for yourself?" She's forgotten Horace's heart, if we haven't. We've seen him struggle up the stairs; we've seen him swallow a pill.

The angry obbligato from above pushes the Hubbards into action. The Union Pacific bonds, borrowed from a "friend" of Leo's for a few months, will provide their salvation. Ben prefers not to know the friend's name, but the bumbling Leo has trouble with secrets. Yet the scheme appears too promising to let scruples interfere. Leo must get the bonds, and Oscar can draw the checks and take the night train for Chicago. Ben will decide later on Leo's reward. Again we are skirting the edges of melodrama, but we know the Hubbards. They are greedy, devoid of ethical inhibitions, willing to risk anything to realize their selfish ambitions.

We still hear Regina's voice, "high and furious," a fist pounding on a door. Alexandra rushes down the stairs pleading with Uncle Ben to make her stop, and then Regina returns. How long can Ben wait for the money? He could wait until next week, but "I can't wait until next week. I could but I can't." He enjoys his joke, enjoys Regina's suffering. He also relishes his fraternal politeness. They won't be on hand for their usual Friday supper: "Oscar is going to Chicago tonight." No wonder the Hubbards slash each other so freely; they've been practicing every Friday night. Regina is desperate. He will have to wait. Ben is not taking orders from her. He leaves, ignoring her clenched fists. Horace has appeared on the stairs, observing the battle. He's been waiting for years to see her cross swords with Ben. So they don't need her; she's not going to have her millions after all.

Regina turns her rage on him, uninhibited by Alexandra:

he hates to think she'll be alive and get what she wants. He's being selfish just because he's going to die. Regina is a superstar in cruelty. Horace clings to the banister, trying to match her: "I'm sick of you, sick of this house, sick of my life here. I'm sick of your brothers and their dirty tricks to make a dime. There must be better ways of getting rich than cheating niggers. . . . I'll die my own way. And I'll do it without making the world any worse. I leave that to you." Her flinty conscience is untroubled; she's smiling as she turns on him: "I hope you die. I hope you die soon. I'll be waiting for you to die." As Addie comes in to shelter Alexandra, Horace starts up the stairs and the curtain comes down.

The sheer raw emotional power of this second act is unsurpassed in the modern theatre. As our hate against the Hubbards is inflamed, we are secretly aware that Miss Hellman has struck at the aggressive impulses that lie below the surface in all of us. We have been hurled into a den of Southern foxes, true to themselves, true to their time, true to their society. They reveal the worst in themselves, clearly, naturally, and shamelessly, and their stark portraits appear more frightening outlined against those of Birdie, Alexandra, and Horace. And in the final moments, Horace alerts us to their more devastating social damage.

As the third act begins, there's a momentary lull in the storm, with Alexandra and Birdie at the piano and Horace, in his wheel chair by the window, listening. Yet the main action is not forgotten. Horace has the safe-deposit box beside him. Birdie recalls their early days when Horace played the violin and she accompanied him, and we recall that Leo found a piece of a violin in the box. Miss Hellman never misleads us with irrelevant information. Addie joins the happy circle, bringing cakes and elderberry wine. It "does the stomach good in the rain." We quickly learn that Oscar is back from Chicago, that neither he nor Ben have appeared since the day of the quarrel. Addie reports that Ben has been spreading the word about the mill: "Every human born of woman will be living on chicken. . . . There ain't been so much talk around here since Sherman's army didn't come near." Only fools may believe him, but "you ain't born in the South unless you're a fool."

Horace calls Cal to go to the bank and tell Mr. Manders that Mr. Horace is much obliged to him for bringing the box, that he and attorney Fowler are to come over after supper. Cal will find Mr. Manders, Mr. Joe Horns, and Mr. Leo around the big table going over the day's business. Cal, straining his brain to understand, gives up. "No, sir. I ain't going to say I understand. I'm going down and tell a man he give you something he already know he give you. . . . I ain't going to understand it, but I'm going to say it." The comic diversion takes the edge off the melodrama.

With the wheels in motion and while Cal is on his errand, Birdie continues her pathetic memories. Her mother had not liked the Hubbards, not because they kept a store, only because she didn't like people who killed animals they couldn't use and who made their money charging awful interest to poor, ignorant Negroes and cheating them on what they bought. Addie echoes her sentiments: "Yeah, they got mighty well off cheating niggers. Well, there are people who eat the earth and eat all the people on it like in the Bible with the locusts. Then there are people who stand around and watch them eat it. Sometimes I think it ain't right to stand and watch them do it." Addie is speaking for the author. No single idea about social responsibility so dominates Miss Hellman's thinking and repeatedly finds its place in her plays. Injustices are perpetrated on the innocents not only because of ruthless villains, but because so many placid, frightened bystanders turn their heads and refuse to become involved.

Birdie persists with her memories. Why did she ever marry a Hubbard? In twenty-two years she's not had a happy day; even her solitary drinking—headache spells to the family—has not saved her. And twenty years from now Alexandra will be in her place, if she does not run before they've tied her to Leo.

Birdie is exhausted, and Alexandra must lead her home, but not before Horace has promised Alexandra that he'll take her away.

He has already laid his plans. He's changing his will to take care of Alexandra; he's even leaving something to Addie. She knows that's impossible. "A nigger woman in a white man's will! I'd never get it nohow." He's thought of that. He's left $1700 in an envelope in the drawer of his armoire with her name on it. She promises to use the money to take Zan away. With that settled, Cal is back with his report. As we expected, the message had its effect. Leo jumped up and tried to leave, but Manders told him to sit down and finish his work and "stop acting like somebody made him Mr. President." Although one of the Hubbards is suffering, we wonder if Horace has the power to rout them all. They are tenacious opponents, and one of them is about to appear. We hear Regina's voice outside. Cal quickly disappears. Addie rolls Horace's chair toward the stairway, but he insists on staying.

Regina is furious. She's divided the house. He's to stay in his part, she in hers, and this is hers. The days since his return have not tempered her inhumanity. But he has a scheme to subdue her. Leo has stolen the bonds. Horace is going to let them keep them, as a loan from Regina. He's changing his will to leave the bonds to her and everything else to Alexandra. She can deal with Ben and Oscar after his death. Leo and her brothers now know that he knows they've stolen the bonds. "They'll be mighty relieved to know I'm going to do nothing and Ben will think it all a capital joke on you. . . . There's nothing you can do to them, nothing you can do to me."

The ultimatum fires Regina's fury. She has not hated him; she's felt only contempt. He was a small-town clerk, and he hasn't changed. She married him because she was lonely and wanted the world, and Papa had left all his money to Ben and Oscar. She used to lie in bed at night, praying that he would not come near. She even convinced him that Dr. Sloan had said that something was wrong with her and he shouldn't touch her. That was when she began to despise him. She's been waiting for this time, never dreaming that he would get heart trouble so early and so bad. "I'm lucky, Horace. I've always been lucky."

Horace collapses under her brutality. He reaches for his medicine, breaks the bottle, pleads with her to send Addie up for the other bottle. Regina does not move. When he tries to scream for Addie, his voice is only a whisper. He pushes the chair back and struggles for the stairs. Part way up he falls. She does not move until he's quiet. Then she calls Addie and Cal. They carry him up and she follows. Addie comes back, racing for the doctor, as Alexandra returns. She runs up to her father, leaving the stage clear for a short moment, until the door bell rings. Melodrama may have set in with a vengeance, but we've been well prepared and we're seeing just what we feared.

When he gets no answer to the bell, Leo rushes in. His frantic calls bring no response. Ben and Oscar arrive; Addie has told them about the attack. Even they ignore Leo until he yells, "*Will you listen to me?*" They hear the full story about the bonds and the box, about Manders and the lawyer Fowler. Horace has them cornered. He's had the box for three days, and he hasn't said a word. Why? How much does Regina know? Leo and Oscar are trembling in their guilt. Ben keeps his head. They must brazen their way. Regina may know nothing, and if she does, Leo is to say that Horace lent him the bonds. They're on shaky grounds, but no other course is possible. They're as ready as they'll ever be when Regina comes down the stairs.

After a quick report on Horace's attack, omitting the crucial details, she drops her bomb. Horace told her about the bonds. Leo and Oscar fake innocence. Ben is smarter. What exactly did Horace tell her? Regina takes the bait: Horace was going to say that he had lent them the bonds. Perhaps, Ben suggests, he made up the story to tease or perhaps to punish her; now he'd better go for Dr. Sloan. Regina won't let him escape. They're safe as long as Horace is alive, but she doesn't think he'll live, and if he doesn't, she'll want 75 percent of the Hubbard's share of the cotton-mill venture in exchange for the bonds. She's playing her advantage. Ben tries to dismiss her with a laugh; she wants so much of everything. Regina is in no mood for games; she'll get what she wants or she'll send the three of them to jail.

Her prospects seem good, as their argument is interrupted. Alexandra comes slowly down the stairs, and then Addie. Alexandra circles the room, asking each if they had loved her father and finally to Regina: "And you, Mama, did you love him, too?" Regina cannot face the question: "I know what you feel, Alexandra, but please try to control yourself." Alexandra is laughing hysterically, stopping only long enough to fire the incriminating question: "What was Papa doing on the staircase?" Even that does not shake Regina. In the morning she'll go to Judge Simmes. If the bare facts are not enough, she'll add what's necessary. They can deny their heads off. A jury will weep for a woman whose brothers steal from her: "You couldn't find twelve men in this state you haven't cheated and hate you for it." If that should fail, she'll go to Marshall. Or she'll just take 75 percent and forget the story forever. When they don't answer, she smiles in triumph. The necessary papers can be drawn up tomorrow. Oscar and Leo exit angrily. Ben is philosophical. He knows when he's beat, or beat for the moment: "The century's turning, the world is open. Open for people like you and me. . . . There are hundreds of Hubbards sitting in rooms like this throughout the country. All their names aren't Hubbard, but they are all Hubbards and they will own this country some day. We'll get along." The Hubbard story is part of a larger story. Like so many writers during the Depression years, Miss Hellman deplored the evils of unrestrained free enterprise, forcing society to live at the mercy of a few greedy men.

Ben will bide his time. Like Alexandra, he's puzzled by a man in a wheel chair left alone on the stairs. Someday he may find out. "When I do, I'll let you know." Regina is still confident; she's recaptured her gaiety. "When you do, write me. I will be in Chicago. Ah, Ben, if Papa had only left me his money." She's finally repaired that injustice. Still Ben is not subdued. He turns to Alexandra, as he leaves. She's turning out to be "a right interesting girl."

The battle is over. Before Regina goes to bed to wait for Dr. Sloan, Alexandra wants her to know that she's not going to Chicago with her, though she is going away, "because I know Papa would want me to." Regina is surprised, yet not totally displeased. Does she harbor some remnants of humanity not seen before, or is it pride in detecting her own image in her daughter, a remembrance of her own past or perhaps only her usual selfishness? Perhaps a bit of each. She wishes she had had Alexandra's spunk at her age. "Do what you want. . . . I'd like to keep you with me, but I won't make you stay. Too many people used to make me do too many things. . . . You have spirit, after all. I used to think you were all sugar water." As she turns to go up the stairs, she hesitates and turns back: "Would you like to come and talk to me, Alexandra? Would you—would you like to sleep in my room tonight?" Alexandra has been offered the upper hand, and she takes it: "Are you afraid, Mama?" If she is, Regina will not admit it. She goes up the stairs slowly, and Addie is by Alexandra's side as the curtain comes down.

Three weeks in the life of the Hubbards have ended. Alexandra may escape, Regina may find a new life in Chicago, Ben may join Oscar as a second-class Hubbard, yet it seems unlikely. We know Ben too well; even Leo and Oscar could upset Regina's scheme; and we cannot completely trust Alexandra's new confidence. The Hubbards are strong people. We cannot believe we have witnessed their final battle.

The Little Foxes is a powerful and fascinating play, a highly charged theatrical experience. Loathsome as the Hubbards are, loath as we are to grant their existence, we know Miss Hellman speaks the truth. Their kind did exist, do exist, and as we stand by and watch, they did and do conquer. Regina is a magnificent embodiment of evil: cold, hard, determined, and beautiful, larger than life, yet grounded to the life that made her. Genetic guidance and the perversities with which they've lived have also formed the others. We believe their evil machinations; and there are few moments when we are not burning with hate, distaste, pity, or love. We sense that we are seeing the old South as it truly was at the turn of the century. Aristocrats like Birdie were enslaved by the new breed of entrepreneurs. Families like the Hubbards did turn on each other.

In reading the play we may be disturbed by the trappings of melodrama: strongboxes, stolen bonds, spilled medicine, death on the stairs. Miss Hellman told a reporter during rehearsals that she kept saying to herself, "*Foxes* is a melodrama." Not in the pejorative sense, which attaches the label to the component parts rather than to the whole, but in the sense that she, like many of her illustrious predecessors in the theatre, wrote strong characters and strong actions. She insisted that if the Marines arrive to save the girl, we are turned off only if the intention is to shock rather than to clarify or solve. Her motive, grounded in the motives of her characters, was to expose and clarify. Dramatic shocks, when they came, were not unexpected or gratuitous.

Most of the New York critics supported her view. The strength of the play derived from its melodramatic qualities, yet in total it was not a melodrama. She provided no reward for virtue, no punishment for vice, the stock-in-trade of melodrama. Nor should she be labeled a sensationalist because she dared to depict unpleasant and mean characters who suppressed their humanity, even in the face of death. Instead, as George Jean Nathan remarked (*Newsweek*, February 27, 1939), she should be praised for "a true and honest play" in which there was "not an inch of compromise, not a sliver of a sop to the comfortable acquiescence of Broadway or Piccadilly." Too many nice-Nelly playwrights have become frightened of the word melodrama and thus have forgotten the power and excitement to be stirred by the genuine drama of character and will. They have shied away from evil and malice and turned their backs on grim and unpleasant situations. Miss Hellman knew that "America was melodrama in 1900," as Walter Kerr remarked, and she capitalized on what other playwrights had neglected.

The critics praised her vivid portraits, "characters etched in hatred," her shrewd, taut, and parsimonious structure, and her fearless exploration of a grim chapter in American social history. Her wily and slate-hearted Regina and her money-hungry brothers and the pitiful Birdie were drawn by a master. Above all, they acclaimed the vigorous emotional drive in her writing and the meticulous, Ibsen-like craftsmanship in her ordering of characters and events. "Admirably written and admirably constructed," the play "skillfully communicated her burning conviction"; it was "a credit to its author and to American dramatic writing."

That Miss Hellman respected her craft and honored her profession is indicated in the successive revisions that occurred prior to the final script. In the earliest version—presumably an earlier one was destroyed—the action pursues a narrative rather than dramatic line, and more characters are employed. As the play opens, Horace is already home and upstairs, being tended by Charlotte, Addie's daughter, a student at Tuskegee. The Hubbards, all living in the same house, come down one by one to reveal the proposed business deal. Leo, though endowed with the same weakling, bumbling qualities of the later Leo, is another Hubbard brother, rather than the son of Oscar. Grover Giddens, a character later eliminated, is a son of Regina and Horace and presumably like his father. He is having an affair with a syphilitic Eva Gritney, a store clerk. Horace has already upset the Hubbard negotiations with Mr. Barton in Chicago. He has refused to invest in the enterprise, though he's willing to lend them the money. Charlotte supports his view, insisting that the proposal would exploit the poor workers. Regina is furious. She hasn't raised her voice in twenty-two years, but she will now: "How dare you bring your nigger into this room, asking her opinion. Your nigger in this room. You heard me." In revenge, Regina consigns Horace to the sewing room on the third floor.

At the opening of the second act we learn that Horace is suffering from lung trouble. Addie doesn't want Zan to go near him. It's all right for her daughter, Charlotte, because "black people don't catch so easy." Southern attitudes toward blacks are prominent in this early version. When the deal with Barton is settled—in the second rather than in the first act—there is much more talk about the hiring of Negroes. There are hints that the relationship between Charlotte and Horace is more than nurse and patient. Leo insists that "it ain't always wise for a nigger girl to talk so much to a white man. Ain't that so, Charlotte?" Tuskegee has given her an audacity her mother doesn't have: "It's only wise, I guess, when you talk to a nigger girl in one of the South Street houses, eh, Mr. Leo?" Miss Hellman's mind was on the Hubbard's Negroes.

As this part of the play is reduced, the complications in the business deal are increased and dramatized. Here Leo simply turns up with the bonds in his pocket, "little Leo that nobody ever thought was worth a nickel." He demands a 50-percent interest for his contribution, but settles for 10. Regina is cut out because she won't permit Horace to lend them the money. Her threat to send them to jail has not yet developed. Horace is still alive at the final curtain, though he appears near death: "Do you know what it is to see your own blood come out of your mouth and to know you're spitting out your life? . . . Get me away from the Hubbards just a few hours to die." Regina obliges by transferring him from the sewing room to an unused slave cabin. The play closes with Ben and Regina alone. He's going to buy her share of the house so she can move out after Horace dies. She still thinks she can turn the tables and buy his share. Ben doubts that. "Let us live in brotherly and sisterly love, in Christian peace, until that day comes. Goodnight."

Although the basic ingredients have appeared, they have not been developed and dramatized. None of the characters has achieved his final portrait, though Ben and Regina are further along than the others. This first draft offers a remarkable testimony to Miss Hellman's craftsmanship. It is not simply a scenario; it is a fully written play, filled with many fine speeches which were later sacrificed. A lesser playwright could not have relegated so much copy to oblivion.

In the next draft Grover Giddens and Charlotte have been eliminated, Leo has become Oscar's son, and the sequence of action appears in its final form, though there is a scene break in Act III, following the death of Horace, denoting the passing of twenty minutes. At the beginning of this second scene, Dr. Sloan announces Horace's death. Dr. Sloan is, of course, eliminated in the final version. In this and the two succeeding full drafts—the last dated "1/9/39, the day the play went into rehearsal"—Miss Hellman sharpens the characters, compresses the action, eliminates excesses, dispenses information by indirection, and perpetually searches for the best word. A few examples must suffice.

Instead of permitting Regina to tell Marshall that her husband is a banker, Ben transmits that information. Horace's revelation of his illness—"Regina, you see, the doctors—I don't know how a man should announce his own death"—becomes, "Well, I suppose they've written you I can't live very long." His "angina pectoris" becomes "heart trouble." The anti-Negro talk and the word "nigger" are radically reduced in each succeeding draft. At one point Oscar talks of lynchings and insists that the "streets will run with hate and blood," if Negro and white work together. This is eliminated. "Cobs" becomes "horses." Oscar's "I haven't hunted" becomes "I haven't shot."

Only one significant change was made after the play was in rehearsal. Originally the play ended with a final scene between Addie and Alexandra in which Addie mocks Zan for not defying Regina and leaving. Finally Zan says, "All right, you hold open the door, Addie, and I'll go through it." And

Addie closes the play with, "That's my girl." Arthur Kober apparently suggested that this scene be eliminated, giving the final moments to Regina and Alexandra. Shumlin liked the original "coda" and hated to see it go. Miss Hellman did not follow all suggestions, not even Hammett's. In the margin of one draft beside the passage in which Regina accuses Horace of contracting his illness from his fancy women, Miss Hellman noted, "Can this come out? Dash thinks it should." It didn't come out. She was her own master, and in her third play to reach the stage, she demonstrated her patient and sure hand in transforming raw domestic and social substance into a powerful dramatic document.

VIII

Hardscrabble Farm and *Watch on the Rhine*

In early March, 1939, with *Foxes* settled into its long run and with the text published, dedicated to Arthur Kober and Louis Kronenberger, "who have been my good friends," Miss Hellman deserted New York for an isolated village in Cuba. She needed a rest and time to contemplate what had been happening in the world while she had been occupied in the theatre. She could not know, as she said later, that this was to be "the holocaust year of the century," yet she knew from what she had seen in Spain and in Western Europe that "the hurricane was somewhere off the coast and death around the corner." And though there was always a bit of "shame and sorrow at the Liberal's impotence in the face of the hurricane," she ought to become as involved as her friends. Hammett wrote on March 10, 1939, praising Dottie Parker's piece in the *Masses*, and announcing that he was "going to get up and type a long letter to Herbert Biberman on the State of the Nation and how to keep from viewing the future through rose colored testacles [sic]."

Back in New York, late in the spring, she determined to escape the turmoil of the city. She was not by nature an activist or a joiner, and the city was seething with worthy enterprises soliciting her membership and support. Political teamplay was not her meat. In late May, she did, however, moderate a discussion of contemporary problems and the problems of the dramatist, part of the New School's Third American Writers' Congress.

If nature had not prepared her for political involvement, strangely it had prepared her to delight in the 130-acre New York farm she bought in May. On Hardscrabble Road, midway between Pleasantville, Chappaqua, and Briarcliff (between the Saw Mill River and Bronx River Parkways), the farm, half woodland, half open fields, had an eight-acre spring-fed lake, a spacious main residence surrounded by a screen porch, a six-room caretaker's cottage, two guest houses, barns, poultry houses, a stable, rock gardens, orchards, vegetable gardens, and grape arbors. "Hardscrabble Farm," as it was called, provided a happy home for the next thirteen years and the workroom in which her next five plays were written. Her days on the farm were the best of her life, reviving misused land, raising poultry, hunting, trapping turtles, and fishing— Shumlin insisted that "she knew what every goddam fish was planning at the other end of the line"—swimming and tennis, afternoons in the kitchen preparing crab gumbo, turtle soup, or some other New Orleans specialty. She delighted in good food and had once even thought of opening a restaurant. The house was constantly filled with visitors, particularly men, all of whom appeared to have been in love with her at one time or another. They sought her friendship, her artistic and business advice. The happiest years with Hammett were at Hardscrabble, though he was not always there. During the war, he was in the army, having enlisted as a private, and after the war his heavy drinking often became intolerable.

In spite of the relaxed and often zany atmosphere at the farm, she worked well there, as did a number of her guests.

Normally she spent three hours at her typewriter in the morning, two to three hours in the afternoon, and again from ten at night until one or two in the morning. When too many helpful guests began invading her sanctuary, she tried writing longhand in bed, but when that didn't work, she posted a warning on her door:

This Room is Used for Work
Do Not Enter Without Knocking
After You Knock, Wait for an Answer
If you get no Answer, go Away and
Don't Come Back
This Means Everybody
This Means You
This Means Night or Day

By Order of the Hellman-Military-Commission-for-Playwrights. Court Martialling Will Take Place in the Barn, and Your Trial Will Not be a Fair One.

The Christmas Court-Martialling Has Now Taken Place! Among those:

Herman Shumlin, former *regisseur*.

Miss Sylvia Hermann, aged three, former daughter of a farmer.

Miss Nora, former dog.

Mr. Samuel Dashiell Hammett, former eccentric.

Mr. Arthur Kober, former itinerant sweet-singer.

Mr. Louis Kronenberger, born in Cincinnati, lynched by me.

Emmy Kronenberger, wife to Kronenberger, died with him.

Mr. Felix Anderson, former butler.

Irene Robinson, former cook and very pretty.

Note: Mr. Max Bernard Hellman, father, is a most constant offender. His age has saved him. This sentimentality may not continue.

Being a Southerner she never much liked fall and winter, but in the spring, "I am like an idiot four-year-old," she once said. "I go around making noises which indicate great contentment with nature. I am in the garden all the time and I get in the way of everyone who is trying to work. I put out seeds on Monday and, one friend says, on Wednesday if plants haven't come up I go out and reseed the whole plot."

From 1939 to 1952, Hardscrabble was home base, and except for brief excursions, she stayed at home base. She lost the farm in 1952, "because," as she later explained, "the hi-jinks of Senator McCarthy and his rivals in the House UnAmerican Activities Committee made it impossible for me to keep it."

On January 10, 1940, she joined Lin Yutang and Edna Ferber as one of the speakers at the Book and Author Luncheon at the Hotel Astor. She welcomed the opportunity to speak her feelings about what was happening in the world: "I am a writer and also a Jew. I want to be sure I can continue to say what I wish without being branded by the malice of people making a living by that malice."

In June she went to the Republican convention in Philadelphia for *PM*. She had been involved with Ralph Ingersoll's paper from the beginning, had suggested the name, and had bought a small share in the enterprise. Her piece, "The Little Men in Philadelphia" (June 25, 1940) did not cover the convention proceedings. After attending a news conference with Senator Vandenburg where "the questions and answers boiled down to simple unspoken cynicism; deals will be arranged and a candidate will be chosen," she roamed about the city talking with a cabdriver, two storekeepers, a shoeshine boy and a watermelon boy. None of them would speak out. When you had to earn a living, it was better not to talk politics, it was "not smart to have ideas." She was grieved that "uptown the party of Abraham Lincoln is making deals in a city in which at least three white men and two black men are too suspicious and too tired and too frightened to exercise their primary right of free and easy speech. And I thought that Lincoln might not like that."

She took a brief turn in Hollywood with *The Little Foxes*, "added dialogue by Dorothy Parker, Arthur Kober, and Alan Campbell." According to Kober, their contribution was insignificant, and he preferred to have his name omitted, but Alan Campbell was "a little guy who needed the credit," so the three names appeared. Most of the original text was retained but the action moved out of the house and around the town, with scenes at the bank and at the railroad station. A touching love story was added, with Alexandra and David Hewitt, a handsome young newspaper man. This and the deletion of Regina's references to Horace's fancy women were the only concessions to Hollywood. Produced by Goldwyn, directed by Wyler, with Bette Davis (Regina), Herbert Marshall (Horace), and Teresa Wright (Alexandra), and with the original Hubbard family—Patricia Collinge (Birdie), Dan Duryea (Leo), Charles Dingle (Ben), and Carl Benton Reid (Oscar)—it opened at Radio City Music Hall on August 21, 1941. If some saw shades of nineteenth-century melodrama in *Foxes*, the full program at the Music Hall was like a nineteenth-century hodgepodge evening in the theatre. The Hubbard saga was augmented with a stage show dedicated to the U.S.O., an Hawaiian fantasy featuring "The Cockeyed Mayor of Kaunakaykai," the Rockettes in navy white, swinging a mean hornpipe. Apparently ukuleles and hulas did not reduce the power of the film. The *Times* (August 22, 1941) called it "the most bitingly sinister picture of the year," Bette Davis at "her brittle best, playing one of those Borgias with a cut-glass brilliance, a serene cupidity, a frightening frigidity."

Londoners saw the film of *Foxes* before they saw the play, and when Fay Compton attempted Regina at the Piccadilly Theatre in late October, 1942, the critics found her an inadequate substitute for Bette Davis. She was too much the stock villainess, lacking in Southern charm. Although Emlyn Williams, the director, had not shaped as convincing a family for *Foxes* as he had for *Watch on the Rhine* the previous May (*Watch* opened in London before *Foxes*), one critic advised "those who think the Archbishop of Canterbury goes too far in criticizing the profit-motive in industry should go see it."

Before her brief interlude in Hollywood, she was already well into her next play. Painfully conscious of the rising fury of the hurricane off the coast and the social ills corrupting life at home, she knew she had to use her strong voice in the theatre to shake her audience from their apathy. She returned to the idea of the titled European couple stranded in a midwestern home. She also thought of dramatizing Zola's *Germinal*. Out of its gruesome scenes in the coal mines, its passionate cry for social reform, she might fashion a proletarian documentary to block out the memory of *Days to Come*. This project was abandoned.

Hammett had been instructing her in his own brand of Marxism, beliefs deeply grounded with him, but her irrepressible skepticism never permitted her to subscribe without her fingers crossed. And in 1940 the Hitler hurricane seemed so much more threatening than economic injustice. The Nazi atrocities, the rumblings of the *Wehrmacht*, the nightmarish horrors of Spain so fiercely remembered, even the dimmer memories, now revived, of Hitler's fair-haired youth first learning their ghastly games, commanded her to raise the danger signals. Smugness, business as usual, the great Atlantic were puny barriers against the Fascist menace.

Knowing what she wanted to say was easier than finding the means. She was not a shouter, though Dorothy Parker once remarked, "When Lillian gets mad, I regret to say she screams." She could not write a screaming play. For her the stage was not a soapbox; she was not a preacher, a propagandist. The play came first; the moral message must be bound to the play.

As with *Foxes*, *Watch on the Rhine* evolved from extensive research: digests of some twenty-five books, pages of preliminary notes, and a series of carefully improved drafts. Although at times she questioned the necessity for so much research, she once said that "I seem to have to do it to be sure I know what I'm talking about."

Her notebook contained lists of possible names: Kabler, Fogler, etc. Items to be checked: "Hamburg speech was '36 or '37?" "Spain during Carlist trouble: Verify." Phrases and words to give the authentic German flavor: "Ten years before (not ago) today." "Depart instead of leave." "I will accompany you." "Not quite very well." "So?" "No?" "Give me fire instead of give me light." A skeletal scenario: "Act One—Anise with mail. Joseph on terrace with breakfast/ Fanny comes down/ David and Marthe/ Teck—Marthe/ All of family/ Sara, David, family; Marthe—Teck/ Maybe Teck and Kurt do not meet until last of act." In another part of the book, Miss Hellman recorded notes for doctoring an early draft: "Say date of play. Anise should not say Balkan nobility. Possible confusion on Emily, who she is. David says 'Mama' too often." Then, "In general: Feel more Sara's coming. 'I'm very excited' —show excitement rather than tell about it. Mention Sara's name more in 1st part. Go back for Bodo's misuse of words." She searched for the means to let the characters show themselves.

On the two earliest drafts, she noted that "Play No. 5" (she was still counting *Dear Queen*) was "started about August 15th [1939] and finished December 27th [1940]," though with two more typed drafts, it was not finally mimeographed for the actors until mid-February, 1941. Even at the earliest stages, she retained only a small part of her original idea, European nobility thrown into an American household. She moved the setting from the Midwest to Washington, D.C., made the Europeans villainous, and centered on an heroic anti-Fascist battling for his life, for his family, and above all for freedom.

Apparently there were other notebooks, now misplaced or lost. Miss Hellman showed Margaret Case Harriman (reported in *The New Yorker*, November 8, 1941) "two or three volumes" of 400 to 500 typed, single-spaced pages each with data on contemporary history, local customs, political events, and with long lists of names and biographical sketches of the characters before their appearance in the play. Such notes appeared as "What was he doing in Germany? Scientist? Trade Union Movement? Maybe China? What was going on 1920–1932? Maybe they have only been here about six months? What was he doing here?" As with the *Foxes* research, a detailed history of the period could be written from her notes.

The action begins in the luxurious living room of the Farrelly mansion some twenty miles from Washington on a warm spring morning in 1940. "Four or five generations have furnished this room." Wealth, elegance, and family continuity are immediately evident, and in contrast to the other plays, the scene is contemporary. The morning routine is underway. Anise, the French housekeeper, is sorting mail; Joseph, the handsome Negro butler, is fussing over the breakfast wagon; and Fanny Farrelly, clearly the commanding matron, appears in an elegant dressing gown and orders Joseph to ring the bell. David is not yet down, and he's scheduled to meet the train. Joseph must push the clock ahead and ring the bell; Fanny likes to disturb folks. The first brush strokes on Fanny's portrait reveal another of Miss Hellman's self-assured, strong-minded, and strong-willed females.

As Fanny thumbs through the mail, anxiously asking the time every few minutes, the identity of the expected arrivals is gradually revealed: Miss Sara, a daughter who's not been home in twenty years, is bringing a husband *and* grandchildren. (How much more dramatic anticipation in this opening than in Miss Hellman's first draft with Sara and her family on stage at the opening curtain and with Fanny still asleep!) The stack of mail provides the spark for more family details. Fanny was deeply in love with her husband, Joshua, whose portrait is on the wall. She could not have looked at another man as Birdie Chase's daughter has done. There are legal advertisements for David, invitations to lower-class embassy teas and bills for the count and countess, "the Balkan nobility" who have camped with them for the past six weeks, and a night letter from some woman in Lansing who is pursuing David. Through all this, Joseph has been furiously sounding the bell and now announces that "the sausage cakes is shrinking."

The bell and Fanny's commanding shriek have brought David down. Mother and son greet each other warmly, though David is irritated by the "air-raid alarm." He'll convert the chickenhouse into a playroom, hung with bells, "and you can go into your second childhood in proper privacy." Marthe de Brancovis appears, though not before we learn that David has been flirting with her and that "the Balkans" have been tolerated because her husband, Teck, plays cribbage with Fanny and tells good jokes. Fanny is concerned about accommodating them and the new arrivals.

When Marthe comes in, Fanny adjourns to the terrace for breakfast after informing David, in Marthe's hearing, about the night letter from the Carter woman. She makes her point. Marthe's jealousy is aroused. (In the first versions of the play the affair between Marthe and David—his name was then Gil—received more attention. David had a wife, Emily, who figured prominently and who harbored an intense jealousy. With David unmarried, Fanny has assumed Emily's jealousy. When Miss Hellman abandons characters, she reassigns their attributes.)

David's mind is on Sara and her husband, whom he's never seen. We sense that two sets of refugees, different classes of refugees, are going to disrupt the Farrelly establishment. In this first encounter we grasp little about the involvement of David and Marthe. They first met as children, when David's father was stationed in Paris. We're eager to learn more, when Teck appears. Miss Hellman frequently tantalizes us with such interruptions.

Teck is a good-looking man, continentally slick and smooth, another of Hellman's handsome people. Again the breakfast bell signals Fanny's impatience and helps to clear the stage. As David joins her, Teck and Marthe reveal their situation.

Although the "countess" title has worked magic in extending their credit, they are badly in debt and have only $87 in American Express checks. They know something of Sara's husband. He's poor, an engineer, an anti-Nazi, and he left Germany in 1933. They don't know if he is a Jew. Teck has connections with the German Embassy, and in spite of his shaky finances, he still gambles there.

(Miss Hellman was fascinated with gamblers and gambling and with playing for high stakes. One night she won $21,000 at chemin de fer and the next morning ordered two ambulances for the Spanish Loyalists. When she lost $19,000 the next night, she did not cancel the order. In Hollywood she was a regular at the Clover Club. In 1937, Hammett reported that the club was about to abandon chemin de fer when she left town. Although she had arrived too late on the Broadway scene to join the Thanatopsis Inside Straight Club which Heywood Broun, F. P. Adams, Alexander Woollcott, the Marx Brothers, Russel Crouse, and the Gershwins made into one of Broadway's noisiest legends, a later club, with some of the same participants, welcomed her to membership. Morrie Ryskind once commented that he was saddened over the low estate of the arts when he found her on the floor shooting dice. She was also an ardent bridge player. Arthur Kober recalls that during the early days of their marriage, he frequently retired while she was still at the table. One time she was invited to a supper party at a London home. "No sooner was dinner ended," she reported, "than I found myself $700 out of pocket in one of the weirdest crookedest poker games in history." She recouped part of her loss by using her London host—he was "a glamorous aristocrat," and not English—as a model for her portrait of Teck de Brancovis.)

Teck and Marthe are precariously at odds with each other. She distrusts the Nazis and knows that if he should lose when gambling at the Embassy, they would be driven out of the country. The risk does not trouble him; he trusts his skill. He is more disturbed by Marthe's flirtation with their host. For the moment they must maintain their composure and not imperil their comfortable and inexpensive quarters; they join the breakfast table on the terrace. We know, better than the Farrellys, how dangerous this pair could be.

The stage is empty only for a moment before Fanny's plans and our expectancy are dramatically disrupted. Sara Müller and her family march in. Dowdy yet neat, they look like immigrants, each carrying his assigned share of the shabby luggage. Sara and Kurt are sturdy, handsome, and serious. The children are stiff, too heavily dressed, and anxious to behave properly. Joshua, fourteen, named for his grandfather, is the platoon leader. Babette, twelve, fusses over her mother's clothes—she wants her to look her best. Bodo, nine, is the talker, undisturbed that he does not yet command the language; he can always shift to German or French. The children are astounded that they're permitted to sit on the couch, that the door was unlocked. Sara is overjoyed to have her family together in a place like this, though she finds it hard to say so without seeming to be critical of her husband. He understands: "You must enjoy your house, and not be afraid that you hurt me with it. Yes?" Miss Hellman has a good ear.

Anise is the first to discover them, to learn that the later train was too expensive. She calls to the terrace. Fanny's embrace is warm and motherly, her welcome to Kurt straightforward and honest, no hint that she might have disapproved of him earlier. As the children are introduced, they bow politely. Fanny wonders, as we have, if they are children or "dressed up midgets." No offense intended, and none taken. Fanny informs Sara about the "titled folk." The countess is the former Hortie Randolph—Sara remembers her. The Müller family is adjusting to their new surroundings. Bodo continues chattering, Joshua and Babette laugh when Fanny puts him down: "If you grow up to talk like that, and stay as ugly as you are, you are going to have one of those successful careers on the lecture platform."

After Anise has taken the children to wash for breakfast, Fanny admits that she likes Kurt; her first impression was wrong. She'll remodel the house, and they'll all live together;

David has already made inquiries about an engineering job for Kurt. Kurt explains that he's not been an engineer since 1933. He is an anti-Fascist, "and that does not pay well." Sara explains that times have been rough, yet they've lived as they wanted to live: "I don't know the language of rooms like this any more. And I don't want to learn it again." In Germany, Kurt explains, he has gone to work and come home every night; they were as happy as people could be in a starved country that was going to pieces, until 1931, when he saw twenty-seven men murdered in a Nazi street fight. That was the turning point: "I say with Luther, 'Here I stand. I can do nothing else. God help me. Amen.'" Now they've been forced out of Germany for their own safety, but they have not given up the fight.

When the play opened in April, 1941, it carried the blazing effect of a front-page headline. It was just a year after the invasion of Norway and Denmark, less than a year after Hitler had overrun Holland and Belgium, the British had been driven to the beaches at Dunkerque, and France had fallen. Britain was now struggling for its life against the German Luftwaffe; within three months the Nazis would invade Russia. Hitler had never appeared more monstrous and invincible, and those who fought against him more noble, particularly the underground fighters who risked themselves and their families. Kurt Müller's charismatic command over the audience in 1941 cannot be overestimated.

In the first version of the play, Kurt's activities were more explicitly detailed. He had led a brigade in Spain; his eldest son, then nineteen, had been killed by his side, "fighting for the people." Kurt has been a member of the anti-Nazi underground, "trying to teach the working mass of the German people." One of their closest friends, the night before he was executed, had smuggled out one thousand pieces of paper on which he had written, "Come and see an anti-Nazi die." The Müllers have lived from hand to mouth all over Europe, most recently in Paris, and then in Mexico before entering

Watch on the Rhine

NEW YORK PUBLIC LIBRARY

the United States without a visa. And all over the world he'd discovered that it was "fashionable to be an anti-Fascist, as long as you do it fashionably." By the final version Miss Hellman had eliminated the eldest son, unburdened the play of the revolutionary specifics, and deleted the allusion to the fashionable liberals.

With the political background established, and more compactly than in the early drafts, David and Sara go to the garden to revive their childhood memories, and Kurt is left to face the "Balkan nobility," with some help from Bodo. Bodo is awed by the "splendorous arrangement of the house, the magnificence and sanitary quality of the plumbing," but not impressed with Teck and Marthe; he's met poor counts and countesses before. Teck and Kurt study each other and spar about their accents, wondering if they've met. Kurt breaks the tension. Looking up at the portrait of Joshua, he recites a passage that Joshua once wrote about breakfast on the terrace. This is for Fanny's benefit, and even when he admits that he memorized it the night before, she is pleased. Kurt has won our hearts and Fanny's. He is honest, unpretentious, loving toward his wife and children, and courageously dedicated to the fight against Fascism.

With the family at breakfast, Teck and Marthe speculate on the Müllers. Teck has sharp eyes, sharper than ours. He's seen the bullet scars on Kurt's face, the broken bones in his hands, and fingering the luggage, wonders why such a beat-up brief case should be locked. He could make inquiries at the Embassy, but he hesitates to "ask questions without knowing the value of the answers." When Joseph conveniently appears in the hall, Teck orders him to carry the baggage upstairs. It will be "more comfortable to look at behind closed doors." Teck is a cool, calculating con man in the old tradition, and we sense that Marthe's plea to "leave these people alone" will be ignored. As Teck follows Joseph, we know that Kurt is not safe, even in his mother-in-law's home. This detective-story close to Act I came late in the play's evolution. Originally the act ended with Teck telephoning a Baron Phillip Von Erner to inquire if he knew a Kurt Müller. The present ending is more chilling.

Quickly, yet naturally, a series of threatening questions have unfolded. What will Teck find in the brief case, how will he pursue Kurt, how will Kurt fight back? Will Teck's jealousy, or even Fanny's, shatter the affair between Marthe and David? Can an heroic anti-Fascist survive, even in a free country? These questions are not simply detective questions. Each is enriched with human consequences. Miss Hellman has made us care about what happens to these people.

When the second act opens, the Müllers have adjusted to the new household. Sara is crocheting, Bodo is repairing Anise's heating pad, Joshua is outside with Joseph learning baseball, Fanny and Teck are at cribbage. David, Marthe, Kurt, and, for a moment, Babette are missing. Political conversation appears to have been outlawed, but they skirt the edges. Bodo cannot understand why comfort and plenty exist for some and not for all. Teck probes for more information about Kurt. Did he stay close to the German border because he thought National Socialism would collapse? Sara hopes that day will come; Teck does not. If he thinks that, Joshua wonders if Teck doesn't find it "most difficult to sleep." Sara shuts him up in German and apologizes to Teck. She can no longer tolerate polite politics: "By this time all of us must know where we are and what we have to do. It's an indulgence to sit in a room and discuss your beliefs as if they were a juicy piece of gossip." Babette breaks the tension, running on from the kitchen with a potato pancake she's been cooking. Again Miss Hellman has broken in. The questions are left to simmer under the surface.

Within a few days Teck proposes to collect his $85 cribbage winnings from Fanny and depart. There are too many refugees in the house; no doubt the Müllers will also be moving on. Teck cannot avoid his inquisitorial probing. Fanny corrects him. The Müllers will not ever be leaving. They've come home to see her die and that will take time. "I shall do a fine death. I intend to be a great deal of trouble to everybody. . . . I shall take to my bed early and stay for years. In great pain." Anise is reminded of an earlier exhibition. When Fanny was pregnant with Sara, she began her labor in the middle of a dinner ball for 200 guests, apparently induced by her husband's dancing two waltzes with an English beauty. After being carried to her bedroom, she agonized for three weeks before Sara was born. By the end of Anise's recital, Fanny is ready to expel her from the house. Sara separates them, forcing each to apologize. Miss Hellman enjoys these play-acting scenes, and so does her audience.

The children help to subdue Fanny, assuring her of their love. Bodo loved her "the primary second" he saw her. And Kurt, back from the garden with David where he's been "exchanging misinformation" with the gardener, also helps to break the strain. For a moment family gaiety prevails. Fanny is planning a party for Babbie's birthday tomorrow. That's why Marthe is in town on errands. The mention of Marthe starts a touchy game. Teck has heard that David and Marthe were seen together in a jewelry store. David admits that much, no more. Fanny attempts to ease the embarrassment by asking if Kurt or Teck ever knew Paul Von Seitz? The name came up because Mellie Sewell had heard from Louis Chandler's child's governess that Teck had won quite a bit of money in a poker game at the German Embassy, a game with Sam Chandler, a munitions bootlegger, and Von Seitz's nephew Philip. Kurt has been playing the piano. He stops abruptly at the mention of the German Embassy. Miss Hellman recognized that live music could provide dramatic punctuation; she used it in *Foxes* and would again in later plays. Teck has his eyes on Kurt. Kurt must have known the young Von Seitz; he was the German military attaché in Spain. Kurt does not duck the question. He knew of him, but the side on which he fought was not where he was stationed. These two men do not fear each other. If a showdown comes, neither is going to back away. Miss Hellman does not deal in feeble confrontations. Kurt knows that if his side had won in Spain, the world would now be different. Sara and Fanny share his view, as does Miss Hellman. Sara recalls that Papa said, "For every man who lives without freedom, the rest of us must face the guilt. . . . We are liable in the conscience-balance for the tailor in Lodz, the black man in our South, the peasant in—" Miss Hellman is reminding us what the struggle is all about, what the play is about. Now it's Anise who tries to ease the tension; she's rounding up the children for their baths. Joshua admits that the "tub is a thing of glory," but the event need not be announced so publicly. Bodo is turning the heating pad over to his father. Teck jumps at this opening. Is his father an expert electrician and "as good with the radio?" Kurt, for the first time, puts a cutting edge on his voice: "Count de Brancovis. Make your questions to me, please. Not to my children." Nerves are tightening, but Teck maintains his composure. He's not yet ready for a decisive battle.

Marthe, unwittingly, helps him back away. She's returned with the birthday dresses for Babbie and for Sara. Touched to see Sara looking so happy, Kurt leans down and kisses her tenderly. More than ever we sense the strong bond that holds them together. It's an appropriate moment for Joseph to announce a long-distance call for Kurt. Sara and Teck watch him intently as he leaves the room.

Marthe tries to get their attention back to the dresses. Fanny has also bought one for her. Teck wonders if Fanny also gave her a sapphire bracelet from Barstow's. David has the answer. He gave her the bracelet, and "it is not any business of yours." Teck does not share his view. He orders Marthe upstairs to pack; the time has come for them to leave. Marthe is willing to depart, though not with him, nor with David. She loves David; David does not yet really love her, perhaps because of his mother. She understands maternal management; it led her to a title and her present predicament. She's now a tough girl and she'll survive. If Teck is leaving today—he says he is—

we must "make sure we go in different directions, and do not meet again." The refugees are abandoning their sanctuary.

When she has retreated and Kurt returns, Sara and Teck know he's troubled, though he insists that it's nothing important; he must simply go to California for a few weeks. Teck has read the afternoon newspapers; Colonel Max Friedank, chief of the anti-Nazi underground movement, has been captured in Zurich. And at the Embassy he learned that Ebber and Triste were captured with him. "They could not find a man called Gotter." Teck plays his advantage immediately. He would like to have $10,000 before he goes. Blackmail comes easily for Teck, and it's a favored device for Miss Hellman. Morris Ernst, the lawyer, once commented that blackmail was the one indispensable ingredient in her plays.

David rushes at Teck, but Kurt restrains him; the blackmail is not aimed at him and Marthe. Kurt and Teck face each other for a showdown. Kurt knows that Teck has rifled his brief case, admits that his hands have been broken, that they shake when he's afraid, that he's afraid now. He recognizes Teck's power. Teck is willing to wait for the answer while he packs.

Alone with the family, Kurt corroborates Teck's report. He knew he was on the wanted list; he did not know his price had reached $10,000. His brief case contains $23,000, "money gathered from the poor who hate Fascism." If Fanny thinks he was careless to carry so much, wasn't it careless of her "to have in your house a man who opens baggage and blackmails?" Miss Hellman sounds her message again: "Fanny, you must come to understand it is no longer the world you once knew." There's no place for innocent bystanders. Kurt and Sara know that he must return home, use his skill and money to free the new captives. The guards at Sonnenburg can be bribed. It's been done before. Teck will not yet have passed his information to Von Seitz; "he's probably only asked most guarded questions." Sara has the final words before the curtain. She accepts what must be done: "Don't be scared, darling.

You'll get back. . . . You'll do a good job, the way you've always done. . . . You'll get home. Don't worry, you'll get home. Yes, you will."

We fear for the Müllers; we cherish their courage. We wish we were like them, knowing in our hearts that we are more like Fanny and David and even Marthe. At no other moment in a Hellman play do we become so passionately involved. What happens to Kurt and Sara is happening to us.

A half-hour later the payoff has not yet been made. Kurt is at the piano, Sara sits quietly on the sofa, David is pacing the terrace. Fanny wonders how bribery can help Kurt. He assures her that though the Fascists are smart, sick, and cruel, they are not supermen. They can be beaten by men "who know what they fight for." Yes, he could abandon the cause, find excuses: his wife, his family. That is not his way.

When Teck appears carrying Kurt's briefcase, David and Fanny explode in anger. He assures them he's touched nothing, he's saving Kurt a trip upstairs, and if they persist in their abuse, he'll raise his price. The "desired list" he got from Von Seitz contains a description of "Gotter" (Kurt) and the record of his subversive activities: border crossings, secret radio broadcasts from Düsseldorf, a raid on a Gestapo chief. Kurt knows Teck and his kind. Fanny and David must try to understand this other world: "All Fascists are not of one mind, one stripe. . . . [Some] come in high places and wish now only to survive. . . . For those last, we may well some day have pity. They are lost men, their spoils are small, their day is gone." We admire, if we cannot share, Kurt's magnanimity.

Teck warns him not to let his "understanding heart" corrupt him; he will not get back if Von Seitz is informed. Kurt knows better. Roumanians, like Teck, might capture him immediately, not the Germans. They'll trail him, hoping to pick up more information before they close in. What's more, the money in his brief case is going with him. He did not touch it when his children were hungry. "If I would not touch it for them, I would not touch it for you." Teck is unconvinced:

"You are a brave one, Herr Müller, but you will not get back." Kurt is confident. He promises to send Teck a postcard reporting his arrival.

Frightened by the impasse, Fanny and David agree to supply the money, if they can be sure that Teck will not double-cross them. Understanding their skepticism, Teck will accept $2500 in cash and a postdated check, giving Kurt a month lead time. If Fanny doesn't have that much cash in her safe, he'll settle for what she has, $1500 or $1600. David goes for the checkbook, Fanny for the money.

With the "new world" out of the room Teck feels more comfortable: "We are Europeans, born to trouble and understanding it." Teck may want to play games; Kurt does not. He knows that Teck has his own backlog of troubles: the Budapest oil deal in 1931, his involvement with Fritz Thyssen and with Kessler. Von Seitz would never give him the money, certainly not for a description of a man who has a month to travel; at most the Embassy would reward him with a visa. And he's not going to get the money from Fanny and David. "You are a gambler. But you should not gamble with your life." Teck has pushed the stakes too high.

Kurt quickly drops his glass, strikes Teck on the side of the face, and as he tries to recover, throws him to the floor. After four heavy blows on the head, Teck is quiet. Kurt calmly takes his revolver from his pocket and starts to lift the body. Joshua appears in the doorway. Although stunned by what he sees, he obediently follows his father's command, opening the door and closing it after Kurt has carried the body to the terrace. Sara has been at the window during the struggle. Joshua understands that they must move again. He'll pack and get the children ready. There's no need; only "Papa is going home." Joshua must go upstairs, take Babbie and Bodo to his room, close the door, and stay there until she calls him. He obeys.*

* Mady Christians, who played Sara, once told me of their difficulties with this scene when they did a command performance in Washington on

Sara calmly and automatically sets the room in order. When Fanny and David return, she's at the telephone booking a flight to Brownsville in the name of Ritter. She assures them that Kurt has done what he had to do; he couldn't take chances with his work to spare them. When Kurt departs, he'll not be coming back. For the rest of her life she'll be alone at night, the dreadful moment in every day. Miss Hellman never lets us forget the human consequences.

Kurt is back onstage. For a thousand years man has been fighting to make a world, so far without success. He has not given up and he alone is responsible for what he's done. "I will do it again. And I will keep my hope that we may make a world in which all men can die in bed." His escape plans are simple. After saying goodbye to the children, he'll pack the body in the trunk of the Farrelly car and drive into Washington. The pistol found in the abandoned car will indicate a quarrel between two Europeans; one was shot, the other disappeared. By that time Kurt will be out of reach.

The final farewell—Sara has brought the children down—is touching and tender. Fanny and David must assume his paternal responsibility for the children; that's his only will. He's robbed them of their childhood, but he had no choice. In a few days they'll know that he's done something bad, yet they will live to see the day when men will cease to steal and lie and kill because "in every town and every village and every mud hut in the world, there is always a man who loves children and who will fight to make a good world for them." Some day he'll come back to them, or they'll come to him, and "I will have ordered an extra big dinner and we will show them

---

January 25, 1942, to celebrate President Roosevelt's birthday. This was the President's first public appearance since the war began, except to attend church and address Congress, and the security was unusually tight. The Secret Service chief knew of the gun business and advised Paul Lukas (Kurt) to substitute a wooden prop-revolver. Lukas protested. He would not tolerate such amateurish nonsense. When he was told that Secret Service men would be stationed throughout the house and backstage and though the chief would do his best some men might not get the word that the gun was part of the play, Lukas accepted the wooden gun.

what our Germany can be like." As the children give him a final hug and return to their rooms, alone in their sorrow, we wonder when and if that happy reunion will ever occur. It's an overwhelming moment, probably the only time tears cloud our eyes at a Hellman play.

The adult goodbyes are short and simple. Kurt knows that "men who wish to live have the best chance to live," and he wishes to live. Sara knows he speaks for her as well: "Come back for me, darling. If you can." As she hands him the brief case, he assures her he will try. We hear the car starting and moving away, and Sara goes to the children. Fanny and David are given a brief coda before the final curtain. They have been "shaken out of the magnolias," as Fanny says, but they'll manage the rough days ahead. "I'm not put together with flour paste. And neither are you—I am happy to learn."

Watch on the Rhine is a warm and compassionate play, as it is also a play of pith and moment. The Farrellys and Müllers are as blessed with love and nobility as the Hubbards were cursed with hate and avarice. Only Teck could have thrived in the world of *Foxes*. The political challenge does not ring with strident battle alarums, drums, uniforms, and party salutes, yet the terrifying face of Fascism hangs like a gargoyle over the Farrelly household. No longer can the Atlantic and Potomac shield us from the Nazi menace. The message penetrates because these people are "human beings not their ideological ghosts," as Louis Kronenberger put it.

Miss Hellman insisted that she did not consciously write a political document. "Good writers have a good look at the world around them and then they write it down. That's all. . . . Writers should not *see* their work. Writers shouldn't have anything to do with words like betrayal or courage or bigness or smallness or sex or Greek or new or old [or propaganda]. You write it down but you mustn't stand back and see it. You do it and go to bed and leave the big words for other people. It just isn't your business to tell people what you're doing or wanted to do." Because she centered on a minor episode in the current history of death and destruction rather than a major world event, because she shunned preachment and pronouncement, her play overshadowed the other anti-Fascist plays. One critic remarked that by comparison Elmer Rice's *Flight to the West* seemed like "embarrassed stuttering" and Sherwood's *There Shall Be No Night*—from the preceding season—like "boyish cheerleading."

The essential substance of the play remained unaltered from first scenario to final draft, though as always Miss Hellman tightened and sharpened. Early in the development Marthe worked as Teck's ally in the blackmailing scheme, and the first scenario placed the killing before the rise of the curtain on Act III. In an early draft Kurt augmented his anti-Fascist sentiments with extended passages in praise of socialism. Miss Hellman wisely decided to focus on the Fascist threat.

In retrospect, except for those who suffered through the Hitler years, the fierce impact of the play in 1941 cannot be fully sensed. If it appears melodramatic now, it appeared melodramatic then, but with a difference: the world was boiling with melodrama. Cruelty and villainy were not figments of the playwright's imagination, and it was almost impossible for a writer to tell us anything we didn't already know or to dramatize atrocities more effectively than events had already dramatized them. Miss Hellman knew that her fiction must do more than demonstrate the strange and awful truth that screamed from the front pages of every daily paper. She tried, if she did not entirely succeed, to shift from the massive melodrama of life to the heroic human story of one family behaving "like thoroughbreds in an agonizing situation," as one critic remarked, by making us aware of the blinders we still wore, blinders the European had long since discarded, by alerting us to our own vulnerability.

Here was a play of burning intensity for every American who cherished his life and his country, who believed that human decency could prevail. And for those who knew Miss Hellman, here was the expected neatness, precision, and dynamic power; here also were the characters in close-order formation, keenly not crudely differentiated, and all of them breathing with life. At the same time, here was a new Hellman with characters from another mold and with a more skillfully manipulated climactic moment. Certainly there was a firmer plausibility in Teck's destruction than in Martha's suicide or in Horace's heart attack.

Most critics pronounced it her most compelling work. In its unforgettable moments—the Müllers arriving out of the darkness of Europe, Kurt's contempt for the idea that "they" are invincible, Frau Müller letting her husband go back knowing she and the children may never see him again—the awful truth of Fascism was brought close to home. If there was too much aimless wandering in the early scenes, if the Marthe-David love affair seemed superfluous, if too much attention was bestowed on the precocious Bodo, if the final farewells were overextended, these were minor deficiencies. No one could deny its honesty nor escape its fearful message, particularly when supported by the "beautiful direction" of Shumlin* and the masterly performances of Lucile Watson (Mrs. Farrelly), Mady Christians (Sara), and Paul Lukas (Kurt). Miss Watson not only gloried in the sure-fire delights of one of Miss Hellman's salty and officious great ladies, she made her a woman as well. Paul Lukas, a native Hungarian who had made some fifty Hollywood movies and had appeared only once before on the American stage in a production of *A Doll's House* with Ruth Gordon, created a truly heroic modern man who, according to Brooks Atkinson, "knew fear a thousand times, but resisted it with modest steadfastness because he believed in the freedom and dignity of man." He was elegant, even in his silences, "one of the great performances in recent years."

Many critics wondered how the play's documentary pertinence might appear a quarter of a century later. Would future readers believe that this was what life in America was like when the Nazi evil began to creep across the ocean? Could we

* The printed text was dedicated to him, with "Thanks and Affection."

hope that by then they would find it "melodramatic and improbable for all its eloquence"? That day has not arrived.

At a dinner at the Algonquin Hotel on Sunday evening, April 27, 1941, the critics honored her with their highest accolade, the New York Drama Critics' Circle Award. The citation read, "To Lillian Hellman for *Watch on the Rhine*, a vital, eloquent and compassionate play about an American family suddenly awakened to the danger threatening its liberty." When the play opened at the Martin Beck Theatre on April 1, 1941, *The Little Foxes* was still sending back healthy profits from its national tour. Miss Hellman has jumped into the front rank of serious and successful American playwrights.

The following January, while the play was still on the boards, Miss Hellman speculated on changes she might have made. Perhaps, as in *Days to Come*,* she had one character too many, but she could not determine which one. She thought her anti-Fascist sentiments should have been more pointed, many speeches cleaner, many things said with more depth and understanding. Yet she was certain that she had done her best at the time the play was written. "Within the limitations of my own mind and nature, my own understanding, my own knowledge, it was the best I could do with what I had. If I didn't hope to grow, I would not hope to live."

Two days before the play concluded its Broadway run of 378 performances on Saturday, February 21, 1942, and prepared to go on the road, beginning in Philadelphia the following Monday, a gala farewell was held in the Martin Beck lounge after the performance. The public was invited to contribute a dollar and join Miss Hellman and the cast, the proceeds to go to the Emergency Anti-Fascist Refugee Fund. Since the play had opened, she had been involved with many similar ventures. She was co-chairman of a Dinner-Forum on "Europe Today" at the Hotel Biltmore on October 9, the money to be used to transport outstanding anti-Fascists from

* During the run of *Watch*, Shumlin contemplated a series of special matinees of a reworked *Days to Come*. The project never materialized.

French concentration camps to Mexico. In March, 1942, she participated in a dinner honoring Paul Robeson.* Her political enterprises were not always so public and solemn. In June, a week before her birthday, she sent a wire to a dozen of her friends: "A birthday present for Lillian Hellman is a blow against Fascism."

In the summer of 1942 an illustrated limited edition of *Watch on the Rhine* was published by the Joint Anti-Fascist Refugee Committee to support their activities. Numbers 1–50, bound in leather, were priced at $50. Everyone involved donated his services, including Rockwell Kent, eleven other artists, and Dorothy Parker.

Miss Parker's foreword, so eloquently echoing Miss Hellman's sentiments, deserves a wider audience than it had:

> The woman who wrote this play and the men who made these drawings give this, their book, to those who earliest fought Fascism. Most of those warriors died; on the stiff plains of Spain, behind the jagged wire of French prison camps, in small echoing rooms of German towns. Few of their names are told, and their numbers are not measured. They wear no clean and carven stones in death. But for them there is an eternal light that will burn with a flame far higher than any beside a tomb.
>
> Many did not die, but they none the less gave their lives. Wherever they are, they bear the battle on. And because they do, death walks behind them daily. No man grows used to that cold follower.
>
> These men, the dead and the living, knew soonest, gave first. Because of them, other men will stand and stretch

* George Jean Nathan wrote: "It is a rare committee formed to improve the accommodations of the Negroes at the Ritz-Plaza, or to make Palestine a future Newport for the Jews, or to improve the quality of impoverished Chinese Peasant's chow mein, or to instruct Tom Lamont in the underestimated virtues of the Stalin economy, or to guarantee the right of free speech to Morris Ernst that does not find her name high up on its stationery." (*Theatre Book of the Year, 1943–44*. New York, 1944, p. 296)

and stride again, will see their women beside them proud and straight of shoulder, will look in their children's eyes and find no fear. Because of them, the world can go unashamed.

They are brave men who lay down their lives and their liberty that men to come may live and be free. This play, these pictures, more shining than marble, more enduring than brass, stand here to the glory of their courage.

Dorothy Parker

During the spring of 1942, Lillian Hellman edited Hammett's screen version of *Watch on the Rhine*. Except for localizing some scenes and supplying more explicit detail for others, the film duplicated the play. At the opening we see the Müllers cross the Mexican border, then in the day coach and at lunch counters on their journey to Washington. These scenes alternate with Fanny in her limousine rushing around Washington to buy tricycles and other necessities for the children. Later the camera tours the Farrelly mansion and the Washington sights, including a view of the Müller children on top of the Washington Monument. It also shows Teck at the German Embassy, talking of spies and anti-Nazis and later procuring a copy of the "wanted" list. But the essentials of the play were not sacrificed to these additions. Apparently at one point the Hays office insisted that the film show some retribution, even if accidental, for Kurt's killing of the count until Miss Hellman wrote to Mr. Breen inquiring if he were aware that it was now national policy to exterminate Nazis. Produced by Hal Wallis at Warner Brothers, directed by Shumlin and with Paul Lukas repeating his stirring performance, it alerted a wider public "to what we are fighting for," and when the critics appraised the 1943–44 film season, it was selected one of the best pictures of the year.

When London saw the play at the end of April, 1942, directed by Emlyn Williams with Anton Walbrook (Kurt),

Diana Wynyard (Sara), and Athene Seyler (Fanny), the critics declared that its harrowing message made it "one of the best and most moving plays in years," a shattering reminder that "we are all guilty, and that if it is now too late to undo what has been done, it is by no means too late to re-make, to create again a world in which decent humanity may live, unpursued and undevoured."

IX

The North Star and *The Searching Wind*

Thoughts of a new play were running through Miss Hellman's head while she was still occupied with Hammett's treatment of *Watch on the Rhine*. Not only was she impatient to get a play underway, she knew she must continue to speak about the state of the world. For several weeks she struggled with a scenario centering on the Versailles Peace Conference. When that failed to take form, she may have thought of Joshua Farrelly, whose portrait had hung in full view throughout *Watch on the Rhine*. In his days in the American foreign service he must have known what was happening in the world. Perhaps now, if he stepped down, he could tell us where and when we failed to see the danger ahead.

In the summer of 1942 she could not have pushed the war out of her mind even if she wanted to. Hammett, though he was forty-eight and his X-rays still showed the tuberculosis he had contracted during World War I, had enlisted as an army private, and from his station at Fort Monmouth, New

Jersey, kept her apprised of America's military progress. He had been assigned to "revise, correct, rewrite, coordinate, deshit and otherwise make sense of three divergent courses in Army Organization." His reports from Monmouth that fall and winter, before he was transferred to Seattle, helped her tolerate his absence. On a slot-machine typewriter—ten cents for thirty minutes—he described his favorite colonel, who said, "He done this and he done that." He sent her to Abercrombie's for a pair of shoes, 10½C, his contribution to the Army's motto, "Keep the civilian population busy with errands." He reported that there were "a great many young men in the army who look, talk, act and snigger like Bennett Cerf" and "a surprising number of finger-nail biters. (Try to keep from relaying this item to Dotty [Dorothy Parker] even if you think it would cheer her to know that Mr. Campbell is among his ilk.)" On December 15, under the heading "Private Hammett reports," he listed sixteen military accomplishments. Among them: "1. That he passed prick inspection last night with flying colors. 2. That he was accompanied by Private Gottlieb, one of your people," to enjoy the delights of the village.

After he was moved to Seattle and then to the Aleutians, in August, 1943, his "Dear Lily" letters continued regularly, always gay and never weighted with the dreariness and frustration he must have felt. From Seattle he sent her instructions for setting the turtle traps at Hardscrabble, announced that he was going to town for a ball game and "to see if any old friends have daughters, and that darling is how we are winning this war." On August 22, from Alaska he wrote, "Your report on the play sounds exactly like a girl named Lillian Hellman I used to know, when she was writing a new play. . . . I still like 'The Searching Wind' for your play, so don't let's have anymore dillydallying about it." In November—apparently she'd been ill—he advised her to "get through that hospital stuff and that stuff with your teeth and then stay all in one piece. You're not supposed to start falling apart as soon as my back is turned. I'd figure that with reasonable care you could be made to last a number of years longer, and I haven't made any plans for replacing you. So cut it out. Much love. S. D. H."

With Hammett in uniform, she had to find her own patriotic role at home. She continued signing her name to anti-Fascist projects, contributed a few sentences to the speeches of Washington politicians, and tried to bring the new play into line. But the play was sidetracked when she agreed to join William Wyler, the director, in preparing a documentary film on the war in Russia. The idea may have originated with President Roosevelt, though Harry Hopkins acted as spokesman for the government. She and Wyler went to Washington to consult with Ambassador Litvinov. He was fascinated by the proposal but wondered if his government could help when they were fighting for their lives. Fortunately his skepticism did not prevail; they had reached the Russian Embassy at a fortunate moment. The next day Molotov arrived and enthusiastically promised to supply a Russian bomber, a camera crew, and whatever else they needed.

The picture was never made. At first it was delayed because Goldwyn proposed that Wyler and Hellman reduce their normal fees, allowing their patriotism and devotion to Russia to count for cash. Miss Hellman reportedly told Goldwyn, "The trouble with you, Sam, is that you think you're a country. You're not." Then Wyler enlisted in the Air Force, and Miss Hellman refused to proceed with another director. But since she had gone this far and was still under contract to Goldwyn, she agreed to work with Lewis Milestone on a semidocumentary along the same lines—documentary because is was to be fully researched, semi because it would be shot in Hollywood, not in Russia.

Her first attempt at an original script did not please her. When she finished writing at the end of December, 1942, and returned to New York, believing she had given Goldwyn an honest film about Russian peasants fighting and dying for their country, she had not reckoned with Lewis Milestone.

Two weeks after she was back in New York she received fifty pages of suggested changes and whole pages of dialogue rewritten by him. A month later another batch arrived. She had not known that Milestone invariably rewrote every script he directed. She protested to him and to Goldwyn, without success, and when she saw a rough-cut version in May, her peasants had become Hollywood slick: clean, noble, and handsome. Their North Star cooperative on the Bessarabian frontier resembled a North Dakota prairie town, and they danced to Aaron Copland's music and sang Ira Gershwin's lyrics as if they were strays from *Oklahoma*. She was so incensed that she bought back her Goldwyn contract for $30,000. When *The North Star* premiered in two Broadway theatres simultaneously on November 4, 1943, the critics echoed Miss Hellman's displeasure. James Agee, for example, thought it represented "the utmost Hollywood can do, within its present decaying tradition, with a major theme." Yet they admitted that its anti-Nazi message was not completely lost on the great American movie audience, and in spite of the Hollywood-Milestone treatment, there were some telling moments. One comes when Dr. Kurin, a devoted scientist and physician, addresses his former student, Dr. Von Harden, and Richter, his Nazi assistant: "Men like you who have contempt for men like Richter are the real filth. Men who do the work of Fascists and pretend to themselves that they are better than those for whom they work. Men who do murder while they laugh at those who order them to do it. It is men like you who sold your people to men like him." Its slickness apparently did not disturb the Russians. In August, 1944, the Soviet Embassy reported that it was drawing capacity crowds in Novosibirsk, Tomsk, Stalinsk, and other Siberian cities. The film still occasionally reappears on late-night television under the title *Armored Train*.

Her frustration with the Hollywood system would have been more distressing had she not had her own new play already in the typewriter. Here she had complete and final authority. She had plunged immediately into writing without the customary preliminaries. Her *Watch* notebooks, her own vivid memories of Germany, France, and Spain, and the front pages of the daily press for the past decade—she was always an avid newspaper reader, sometimes reading as many as six a day—provided all the details she needed. The human story, geared to her audience, had been sparked by Joshua Farrelly's portrait, and the title was supplied by a maid who had frequently reminded her that "it takes a searching wind to find the tree you sit in."

Miss Hellman knew her Broadway patrons: upper middle-class, comfortable and secure in their elegant apartments and suburban retreats, convinced of their invulnerability. They were neither cold nor heartless; they wept for their less fortunate brothers, wrote checks of condolence, flaunted their liberality. Yet few perceived their share in the world's guilt. Even at this late moment, she might shatter their innocence, reminding them that they had hugged the sidelines, watching the gathering storm with their fingers crossed, convinced that it would blow itself out.

As usual she put four or five versions through the typewriter before she satisfied her own quality control with a draft for Shumlin in August, 1943. Even after that she did considerable doctoring before the play went into rehearsal. The changes from draft to draft were not radical, though she once said that this play took more work than any of the others. Only two minor characters were dropped as she went along. Some names were changed: Moses Taney began as Moses Bowman, Emily Hazen as Alice Hazen, and Catherine Bowman as Catherine Wondell. She abandoned the tight three-act structure, freely shifting the action from Washington to Rome to Berlin to Paris and from 1944 to the twenties to the thirties and back to the forties. After she submitted the play to Shumlin, she told a friend that "he's probably mad at me for putting in so many sets and so many people, but I couldn't help it." She was right. Shumlin had recently been burned by an expensive and unprofitable multiset play and had vowed never to undertake a production that required more than a single interior. In his first conference with Howard Bay, he demanded that he see fully detailed models of every setting; once the scenery costs were fixed, not a penny more would be available.

Shumlin's economy was not apparent when the curtain went up. *The Searching Wind* opens in an elegant drawing room in the Hazen house in Washington, with the same fine proportions, the same rich furnishings, and the same terrace as the Farrelly residence had. No portrait surveys the room, however. Instead a handsome man of seventy in evening clothes, reading a newspaper, appears in command. Across from him a young man in uniform, his leg propped on a chair, a cane beside him, is also reading a paper. Grandpa Moses has given up publishing, though he still owns the newspaper. Like all former thinkers, he's writing a book. When Sam is free, if the leg gets him a discharge, he can take over the newspaper and spend the rest of his life "acting important and misinforming folks." He's qualified even if his international parents wasted his time learning foreign languages and gave him only one year at Harvard in which to learn to read. Moses is a caustic skeptic. Fanny Farrelly's husband must have been like him.

Moses and Sam have jumped the generation gap. They're frank and open with each other. When Grandpa Moses attempts to read an article from Italy written by Ambassador Alexander Hazen, Sam refuses to listen. He can read his father's articles by himself. Moses persists, annoyed by the bad writing: "People on newspapers write English as if a rat were caught in the typewriter and they were trying to hit the keys which wouldn't disturb it." Miss Hellman reserves her figurative whims for the secure and crotchety oldsters: Mrs. Tilford, Cora Rodman, Fanny Farrelly, and Moses Taney. Moses cannot tolerate diplomatic doubletalk. Three thousand words to say "that sometimes democracies have to deal with people they don't approve and sometimes, in order to save something or other, you have to do something else or other." The hollow phrases have a familiar ring. Already we know that Miss Hellman is tracking serious matters.

More background is laid before the rest of the household moves in. Sam has always been conscious of being the son of a famous father and famous grandfather. His friend Leck, who was killed in Italy, did not suffer from that affliction. His father was a baker in Jersey City. Moses also has memories of Italy: the day, twenty-two years ago, when Mussolini marched into Rome. Miss Hellman may have chosen a wider panorama, but she has still compacted the details tightly and neatly.

Before introducing the other principals, she entertains us with a comic interlude. Ponette, in an ill-fitting butler's uniform, wanders in with a tray of bottles and glasses, dropping a glass as he settles the tray on the edge of the table. He's as troubled with the language as he is with his role: "Pardon. You think that Madame Hazen tonight wishes here, or table terrace?" Hearing the commotion, Sophronia, the Negro servant, wants to know, "What spilled tonight?" Moses plays Tambo to her Bones: "It's not spilling night, it's dropping night."

The Hazen establishment is moving into action for the evening. Something special is in the offing. We've already noted Moses Taney's evening clothes. Now Emily enters, a handsome woman in her early forties in a dinner dress, nervous and apprehensive. Catherine Bowman, whom she hasn't seen in twenty years, is coming to dinner. She hopes Moses and Sam are not proposing to join them. Moses had not intended to stay, but "any dinner at which you aren't wanted is always a little less dull than one at which you are." Emily is in no mood for jokes; why doesn't he take an apartment at the Shoreham and come in for Sunday tea? He reminds her that the house belongs to him and that he intends to leave it to Sam, not to her. She and her husband don't need a house; they'll "always be busy ambassadoring in Europe, talking away in eight languages, in that diplomatic basic English." If Sam turns out to be a diplomat, he'll be scratched from the will. It's the opportune moment for Alexander Hazen. He's a good-looking man of fifty in dinner clothes, the uniform of diplomacy. He and his son are on easy terms. He understands Sam's lack of enthusiasm for the foreign service, his differing views on Italy. At the moment he's more concerned that someone saw Sam going into the hospital. As Sam brushes the question aside, his evasion is helped by a cab coming up the drive.

Alex had hoped they would be dining alone. Instead they're to be joined by Cassie Bowman. When Emily heard she was in Washington, she invited her. After all, they grew up together; Moses had escorted the two of them around Europe when they finished college; Cassie has never seen Sam. She's speaking too rapidly; Alex is stirring the martinis too vigorously. He has seen Cassie last week. Moses tries to relieve their distress: "This can't have the historic importance of the reconciliation of General Grant and General Lee."

Cassie is also a beautiful person, though her dinner dress is plain. Her first impulse was to enter from the terrace, as she did when they were kids. The greetings are warm and polite, if uncomfortably soft between Cassie and Alex, and Cassie unwittingly increases the tension. Sam must know how proud his father is of his ribbons: "He told me last night that your leg was getting better." Perhaps the cocktails will see them through, though Moses is sure they'll "fall flat on each other's faces." The ladies struggle with past history: Cassie's teaching and a survey of Hazen's diplomatic assignments which Cassie already knows from Alex. Emily tries to maintain her composure, though she's burning with jealousy. She heard the "last night"; she had thought it was "last week." (Not before, nor later, did Miss Hellman center on the embattled triangle, though she knew the tortures and techniques of the jealous female. In her early days with Hammett she was regularly on the "find-out kick," hounding him for details about his amorous adventures.)

Again Moses rescues them, with political talk: "Who are we sending over, Alex, to take care of those elderly clowns who call themselves governments-in-exile?" Alex, true to his calling, doesn't think they're clowns; we must work with the leaders. Moses knows it's a dangerous game, the game that Woodrow Wilson played, assuming "that bad men are stupid and good men are smart, and all diplomats are both good and smart." Again they're propelled into the awkward past when they were all in Rome together, the day Mussolini took over the city. As they go in to dinner, the ladies are still sparring. When Cassie drops her purse, Emily reminds her that before exams at college she invariably dropped everything. Cassie can match her: "Everybody does something when they get nervous: You speak more slowly. You always did. You're doing it now." They're on even terms as the curtain falls. Something happened in Italy, and while they're troubling their dinner with the memories, we will see the day in Rome as it was in 1922.

Originally the second scene was set in a Paris hotel, then in the Excelsior in Rome, and finally in the Grand Hotel. The room is crammed with trunks; there's a news ticker on the table; Sophronia is crowded into a corner, ironing. Scattered gun shots can be heard as the phone rings. It's Hazen. He wants Taney and the girls to move to the Embassy until their boat leaves. When Sophronia transmits the request to Taney in the next room, he shouts from behind the door, "Tell Alex to tell the Ambassador to go to Hell." Sophronia makes a diplomatic translation, "Mr. Taney says to thank the Ambassador, but we'll stay here." A waiter arrives with a breakfast cart, assuring Sophronia that the manager will call on all the guests to tell them not to be frightened by guns. Taney, in a dressing gown, heads for the news ticker and reads, "The government is in control. King Victor Emmanuel returned this morning from bathing in the sea. The stories of Mussolini's armies are lies." Taney can read behind the news; Signor Mussolini will be in the city in a few hours. Moses tries to understand how and when things happened, when he should have first known. The waiter knows only what he's seen: "For me, for many Italians, it was there in 1919, three years ago. Your President Wilson came to tell us what to do, tell us how to make a free country." But Wilson wasn't allowed to speak to the people. In 1919, Moses had guessed wrong or he might have helped. Wilson was a man who liked fancy words and fancy names. "That's one of the things I didn't know in time. I am sorry for that." We may be waiting for the personal story of Emily, Cassie, and Hazen, but the political life of *The Searching Wind* comes first.

As the guns become louder, Emily and Cassie enter in their dressing gowns. Twenty-two years have been stripped from them since we saw them a few moments ago in the Hazen drawing room. It's the only time Miss Hellman employs such a theatrical tour de force. With the political groundwork laid and with Moses out of the room, the girls take up the personal story. They're about to return home, Cassie to teach English at $1500 a year. Somehow she's neglected to share this news earlier; nor did she give Emily the straight story about last night. When she left the party, where everyone was praising Mussolini, it was not because of a headache. She left with Alex. Emily is shocked; she had thought they did not get along well and of course she had expected to marry him herself some day. Already we sense that the marriage must have been engineered by Emily. She had money; her father was an important person. That must have counted heavily with a budding diplomat.

As Emily goes to pack and the manager appears to assure them that the Grand Hotel will be protected, Alex comes in. Contrary to our expectancy, he and Cassie do not share the same wavelength, at least on political matters. He is certain that the soldiers have orders to admit Mussolini. The Ambassador can't do anything; it's not his job. Cassie is distressed, as she has been before, that Alex thinks and talks like the

Embassy. Her attack is too strong for him: "For God's sake, Cassie, if you disapprove of me so much, why did you sleep with me?" Isn't she in love with him? She thinks she is, yet she can't stay with him in Rome. She needs to be alone to think; she's told Emily about them. Cassie deals in half-truths. She does not tell Alex that she's taken a job; she's not told Emily that they slept together.

In spite of their differences they manage an embrace which Moses interrupts. The shooting and shouting outside is rising in intensity. The manager and two Fascist soldiers have come in to certify the guests. Moses tells the manager to shut up, as he reads the ticker tape: "A proclamation has been given to the press. King Victor Emmanuel has asked Benito Mussolini to form a government." Moses is not intimidated by the military presence; he orders the soldiers out. Alex warns him not to be too daring: "The Ambassador feels that we cannot take sides in an internal uprising." The two men see the events in a different light, and Alex is annoyed with Taney's power. "You've been ragging me for years, Mr. Taney. I don't usually mind it. I do today . . . another few months of the kind of misery and starvation they've had, and there would be a revolution. If Mussolini can put it down that doesn't make me like him, or the money behind him, or the people." Alex may echo the American line, but Moses doesn't "like to see them put down by gangsters who make a job of doing it for those who want it done. . . . Whenever such things happen, the rest of the world some day pays for them." That is how the world stood in 1922; how Alex saw it; how Taney saw it. Moses retreats to his room; he'll not share his views with the reporters who are waiting for him in the lobby.

The personal story now comes back in focus. Emily has her turn with Alex, though Cassie is within earshot in the next room. Emily has decided to stay on in Rome, for her music. She's now a great heiress and can do as she pleases. Alex can beau her around. At the moment he's too occupied with his duties to think of the future. He must return to the Embassy.

When Cassie reappears, Emily is idling at the piano and the guns are pounding again. Emily wonders if Cassie has told her everything. Even when they were little girls, she recalls, Cassie was not always truthful. Perhaps after all it is best for Cassie to go home, while she stays in Rome. We are not surprised when Cassie drops the box she's carrying. Human history repeats itself. "What's the matter, Cassie? . . . What is there to be nervous about or to hide?" Cassie is picking up the box as the curtain falls. Miss Hellman has not abandoned Ibsen. Ranging over twenty-two years in multiple scenes has not reduced her compulsion to make everything count.

Back in the Hazen drawing room after dinner, we observe the characters in a new light. Cassie may have loved Alex, but Emily had the power and the will, and Alex was ready to obey whatever wind might forward his career. Vaguely we sense that the human story mirrors the political story.

As in the opening scene of *Foxes*, the principals are still at dinner. Sophronia and Ponette are preparing the coffee and brandy in the drawing room, giving the actors time for their age transformations backstage. When the Hazens and their guest return to the stage, their tabletalk is clearly hanging heavily over them. Cassie has a headache. Moses is still trying to brighten the evening. He thinks Emily is now old enough to be told that he never liked her mother. He felt sorry when she died but did not think she should have taken such extreme action to accommodate him. Alex's father, similarly burdened, escaped by falling "in love with the State Department and that's nothing to climb into bed with on a winter night."

We have not been cheated by not joining them at dinner. They have been on the same track, worrying over the meaning of that fateful day in Rome. If Alex had seen things straight, Sam might never have had to fight in Italy. Their generation has made the mess for him. Moses grants the point, but it takes more than seeing to be smart. Perception without action accomplishes nothing.

When Emily leads the way to the terrace for coffee, Cassie and Alex are left behind. Why did she accept the invitation, why have they dwelt on the past, why did Cassie say they had dinner together last night when it was last week? It was a slip, and she's hurt by his sharp questions. He's touching her hand, saying he's sorry, when Emily returns. Cassie wants to escape. The reunion was a mistake. Emily doesn't agree. "This has been coming for a good many years. We've started it; let's finish it." Cassie thinks it's futile to talk of what might have been. Alex would prefer to leave the argument to the ladies; Sam, in the doorway, prefers to listen. He has a feeling he's involved. Emily is not sure where the truth game will lead, but she persists and is in command as the curtain falls. Again we will not share their confessions; we'll see the story unfold as it happened. However disturbing Cassie's present visit, the dramatic substance is in the past.

As the second act opens, Alex is at a restaurant table. Place and time are quickly revealed: Berlin, 1923, a year after Mussolini's march into Rome. The Hazens are now married and Alex holds another diplomatic post. Inflation is destroying Germany. Only the Americans and English can afford the drinks that cost more than a German can earn in a week. At a distance and then on the street outside, we hear an angry mob shouting, "Juden. Judenstrasse. Juden." It is the *Freikorps* bound for the Jewish section. The doors and windows of the restaurant must be closed. Eppler, the manager, enlists Hazen's help to translate and clarify the situation for his frightened patrons. Alex talks as he did in Rome: " . . . there has been a disgraceful riot of hoodlums against the Jewish section. . . . There is nothing to be done now except by the police." Alex still believes the situation can be controlled.

As the shouts fade, someone is beside him saying, "Hard to believe that we would live to see a pogrom in the year 1923." At first he does not recognize Cassie. They have not met since the wedding, though Cassie has followed his travels. Apparently he and Cassie quarreled before the wedding; she wonders if it's a good marriage. It is; and though the question troubles him, he's glad to see her. If their love is reawakening, they'll have to wait.

Emily rushes in with a young man. They've had a frightening experience. As they crossed the Judenstrasse, a man was being dragged through the streets, an old lady beaten on the head. When they tried to help, "the crowd began to scream at us and push us back . . . we were dirty Americans" and should mind our own business. Only after telling her story does she recognize Cassie with a casual "Hello." Halsey, the young man from the Embassy, believes the *Freikorps* people and the Young People's League are responsible. "There's no question now it's tied up with the Bavarian trouble. The story around is that somebody from Thyssen put up the money for Ludendorff and for those clowns outside." Alex can't believe that a man like Thyssen would support such horrors. Cassie is shocked that Alex refuses to recognize "the proof outside the door," that he'll protest only to protect the Americans in Berlin, not because "it's a horror and a disgrace." When Eppler assures them that the police are in control, Alex and Halsey return to the Embassy.

When Emily and Cassie spotted each other in the restaurant several days earlier, neither had spoken. They have not communicated since the wedding, though Cassie has secretly written to Alex. Emily insists that Cassie has never been a problem; the marriage has worked out very well; she's expecting a baby in March. Cassie refuses to believe her. When your best friend marries your beau, the damage is not repaired so easily, at least not for her, even if she did quarrel with Alex. She came to Berlin because she needed a vacation and wanted to "find out if we could be as good friends as we used to be." Now it seems best not to meet again. Emily agrees, though she's sure they'll meet. Cassie will marry and have children and sometime they'll sit on the porch of a summer hotel and watch their kids playing together and "laugh that it could ever have been any other way—"

In the next scene, instead of returning to the Hazen drawing room, the action is transferred to the living room of a suite in the Hotel Meurice in Paris. James Sears is identifying himself on the telephone as Ambassador Hazen's secretary. Hazen has moved up in the diplomatic world. The caller is a Count Max von Stammer who happens to be in Paris and wishes to visit the ambassador. Alex, entering from his room, agrees to an unofficial social call. He too is vacationing in Paris. France is in turmoil. Children are to be evacuated from Paris tomorrow; everyone who can afford it is departing; Beneš is reported to have called London yesterday morning; intelligence insists that Russia is not prepared to fight Germany. Sears is reading from Halsey's latest confidential report. Bonnet has met with Litvinov in Geneva; Litvinov has promised aid to Czechoslovakia; Halsey is positive Bonnet lied in his report to the French cabinet; rumor about the Munich meeting is still in the air. Alex still cannot believe the Nazis. How can he sift the true from the false and prepare his report that should have gone to Washington five days ago?

With the political moment established, Emily brings the domestic story up to date. Their daughter Sara, whom we never meet, is off to an art gallery. Sam is out walking with Mr. Taney. The Hazens come to Paris every summer to meet the children, "then Father arrives and that's the last we see of Sam." Cassie is also in Paris and Emily has invited her to tea; she has not seen her since that day in Berlin in 1923, though Alex has. In fact he saw her last week. Emily knows, if not from him. Cassie is still troubling them, though they've chosen not to talk of her, and Alex prefers to keep it that way.

When Emily leaves, Count von Stammer is announced. He is an old man who has met Hazen once before, in Genoa in 1922, and now represents von Ribbentrop. They know that Hazen is about to send a report to Washington; the news leaked at a dinner party. Hitler wants the Sudetenland; France and Britain are ready to agree to his terms, and von Ribbentrop wants to be assured that the United States will not pressure them to resist. Alex is angered by the proposal. He does not make the policy of his country: "No one man makes it, thank God. And I am an unimportant man sending back an unimportant report." Von Stammer has more to offer. Hitler will be satisfied if the Sudetenland is ceded; he'll then turn east and "rid Europe of the menace of Russia." Alex will not make deals. Von Stammer is shocked that Hazen doesn't realize what's happening: "By the end of this week I would guess that a journey will be made and a conference will be held. And if there is no meddling from your side of the world, all will be settled." Now that he's performed his duty, von Stammer admits that he does not always see eye-to-eye with his government, yet he does what has to be done. Miss Hellman reminds us that not all Fascists were fanatics. Their cynics were not unlike Moses Taney, their dutiful servants not unlike Alex Hazen. On both sides these silent partners might have prevented the catastrophe.

While Alex is still brooding on what he's been told, there is a knock and Cassie enters. It's not the right moment for a reunion. Always before, he has been able to send his dispatches, satisfied that he had done his best. This time he doesn't know what's best, doesn't know what to say. Why don't they escape to the country for a day? At first Cassie refuses, but when he insists that in spite of his love for Emily, he's only been "in love" once, she agrees to meet him at the small hotel in Fontainebleau. He kisses her goodbye and returns to his desk.

Fumbling aimlessly through his papers he discovers a newspaper clipping Sears has marked for him, a gossip item about Emily and her high-society friends. When she returns, upset by what she's seen in the streets (people running away from their country), Alex wonders if perhaps she too has been running away, blinding herself to what's happening by continuing to associate with the "fashionable society trash." She should know that one can no longer go to dinner where one went a few years ago. She's been hearing the wrong things from the people who are trying to protect their wealth and hers. She insists that her friends may be right, perhaps if Hitler got what he wants now that would shut him up for good. She too hates the Nazis, but she doesn't want a war; she wants Sam to be happy in a peaceful world.

Three times Alex attempts to tell her that Cassie has been there. Emily appears not to hear, then admits that she's seen Cassie and waited in the lobby for her to leave. He might think she's afraid of nothing; it's not true, but before she can utter her fears, Sears is in the room turning on a broadcast from London: "The announcement has just been made that Prime Minister Chamberlain and Premier Daladier will fly to Munich tomorrow morning. There are already hints of cabinet resignations. . . ." Alex snaps off the radio and turns to Emily: "Well, there's your peace." No one in the theatre could escape the impact of that moment. Everyone had his own mind's-eye image of where he was and what he was doing when he first heard the news. Emily is angered by Alex's attempt to tie the appeasement game to the "decadent trash in the society columns." Having contempt for them doesn't automatically put him on the other side. And he's wrong to think this is the time for a personal showdown. She'll order dinner for him and Sears so he can concentrate on his report.

Sears is at the typewriter as Alex dictates. He does not believe that the Sudetenland will be Hitler's last demand, that his talk of attacking the Soviet Union should be taken seriously. But Chamberlain should not be judged too harshly; he's working for peace while many selfish and unpatriotic men are sacrificing their countries for private gain. Alex is tempted to say something about sparing our sons, saving a generation from war, but he finally resists. Much as he deplores the Munich meeting, to label it a complete capitulation would be "a harsh and unwarranted judgment based on inadequate facts." To himself he admits his own uncertainty and takes refuge in knowing that whatever an ambassador says will make little difference. It's a fearful reminder of how history was made.

The London announcement, Hazen's report, the exodus from the city have not disrupted Paris's night life. Moses has been commandeered to the opera with Emily and wants to borrow a white tie from Alex. While Alex gets the tie, Moses reads the report on the desk and calls to Alex, "There's nothing like a good compromise to cost a few million men their lives. . . . Sad world, eh, Alex?" The curtain comes down as Alex slams the door and Moses repeats, "Very sad." Moses has sensed the sorrow engulfing the world, yet he too avoids action, still believing he can find sanctuary at home.

While we have been absent from the Hazen drawing room, they have been torturing each other with memories of what we have seen at firsthand. Emily wonders why Cassie picked the hotel at Fontainebleau for their rendezvous, the hotel where Moses had taken them as children. Sam wants to know if his father really recommended appeasement. Cassie admits that she's always been fond of Alex, yet she's been haunted by Emily. She was envious and angry when they married and wanted to punish Emily, to try to take Alex away from her. She has not really known that about herself until tonight. Now before she leaves she hopes that Sam and his new generation will see things clearly and not deceive themselves.

With Cassie's departure, the attention turns to Sam's question. Alex insists he didn't even know the word appeasement, though he never subscribed to Moses's cynical view of history. Moses had once written to Sam that "history is made by the masses of people. One man, or ten men, don't start the earthquakes and don't stop them either. Only hero worshippers and ignorant historians think they do." Moses may be right, but skepticicm should not become "an excuse to just sit back and watch." Sam doesn't belong to their world, though he doesn't yet know where he belongs. With his one leg, he'll have to find his place. He's been told at the hospital that his leg must be amputated. Moses is shattered by the news: "I hope you won't laugh at me but I would have given my life if I could have saved you any—" He's crying as he touches Sam's arm; there's a warm heart beneath the cynical facade.

Emily and Alex now must suffer even more. Sam had found his place with his friends in the army. Before four out of nine of their men had been killed at "Bloody Basin," they had spent hours talking about their families. He had proudly told them about his father until one day one of his friends produced a clipping from home, a woman columnist's report about an international party with Mrs. Alexander Hazen among the guests. "I looked around the table," the columnist wrote, "and I thought, 'Europe isn't dead. These people will go home some day and once more make it the charming, careless, carefree place I knew so well.' " His buddy gave him the clipping and said, "Glad to be sitting in mud here, Sam, if it helps to make a carefree world for your folks." It was Leck, the baker's son from New Jersey, who explained about " 'the old tripe who just live in our country now and pretend they are on the right side. . . . My God, Sam,' he said, 'if you come from that you better get away from it fast, because they helped to get us where we are.' " The next day Leck was blown to pieces.

Yet now, in spite of his disillusionment, Sam still loves his country and his parents. He speaks with great passion. "I was ashamed of that clipping. But I didn't really know why. I found out tonight. I am ashamed of both of you, and that's the truth. I don't want to be ashamed that way again. I don't like losing my leg, I don't like losing it at all. I'm scared—but everybody's welcome to it as long as it means a little something and helps to bring us out some place. All right I've said enough. I love you both. Let's have a drink." In 1944 the audience tolerated Sam's heroics. Now an actor would edge them with irony. The hope invested in the new generation has not been fulfilled. They have been trapped by the force of events, just as Moses and Alex were.

The Searching Wind, even more than *Watch on the Rhine*, derives its strength from its immediacy. With Eisenhower's invasion of France two months away, with the Nazis still threatening, we struggled to know where we went wrong in bringing the civilized world to the edge of disaster. More than in any other play Miss Hellman relied on her audience. They remembered Mussolini's march into Rome, the first hit-and-run attacks on the Jews in Berlin, the tense days before Munich. She flashed the scenes as they had happened. Well-intentioned, liberal-minded Americans had been trying to grasp what they saw, unable to comprehend fully and unable to act. The big question was inescapable: Could the catastrophic course of history have been altered if Alex or Moses or someone had spoken out?

The ultimate power of the play rests with the bitter-sad indictment of the appeasers and with the documentary reminder of Munich. The personal reflections from the world mirror are too hazy: Alex bending to the will of Emily and Cassie as he bends to the diplomatic winds; Emily using power tactics to win Alex; Cassie, one of the have-nots, relentlessly seeking revenge for the wrong done her in Rome (her Versailles!) Instead the rendezvous of the unhappy triangle seems simply to coincide with the momentous events; and with the world falling apart, they appear banal and inconsequential. Nor do the characters assume any stature. With the possible exception of Moses Taney, the portraits are little more than line drawings. Full renderings were impossible with the multiple-scene scheme. The segmented structure—one critic called it "loose as a haystack"—also reduced the firepower of the political message.

Although the critics praised the play sparingly, their Critics' Circle gave it six of their thirteen votes for the best American play of the season. (It was too late to be considered for the Pulitzer.) They commended her incisive dialogue, her provocative ideas. Above all, America needed to be awakened to the past and future dangers of appeasement, and she had done it more compellingly than any other dramatist. It was unfortunate that she tried to do more. By the second act, the repetitive meetings of the troubled trio seemed silly and the disposition of their problems too glib. With two stories, why hadn't she written two plays or one novel? And must she have made Sam's final appeal to the love of country so "simple-hearted, not to say simple-minded"? George Jean Nathan found the play "pretentious" and Stark Young called it "more windy than searching."

During the rehearsals she and Shumlin questioned each other more than usual. For the first time in their partnership she suggested that his direction might be improved and he insisted her script could be better. Still Shumlin provided an expertly detailed production and a strong company. Dudley Digges (Moses) and Montgomery Clift (Sam) were most favored by the critics. For Digges it was the outstanding performance of his career, for the newcomer Clift, "one of the year's best acting jobs." The ladies, Barbara O'Neil (Cassie) and Cornelia Otis Skinner (Emily), handsome as they were, had limited opportunities, and Dennis King (Alex) came dangerously near a burlesque of the diplomatic stuffed shirt. Even if, as Miss Hellman suspected, American audiences were unwilling to face the truth, they kept the play running for 318 performances. It might have held on even longer if she had not tried so hard to write two plays at once, one political, the other personal.

X

Russia and *Another Part of the Forest*

After seeing the text of *The Searching Wind* into print, dedicated to Dorothy Parker, Miss Hellman began preparing for a trip to Russia. That summer she also bought one of New York's smaller mansions at 63 East 82nd Street. Since *Watch on the Rhine* she had rented two rooms and a kitchenette on the third floor of the old Henry Clews house at 5 East 82nd Street; now she moved up the street, and for the next twenty-six years number 63 was her New York home.

Miss Hellman has given two accounts of the Russian adventure. The first, "I Meet the Front-Line Russians," appeared in *Collier's* (March 31, 1945), the second, much more vividly detailed, in *An Unfinished Woman*. Traveling as a "cultural emissary," a guest of the Soviets, she flew by way of Fairbanks, Alaska, in September. The rugged flight across Siberia, scheduled for three days, took fourteen. In Moscow she was met by Sergei Eisenstein and had tea with him almost daily. She was given quarters at Spasso House, Ambassador Harriman's residence, and a room, when she wished, at the National Hotel. She saw many dreary Russian plays, sat in on rehearsals of *The Little Foxes* and *Watch on the Rhine* but never saw a performance because they were not ready until the following February, spent an evening at an official reception talking with her old friend Maxim Litvinov, attended Harriman's Christmas party, and enjoyed many extended dinners and late suppers with the foreign journalists and exotic internationals who inhabited the Metropole Hotel. She was repeatedly besieged by official emissaries begging her to say whom she would like to see, where she would like to go. Unconvinced that she had no special requests, they supplied them. Certainly she wanted to see Stalin, though that request probably could not be honored. A visit to Leningrad might be possible. When she discovered how the other foreigners envied her privileged status, she accepted the invitation to go to Leningrad, and when she received the unbelievable summons to prepare for the front, she hastily assembled the heaviest woolens she could find.

She was to be ready at a moment's notice any day after December 20. For a week she waited for flying weather, then she and Raya, her interpreter, were instructed to report to the railroad station. The tall blond major who was to be their escort informed them that the journey would take two-and-a-half days—it took five—and that no questions about their location, about their destination, or about military operations would be permitted. They went south via Kiev and then back northwest to Lublin, Poland, where they were met by a Major Kazakevitch. After five days of little water, less heat, and a diet of sardines and "elderly sausage," they luxuriated in the comforts of a small hotel, where they were the only guests. Later she learned that the hotel was Marshall Zhukov's headquarters. The next morning they headed for the Vistula-Warsaw front, stopping for a painful visit to the Maidanek concentration camp which had recently been captured from the Germans. The ovens were still warm and large bins were filled with shoes carefully sorted according to size. That evening at dinner in a

Warsaw suburb she was entertained by the general and his officers, the best dinner she had had in Russia. They talked freely about the war and about their battle plans.

During her two weeks at the front she visited General Chernov's dugout where the locale maps were carefully explained, and she was allowed to take the glasses and scan the German lines across the river. Another dinner with the officers was climaxed with repeated toasts to victory, to peace, to Roosevelt, to Stalin, and to Churchill, and one officer invited her to join the march into Warsaw and on to Berlin. The day before her departure her hosts gave her farewell gifts: a cigarette case inscribed, "For Lillian Hellman, given in friendship by the men, officers, and generals of the First White Russian Army on the Warsaw front," and a "cigarette lighter made from a gun barrel. Carved on it, in awkward Latin letters are the words, 'From the first White Russian Army as a pleasant memory of your visit, January, 1945.' "

On the 14th of January, back at Spasso House, she received an urgent call from the Prime Minister's secretary regretting that Stalin could not see her on the date she proposed—a proposal she had never made—but he could arrange an appointment for the 2nd or 3rd of February. Unfortunately, she informed the secretary, she would then be on her way to England. That same afternoon she heard the Kremlin guns saluting a new victory. Warsaw had fallen, on schedule, as she had been told it would at the front.

She returned to New York on February 27, 1945, via Cairo and London, and at a press conference three days later declared that she had found the Russians a terrific people, polite, puritanical, romantic, and brave. The generals at the front had assured her that they would take care of Fascism on the European continent and hoped we would do the same in our part of the world.

With her extended absence from the typewriter, she eagerly returned to work, completing a first draft of the movie script for *The Searching Wind* in August and, incorporating the suggestions of her producer Hal Wallis, a final script in December. Most of the original was retained, though documentary locales were added: Fascist bombs dropping on Madrid in 1936, a battle scene involving Sam's platoon, and a dinner party with the "International White Trash Set." When the film was released in August, 1946, the critics again objected to the strained commingling of politics and love, and they thought Miss Hellman "too belligerently intolerant of the human mistakes in judgment when the world was whirling from one war to another." Only the five-minute vignette of Albert Basserman as the German count received uniform praise.

Even before completing the Hollywood assignment, she began work on "Play Six," a return visit with the Hubbards. While working on *The Little Foxes* she had vaguely contemplated a family trilogy: a first play to dip into the post-Civil War years, then *Foxes*, then a third, never to be written, set in Europe in the 1920s, showing Alexandra as an angry and disappointed spinster. When she found the audience at *Foxes* seeming to derive a kind of hypocritical feeling of moral superiority to the Hubbards, her own "graveyard affection" for them increased. According to one interview, she cherished them "as one would cherish a nest of particularly vicious diamondback rattlesnakes, and it seemed worthwhile to look into their family background and find out what it was that made them the nasty people they were." Now with her *Searching Wind* exercise in showing the past shaping the present and perhaps reminded of the Hubbards when General Zhukov's aide told her how much he had learned from the Civil War, she began probing the hidden horrors that had nurtured their villainy.

With Hammett back from the Aleutians and out of uniform, with two happy homes in which to work (on 82nd Street and at Pleasantville), and in the company of characters who willingly confessed their most damaging secrets, the play moved along rapidly. By midsummer the sixth and final draft was completed, rehearsals began at the end of August, and *Another*

Part of the Forest opened at the Fulton Theatre on November 20, 1946, produced by Kermit Bloomgarden and directed by Lillian Hellman!

The play chronicles the life of the Hubbards in 1880, twenty years prior to their *Little Foxes* incarnation. Twenty years does not transport them to the age of innocence; their evil natures are already well cultivated. Regina, Ben, and Oscar claw at each other, seeking favor with Marcus, their father. And Regina and Ben, when not slashing at each other, join forces against Oscar. Poor stupid Oscar whines and begs like a whipped dog. Lavinia, their mother, resembles Birdie in *Foxes*. Driven into a dream world, pitifully pleading for attention from Marcus, she finds her only solace among her friends in the "nigger church." The Oscar we know in *Foxes* learned from his father how to treat a wife and son. Birdie Bagtry, his future wife, Birdie's mother, and her cousin John Bagtry occupy Lionnet, though they live on the ragged edge. Pride will not pay bills; Bagtry family treasures will probably have to be sacrificed. Horace Giddens, Regina's future husband, never appears, though Ben has spotted him in Mobile as a likely prospect. Regina has her own prospect, the glamorous and dashing war hero, John Bagtry. Although the play has its own independent life, it is remarkably enhanced by our foreknowledge of the despicable and fascinating Hubbards.

With the curtain opening on the spacious portico of a Southern Greek mansion, French doors leading into the living room —Miss Hellman likes French doors—the heady affluence of the old South is more immediately apparent than it was in *Foxes*. At one end, under a second-story porch, doors open to the dining room and to the kitchen. The lawn slopes away at the other end, toward the main street. Obeisance to the Greeks is augmented by twin heads of Aristotle on high pedestals, and, as we learn later, Marcus Hubbard further honors the Greeks by reading the ancient authors in the original.

Regina, a handsome girl of twenty in a pretty negligee, stands on the portico looking down at John Bagtry. Recollections of Alexandra flash through our minds. Bagtry, thirty-six and with a "sad, worn face," wears a riding shirt and Confederate cavalry pants. We quickly learn that their clandestine meetings are not uncommon, that Bagtry had missed a rendezvous last night, that staying at home with his Aunt Clara and Cousin Birdie is an unacceptable excuse, that his family outranks the Hubbards on the social ladder. Regina, the cold and calculating aggressor in the relationship, angrily reminds him that her father could "buy and sell Lionnet on the same morning, its cotton and its women with it." John smothers her tirade by jumping to the portico and taking her in his arms, and she apologizes. She has a plan, not yet revealed to her father. John too has a plan, to fight in Brazil; he's never been as happy as he was in the war, even though the Confederates lost.

Before they can expand their stories, Lavinia Hubbard and her Negro servant, Coralee, enter from around the portico. Miss Hellman has returned to her old system, whetting our curiosity and then making us wait. Mrs. Hubbard is a delicate woman of fifty-eight with a sweet high voice and "a distracted, nervous way of speaking." She's been to church, where the colored folks said a prayer for her and sang a little song to honor her birthday. She recalls the day when John went off to the war and she blew him a kiss. Of course, they were then living in their little house, and he didn't see her. The Hubbards have come up in the world since the war.

Pushing her mother into the house, Regina attempts to recapture her privacy with John without success. The household is beginning to stir. Bagtry ducks out of sight as Marcus appears from his bedroom on the upper porch, "a strong-looking man of sixty-three with a soft voice of tone and depth." He asks Regina to wait and join him with her first coffee. When Marcus returns to his bedroom, we learn that John and he have never met socially, only at the Hubbard store. No Bagtry has condescended to enter the Hubbard house. Before he departs, he accepts Regina's command to meet tomorrow night, and he takes her in his arms again, kissing her with great feeling.

Sexual passion usually receives short shrift, but here, if fleetingly, we see its power.

With John hurrying away, we're ready for Marcus. Instead, Ben enters from around the house with Jacob, a Negro servant, carrying a valise and three boxes. Ben is thirty-five, "a powerful, calm man with a quiet manner," a carbon copy of his father. The boxes are from Chicago, addressed to Regina. Ben has caught sight of Bagtry and disapproves. Regina is not intimidated. She'll meet a man on the porch in her wrapper if she chooses.

Again Miss Hellman cuts the scene short, giving the flow of real life. Marcus, reappearing above, orders Regina to brew the coffee while he teases Ben. Ben couldn't have been called home to examine the books; Marcus would never allow him to touch the books in his library. Ben squirms like a child. He's returned to examine the books in the store, not in the library. He had wanted to stay in Mobile to invest $2000 in Birmingham Coal, but Marcus wouldn't give him the money. Marcus has a final humiliating command before he returns to his room: "Carry your own valise, son. It is not seemly for a man to load his goods on other men, black or white." What a perverse household this must be with a grown son suffering such indignity. We clearly see where Regina and Ben learned the sadistic techniques they later use on Oscar.

When Marcus reappears on the lower porch, Lavinia announces that a Colonel Isham wants to see him. The colonel, clearly uncomfortable in the Hubbard household, reports that a Sam Taylor in Roseville has been beaten up by the night riders. Oscar was with the riders and would have been strung up if Isham had not protected him. Any man in the county would be happy to string up a Hubbard. Apparently Hubbard problems are not confined within the family. Marcus shouts into the house, ordering Ben to rope Oscar and bring him out. When the sons appear, he throws a wad of bills at Ben; $500 is to be counted out to take care of Taylor. Oscar's protests of innocence and Ben's feeble attempt to provide an alibi are ignored, as is the colonel's protest that five hundred is too much. Marcus won't accept "lectures on propriety."

With the colonel dismissed, the family assembles for Sunday breakfast. Ben is angered by the gift for Taylor; he earns only $20 per week and had only $6 for his trip to Mobile. Marcus advises him to take the long view, though even that might not pay off: "I may not die; did I tell you, Benjamin?" Marcus is kinder with Regina, clearly his favorite. He admires her new dress and wants to hear about the others he hasn't seen. He has less tolerance for Oscar than for Ben. When he reappears chewing on a roll (Leo in *Foxes*, learned his table manners from his father), Marcus announces that Oscar owes him $500.

As Oscar mops up his spilled coffee, more family details are revealed. Ben has seen Horace Giddens in Mobile, a good match for Regina, good society and "solid, quiet rich." It's time she married. Doesn't Lavinia agree? Lavinia does not risk her own opinions: "I really don't know, son. I really couldn't say." Regina can say. She doesn't like Giddens and she's not going to marry for money to please Ben. What's more, she knows such talk worries Marcus and she's not going to have his Sunday spoiled. Regina knows her way with Marcus. She suggests they desert the others and take a picnic lunch, "just you and me. We haven't done that in a long time." Regina may not be as devoted as she pretends, but there's warmth and love between father and daughter. It was a relationship Miss Hellman knew in her own life.

Marcus quickly concludes a bad morning. Oscar's $16-a-week salary will be reduced to $11 until the $500 is repaid. Ben can forget his sister's future and get busy with the store books. If they're short of cash, he can "call in some cotton loans or mortgages, then go to church." Mention of church encourages Lavinia. Marcus promised her they'd talk today. Last year he promised "that on her birthday this year they would talk." What a pathetic creature she is, forced into silence for a year —and now Marcus is again too busy, ordering her to help Belle with the picnic lunch while he selects a bottle of wine.

With the porch to themselves, Regina, Oscar, and Ben unravel their fraternal barbed wire. Regina will not lend Oscar $500. If he weren't so stupid, he'd get it by telling Papa that Ben didn't want him to have it. If Regina doesn't know where her power over Marcus is leading, Ben can tell her: "He's going to keep you right here with him, all his long life." It's not Horace Giddens who angers Marcus; it's any man. Ben wants to be out of the house the day that Papa hears the gossip about her and Bagtry, or is Bagtry to be enticed to Chicago? Chicago is already in Regina's dreams, as it will be twenty years later, but she has more immediate concerns, she must help with the picnic. She warns her brothers not to start anything about Bagtry, or they'll be in trouble.

When Regina's gone, Ben takes command. Did Oscar ride down Sam Taylor because Taylor was after Laurette, "the little whore you've been courting?" When Oscar reaches for his gun, the only authority he trusts, Ben shoves the gun aside, reminding him that their neighbors have not forgotten that Papa made too much money out of the war, that the Hubbard name is odious enough in the county without Oscar making it worse. Oscar's mind is on Laurette; he wants to marry her. She's reformed, hasn't looked at another man for a year. If he could only get an advance on his inheritance, they'd ship off to New Orleans. Ben gleefully reminds him that his prospects are not good. Papa may have spent $40,000 in the past six months, but he'd never subsidize Oscar. Laurette had better return to the security of her profession. Fraternal kindness does not inhibit the Hubbards.

Again, time is called when Birdie Bagtry appears. She is "a slight, pretty, faded-looking girl of twenty," in seedy clothes and with a worn and frightened face, as ill at ease as she will be twenty years later. Left alone with Ben, she timidly reveals her mission. The Bagtrys are desperate. Her mother has gone to Natchez trying to borrow money on their cotton or to sell some pictures. Birdie has come on her own, with her own humiliating question. Would Ben and his father lend them money on their cotton or on their land, perhaps $5000? Ben senses the opportunity, yet he proceeds cautiously, knowing that she'll inherit Lionnet, that she could not yet sign a note, that his father makes all the loans. Perhaps she might join them tomorrow evening at his father's concert and bring Captain Bagtry with her. And now he'll call Oscar to escort her home. Oscar rebels but agrees when Ben assures him that he's discovered a scheme for lending him $500. Money talks with Oscar, as it does with all Hubbards.

When Marcus appears with his bottle of wine and his Greek text of Aristotle and Regina appears in a different new dress, with her parasol and steamer rug, ready for the picnic, Ben drops his bombshell. Marcus is shocked and then intrigued by the proposal. It might provide an amusing hour to see the Bagtrys beg. How much does she want? Ben says $10,000. We can imagine the storm when Marcus learns the truth.

Another threatening cloud appears when Marcus wonders why Regina appears so anxious to have the Bagtrys at the concert. Regina acts the little girl: "What have I done? Just said I'd like to have a few people to listen to your old music. Is that so awful to want?" She hits the mark, as she knew she would. Marcus agrees to be charming to the visiting gentry. His dream has gone well beyond Ben's: "Be kind of pleasant owning Lionnet. It's a beautiful house. Very light in motive, very well conceived—" If not born to the purple, Marcus has learned to appreciate the finer things.

Before the picnickers depart, Lavinia tries again to persuade Marcus to talk with her. If not now, she can get the Bible again and have him swear to talk to her tomorrow. She's stretched his patience too far: "Try to act like you're not crazy. Get yourself in hand." Lavinia is left alone with her religion and her pretend world. She's sure she's been living in sin for thirty-seven years; now she'll redeem herself by teaching little black children. She doesn't know much, but she'll try to remember what she once knew. Coralee leads her to the kitchen as the curtain closes. In none of the earlier plays had Miss

Hellman weighted a first act with so many ominous forecasts. Everyone is vulnerable.

When the curtain opens on Marcus's evening musicale, the action has shifted into the living room we had glimpsed through the French doors. Although less sumptuously furnished than the *Foxes* room, it is conspicuously decorated with Marcus's Greek art: a vase on a pedestal, a statue, Greek battle scenes on the walls. The family and Marcus's two musicians, Penniman and Jugger, hired from the conservatory in Mobile, are drinking after-dinner port before embarking on a new trio that Marcus has composed for the occasion. Lavinia is wandering aimlessly, smiling vaguely at everyone, humming the new score and reciting the menu for the end-of-the-evening collation. Regina is wearing another of her new Chicago dresses. Oscar, at his oafish best, thinks she looks "like the decorated pig at the county fair." He pleads with Marcus to let him invite Laurette; she loves music. What's more she would amuse Marcus and it would "be a good joke on Ben." Marcus agrees, though he shudders at the prospect, as do Regina and Ben. Having the Bagtrys in the house is risky enough without adding Oscar's floozy.

Marcus insists on starting the music, and as they all move to the porch, the room is left clear for the Bagtrys. However, Oscar has quickly returned with Laurette Sincee, who must have been stationed outside. She generously fulfills our expectation. She is "pig-face cute," squeals like Shaw's Eliza Doolittle as she surveys the room, calls him "Oskie," and is perplexed by the "noise" from the porch. Laurette is delighted with Oscar's plan to take her to New Orleans. She has a friend there who does embroidery, and she's always wanted to do fancy embroidery "instead of whoring." Flustered by her loose talk, Oscar insists that she must pretend to be just as good as his family. He can't say the right thing, even to Laurette. "Pretend I'm as good as anybody called Hubbard? Why, my Pa died at Vicksburg. He didn't stay home bleeding the whole state of Alabama with money tricks, and suspected of worse." Even

Another Part of the Forest GRAPHIC HOUSE

Laurette knows about Marcus. Lost for words, Oscar tries an embrace.

It's an appropriately awkward moment for the Bagtrys' arrival. Ben has heard the bell and comes to greet them, followed by Regina and Lavinia. The awkwardness is compounded. John Bagtry is acquainted with Laurette; Lavinia mistakes Laurette for Birdie. As they move toward the music, Ben assures Birdie that he's arranged the loan for $10,000, five of which he'll hold in reserve for her. She shouldn't say anything to his father: "He's a man of such culture, as you say, that talk of money would disturb him on his music night."

For a moment Mozart relieves the tension, though not for long. Oscar comes back for a drink; Laurette is getting restless. Ben understands her distress: "She's not accustomed to a sitting position!" Bawdiness is not common with Miss Hellman; with Laurette it is irresistible. As the concert concludes, everyone drifts toward the punch, Laurette augmenting hers with a shot of brandy "to make it mean more." Intrigued with Oscar's guest, Marcus makes a stab at conversation. It turns out that Laurette's great love of music was fostered by an uncle who played a little drum. Marcus quickly shifts to Captain Bagtry. Perhaps the captain could advise him about Europe; he's thinking of taking Regina there. Bagtry has no memory of Europe; his memories center on the war. This is touchy territory. Bagtry was happy in the war; he did not fight for slavery, he fought for a way of life. Marcus cannot respect such nonsense: "Your people deserve to lose their war and their world. It was a backward world, getting in the way of history." And now everyone must go in to supper. Regina is not ready. She "didn't ask John here to listen to you lecture and be nasty and insulting." The blow hurts. Marcus did not know that she had invited Bagtry.

While the others adjourn to the dining room, Regina restrains John. She's going to Chicago; a month later he'll join her and they'll marry. Her father will have a fit, but after a while they'll return and she'll talk him out of his fit. John's plans don't coincide. He wants to go to Brazil, and he thinks Birdie is going to get the money for his trip. He knows Regina better than she knows herself. She thinks she's in love with him, because she's lonely and he's the first man she's liked. That's not enough. Regina insists that she does love him, but she suspects that Birdie is trying to get rid of her.

As Bagtry joins the others at supper, Marcus returns. Regina wants to know if he's agreed to Ben's loan on Lionnet. He has, though not because of Ben, simply because "it is good for me and bad for them." Regina begs him not to make the loan. Doesn't he realize that Birdie has "come here tonight to make fun of us?" Does he know that Ben is giving them $5000 and keeping $5000? Again Miss Hellman interrupts the scene before Marcus can reply. The musicians have returned from supper, followed by Lavinia, Laurette, and Oscar.

Laurette has laced her punch with too much brandy. She bumps into the furniture and bangs the piano with both hands. Grabbing Marcus's arm, she wants to know how he expects Oscar to live on a "stinking slave salary," how he can talk to his son as if to an animal. She's heard tales about Marcus ever since she was born: "You old bastard. . . . Everybody in this county knows how you got rich, bringing in salt and making poor, dying people give up everything for it . . . and I heard how they suspect you of worse, and you only just got out of a hanging rope. Why the first night Oscar slept with me, I didn't even want to speak to him because of you and your doings."

Marcus holds command in spite of the humiliation. He orders Oscar to remove the girl and come back quickly. Only Lavinia dares mutter a word; as if in a trance, she defends Laurette: "The girl only told the truth. Salt is just a word, it's in the Bible quite a lot." Marcus orders her to her room and turns on Bagtry. "You came to beg a favor, and you stayed to be amused. Good night." John will not be intimidated. No one in the county would be so dishonored as to ask a favor of Marcus. Birdie's desperate attempt to restore order adds fuel to the fire. She recalls that John's twin was killed the night of the massacre, yet she hoped their families could be friends. Birdie has cut deeper than Laurette. Marcus cannot forget that Mrs. Bagtry has not nodded to him in the forty years he's lived in the town. He's changed his mind; he'll not make the loan.

With the guests dismissed, the in-fighting explodes. When Oscar accuses Ben of pouring liquor into Laurette, of using him as bait to get Birdie and Lionnet, Ben laughs at his whining. Why shouldn't Oscar marry a silly girl who owns cotton instead of a silly girl who doesn't even own her mattress? As Oscar charges at Ben, Marcus shouts him away. If his blood is throwing clots into his head, he'd better "go outside and shoot a passing nigger." No holds are barred when the Hubbards open up. Marcus knows about Ben's scheme for the extra $5000. If he tries anything like that again, he won't even have his job as clerk. Is this what a father deserves after working in the fields and saving his money, teaching himself Latin and French and then Greek? "Think what I must have wanted for sons. And then think what I got. One unsuccessful trickster, one proud illiterate." If they think they've been cheated, what about him?

In the morning Oscar will find $1000 on the table. He should get on the early train for New Orleans and "send a Christmas card each year to an aging man who now wishes you to go upstairs." Oscar will accept the offer if Ben comes to the station to apologize to Laurette, and he draws a pistol to enforce his demand. Ben is not frightened, but he knows that Marcus is. "You've always been frightened of guns, Papa. Ever since that night, wasn't it?" Not only guns, Lavinia remembers: "They had hot tar and clubs and ropes that night—" Marcus is nearing the breaking point: "*Stop your crazy talk, Lavinia.*" But Ben continues the torture: "He's just upset, Mama. Old fears come back, strong."

Regina pleads with Ben and Marcus to strike a truce. They must because they'll be alone together after she and Mama leave. If she subdues one flame, she starts another. Marcus plans to join her later and take her to New York and Europe. Ben anticipates a different future and wishes he could watch Marcus's face when she produces the secret bridegroom. Doesn't Marcus understand that Regina persuaded him to cancel the loan because Bagtry was going to use the money to escape? More than that, doesn't he know the awful truth about himself and his daughter? "Go to him, Regina, put your arms around him. Tell him you've never really loved anybody else, and never will. Lie to him, just for tonight. Tell him you'll never get in bed with anybody ever again—" Ben has gone too far. Marcus slaps him sharply across the face, a blow that Ben will not forget "as long as I live." Their evil souls have been completely bared. And when Marcus orders Ben to leave in the morning and get a modest job, "because wherever you are, I'll see to it that you never get another," Ben accepts the sentence. "I was trying to outwait you, Papa, but I guess I couldn't do it." They both realize they've reached the point of no return.

Marcus may have disposed of Ben; he has not dispelled the torture, and he must know the worst from Regina. "When did it happen? How could you—When did it happen?" It's incomprehensible that she would submit to "a foolish man, an empty man from an idiot world. . . . A man who believes in nothing, and never will." Regina knows the time for protest has passed. Even after she's married, "there'll always be you and me." Later they'll take a trip to Greece, just the two of them. She has never seen her father weep before. As she kisses him goodnight, she tells Lavinia to start getting ready for Chicago.

The storm has passed. Marcus wants to be left alone. He doesn't want to hear about Lavinia's sins, about her plans for redemption. The whole town knows she's crazy. "If you worry me any more with it, I'll have to talk to the doctor and ask him to send you away." As Lavinia runs out calling for Coralee, the curtain closes. Marcus may not have loved his sons, but they were a part of his world. He did love his daughter. He's now lost them all. Lavinia he lost years ago. With a morning-after yet to come, with the night of the massacre yet to be revealed, Marcus's ordeal has not concluded.

For a final view of the Hubbards the action returns to the portico the following morning. Lavinia is carrying a Bible and singing a hymn. Ben enters with his valise, ready to depart. Lavinia has been awake all night wanting to talk to Ben. She now knows that she should have told the truth that fearful night, even if it meant sending her husband to a hanging rope. Ben, sensing a trump card, demands the full story, and Lavinia leads her mind through the labyrinth of her memory, wandering from past to present. Marcus was on the well house that night; she and Coralee saw him. Perhaps she should get the envelope of money and tear it up in front of Marcus. Throughout the war Marcus dealt with the enemy, running the blockade with salt and selling it for $8 a bag. One night twenty-seven Confederate boys in training were massacred by Union soldiers; someone had led them to the camp. That was the night Marcus was on the roof. He then disappeared for two days and came back with passes, showing he'd been away, through the Confederate lines. She knew the truth and she recorded it in her Bible.

Ben's spirits are reviving. He wants the envelope and the Bible. The envelope is in the left-hand drawer of the desk; he'll have to break it open. He's eager to break anything, and while he's at it she must call Marcus out to the upper porch. Amazed at her own daring, she does. When Marcus appears, Ben is back with the envelope and the pistol he used to knock off the lock, and when Marcus orders him to put the gun on the table and bring him the envelope, Ben ignores him. He transfers the money to another envelope, calls Jake, and tells him to take it to Birdie Bagtry and on the way back to buy two tickets on the sugar boat. Marcus, still trying to hold on, says he's going to be sorry to have a son in jail. Ben replies with the details of the massacre. Marcus warns him that no one will believe the story of a crazy woman; the doctors know her.

They'll believe when Ben shows them the Bible. Ben is intoxicated with his new power. If there's a lynching, he'll do his family duty: "I'll come tomorrow morning and cut you down from the tree and bury you with respect. How did the Greeks bury fathers who were murdered?"

Marcus, still not surrendering, wants to see the Bible. Could Lavinia have written a lie in the Holy Book? Ben won't be tricked. Marcus tries another tack, as he comes down from the porch. He'll gladly provide funds for her school, honoring any "practical message from God" she happens to get. Ben warns his mother that if she doesn't want Marcus to commit her, she'd better escape now, on the sugar boat. Lavinia takes her Bible and departs.

If Ben needs Lavinia and the Bible, he can bring her back. Now he's ready to dictate terms. Marcus must write a statement confirming the sale of the store for $1 and a note instructing Shannon in Mobile that all stocks, bonds, mortgages, all assets of Marcus Hubbard, Inc., are to be assigned to him. The Hubbards are not merciful victors. "Ever since you started your peculiar way of treating me, many years ago, I have had many ugly dreams. But this is better than I ever dreamed—Go in and start writing now. I consider you a lucky man; you'll die in bed."

The rest of the household now comes alive: Oscar racing through the house, shouting for Papa and searching for his money; Regina on the upper porch, in riding clothes, hoping they'd all have been gone before she got up. She's shocked to see Ben in "Papa's chair, eating breakfast at Papa's table, on Papa's porch." Oscar continues his screaming until Marcus reappears. Even in defeat he sharpens his tongue on Oscar: "The money isn't there, Oscar, because I didn't put it there. . . . An unhappy event interfered. I am thus unable to finance your first happy months in the rose-covered brothel about which you have always dreamed."

As he goes in to continue writing, Regina reappears. After toying with her curiosity, Ben announces that she's not going to Chicago, that Papa no longer has any money, that it's been given to him. Regina is sure that Ben's been sampling the new drug she's been reading about. She runs inside to her father but, getting no explanation from him, returns to Ben. He only tells her that she could pawn her pearls and go with Bagtry to Brazil, though he advises against it: "You're not in love; I don't think anybody in this family can love." The Hubbards don't often strike so close to the truth about themselves.

When Marcus returns with the two papers for Ben, he still refuses to explain to Regina what's happened. Oscar is back, dejected and rumpled. Laurette has departed without him; she spat in his face as he tried to pull her off the train, with everyone on the platform laughing at him. Regina may laugh, but her love, "looking like a statue of Robert E. Lee," departed on the same train. Ben ignores their fleeting sorrows. Oscar can get a job loading bananas or settle down in his old job and marry the girl Ben picked out for him. Regina may not have lost her prospect. If Papa is the only one in town who didn't know she had been "sleeping with the warrior," perhaps Horace Giddens doesn't know. Ben has assumed the patriarchal duties and, with Miss Hellman, is making the family arrangements for *The Little Foxes.*

Ben supplies an additional prelude for the later play: "Big goings on all over the country. Railroads going across, oil, coal. I been telling you, Papa, for ten years. Things are opening up. . . . But ever since the war you been too busy getting cultured, or getting Southern." Oscar is fascinated with Ben's dream: "Think we've got a chance to be big rich, Ben?" Of course they have with him in charge, and he might even give Regina and Oscar a share of the future.

Lavinia has returned with Coralee, ready for her journey and with parting gifts for all of them: her pin for Regina, her prayer book for Oscar, her Papa's watch for Benjamin, and for Marcus, her wedding ring. Ben and Marcus would rather have her Bible, but that she'll take with her. She'll pray for all of them. As the curtain closes, we see a new family portrait.

Regina pours coffee for Marcus, but when Marcus pulls out the chair beside him, she crosses and sits beside Ben. Although the Hubbards may accept the new facts of life, their reservoirs of bitterness and greed cannot have been exhausted. There must have been many stormy days during the twenty years before they reappeared in *The Little Foxes.*

Another Part of the Forest does not match the earlier play in concentrated power. Miss Hellman has followed too many paths. If fewer crises had been packed into the two days, if the voices had been less strident, if the massacre had not repeatedly haunted them and us, if the action had centered less on the detectivelike pursuit, the Hubbard and Bagtry portraits could have been more fully realized, and our hearts might have become more committed. Miss Hellman's taut web does not snare us as it snares the Hubbards. We follow their greedy machinations with a cold eye as if watching a Brecht-like epic.

Miss Hellman has mined a rich lode from the Hubbards' history, perhaps too rich in dark deeds for a single evening. Yet even if overloaded with villainy, *Another Part of the Forest* is a strong and exciting play. If the harsh clang of melodrama rings loudly in the final moments when Marcus, crushed to tears, is forced to abdicate, we have seen enough of his black perversities to believe the massacre story, enough of Ben's tutoring in treachery to know he could strip his father bare without batting an eye. The playwright knows these monsters and the dark labyrinth they inhabit, and she does not hesitate to show them at their worst.

She has been more sparing of documentary details than in *The Little Foxes,* though the early drafts contained many more items of Confederate and postwar history, such as an elaborate story about "Old Lena," a boat from the siege of Mobile that was tied up downriver. Russian audiences apparently deplored the absence of documentary truth when *Another Part of the Forest* was done in Moscow in November, 1949, under the title *Ladies and Gentlemen.* One reporter said that it "failed to present a merciless and scornful exposé of the awful capitalist reality"; it merely depicted the conflict between two swindlers.

American critics did not speak with one voice. Some found it "one of the finest dramas by an American author," "one of the most fascinating plays of the contemporary theatre," filled with indomitable force, vibrant, full-bodied, and packed with dynamite. Few dramatists could equal her box score: "She has now turned the trick five times out of six." Others thought the accidental skullduggery and the raging violence did not proceed sufficiently from within the characters. The "Hubbards work so hard to illustrate Miss Hellman's point that they defeat it." George Jean Nathan felt as if he had been listening to a "jammed automobile horn." Her company of Simon Legrees of both sexes, minus only the bloodhounds, "comprised the most odious lot seen on stage since Pollyanna." Wolcott Gibbs thought it an "untidy sequel to an infinitely superior play." If critics disagreed about the play, they agreed that the cast was almost perfect, and Percy Waram (Marcus) most perfect of all, "the best performance of his career." Jo Mielziner's setting ranked with his best, and Miss Hellman's directing was firm and incisive. One critic thought she had achieved the same flaming intensity that Harold Clurman had injected into *Awake and Sing*. Even Herman Shumlin, who had staged all the earlier plays, thought she had done a fine job.

Most of the critics who spoke unfavorably qualified their disapproval. Many thought the sardonic and ruthless Marcus the most interesting character she had ever drawn. Although Brooks Atkinson found her "indictment of the Hubbards a witch's brew of blackmail, insanity, cruelty, theft, torture, insult, drunkenness, with a trace of incest thrown in for good measure . . . a deluxe edition of a dime novel, she can write individual scenes of great theatrical intensity, . . . scenes of madness, desperation and venom that have tremendous impact in the theatre."

Frequently Miss Hellman had been invited to reply to the

critics. She had always refused. This time, accepting the invitation of the New York *Times*, she wrote, "I believe that all writing is contrived; some of it is contrived badly." She believed that violence and evil had always been the true materials of drama and always would be. "I will go on writing plays and Mr. Atkinson will go on frowning down on them. And that is the way it should be. Disagreement between writer and critic is hereditary. . . . It is in the great tradition." She once said that though she was not pained by criticism, she found that the only helpful criticism came from other writers.

At the opening night on November 20, 1946, according to one observer, her father had his pockets crammed with new $1 bills, and when Ben Hubbard counted out the money to pay Colenel Isham, Max Hellman followed suit, rustling through his bills and annoying those around him. When the curtain closed on Act I, as if to placate his neighbors, he stood up and announced: "My daughter wrote this play. It gets better." At the opening night party Gregory Zilboorg, Miss Hellman's friend and psychoanalyst to whom she dedicated the play, told her that her father was suffering from senile dementia. Six months later he collapsed and from then until his death in 1948, his mind was never clear. Such accidental ironies from life would not be tolerated in dramatic fiction. It was the first time, perhaps stimulated by her sessions with Dr. Zilboorg before and after her trip to Russia, that she had probed deeply into the relationship between father and daughter.

The play ran for 182 performances, closing on April 26, 1947. It received four votes in the Critics' Circle balloting, placing third after the winner, *All My Sons,* and the runner-up, *The Iceman Cometh*. In the early fall, after a vacation abroad and a meeting in Paris with representatives from fifteen countries gathered for the sessions of the International Theatre Institute, she rehearsed the road company for a national tour. When the play was transformed into a motion picture by Universal-International, it was adapted by Vladimir Posner, not by Miss Hellman, but when it was released in May, 1948, she received the critics' praise for "her terrible knack of investing characters with every deadly sin without straining one's credibility."

If she had ever thought of adding an even earlier chapter to the Hubbard saga, Patricia Collinge beat her into print. Miss Collinge not only knew the Hubbards from *Another Part of the Forest,* she had played Birdie in *The Little Foxes.* Now turning from acting to writing in a *New Yorker* piece (March 15, 1947) entitled "Another Part of the Hubbards," she dealt with Ben as a teenager, Regina at eight, and Oscar as a baby. Ghoulish games are their chief delight. Their Grandpa died tripping over a string that Ben had laced across the stairway. Oscar crawls the floor playing with a cat whose claws are poisoned. Alabastra, singing and ironing Oscar's diapers, reports that he is a slow learner, but "once he gets hold, he don't never let go." Regina and Ben, plotting to blot out Grandma, tell Oscar they'll give him a fly—Oscar loves flies—if he lets Grandma play with his cat. If that doesn't work, Regina has a back-up plan: she'll stick Grandma with a poison pin. The presence of the cat will clear her of suspicion. While the cat scratches Grandma and she dies, Ben and Regina eat their supper, Regina reminding him that it's called dinner in Chicago. Ben and Regina's greed is already well developed. Ben steals from the collection plate. Regina has killed Grandma because Grandma hates Mama because she married Papa. With Grandma dead, Papa will get her money and Regina can get it from him. Miss Hellman did not accept this early history as the final segment in the Hubbard chronicle. She continued to contemplate a sequel to *The Little Foxes,* but it was never written.

With *Another Part of the Forest* Miss Hellman had made two radical changes in her theatrical life: she took on a new producer and a new director. Heretofore Herman Shumlin had performed both duties. For producer she now cast Kermit Bloomgarden, Shumlin's right-hand man since 1935, and for director, herself. When she brought her finished script to

Bloomgarden in the summer of 1946, he assumed that she was simply soliciting his reactions as she had often done before. When she called a week later to talk about the play and about actors, his responses apparently struck her as vague and unenthusiastic. Ten minutes later she called again, asking why he didn't want to produce her play. Her approach had been too subtle. When he realized what she proposed, he jumped at the chance. Who could refuse to begin his producing career with a new Hellman play?

Bloomgarden, after more than ten years of apprenticeship with Shumlin, was wise to the ways of Broadway. He was also blessed with an innate gentleness and good taste. Miss Hellman had been less well tutored for her task. She had learned about directing from observation, not from practice, and though she had a good eye and ear for what was wrong, she had not acquired that special skill for cajoling, flattering, inspiring, and molding actors to a director's will. Her rehearsal notes read like those of a novice: "beginning too fast," "all movements bad," "too much action in center of stage," "people don't move quite enough." Fortunately for her directorial initiation, she had first-class actors skilled in their profession who covered her deficiencies. And her first attempt turned out so well that she decided directing was no great feat. Her conviction lasted through her next play.

In an interview with Murray Schumach (New York *Times*, October 23, 1949), a week before the opening of *Montserrat*, she explained that she had taken over the staging of her plays because she knew her characters better than any director, that she was good enough to get by, and that most directors had become experts by camouflaging their ignorance with technical jargon. They invariably resolved a play into a basic theme, assuming that the author worked from that premise. That formula did not fit her writing, not even in *Watch on the Rhine*. "I know the people in the play and those people have to say and do what they have to say and do." Very few directors added creative touches, and those who did—Jed

Harris, Elia Kazan, and Herman Shumlin—would flounder without a good play. What's more, she worked out the stage business in her plays so carefully that "something less than genius" was required to direct them. She abhorred directors who talked about "handling performers." That was "playing God in the wrong way," a role she refused to assume. And if she was obliged to tell her casts that she was going to fumble, her fumbling worked for *Another Part of the Forest*, if not for *Montserrat*.

Now that she had become a star playwright—the billing read, "Kermit Bloomgarden presents Lillian Hellman's New Play"—she felt compelled to become more completely involved, from auditions to opening night. In the past she had been available to director and actors during rehearsals, though she had never been entirely comfortable with them. As she once said, "The glamour of theatre people was never to mean anything to me, which was forever to make me difficult for those who have the right to think it should." She had been repeatedly annoyed that once a play was in rehearsal everyone assumed that he knew more about it than the playwright. In her introduction to Chekhov's letters in 1955, she wrote, "If the literary world has a handful of interpreters who mistake themselves for the author, the theatrical world has only a handful who do not mistake themselves for the playwright. We all need to see ourselves as a little more important than we are, but people in the theatre need to see themselves as a lot more important than anybody else."

She knew that actors had to polish their egos, and on an individual basis she found them tolerable. It was the assemblage of theatre egos that distressed her, particularly when—and this seemed always—they battled for position with the latest shop talk and gossip. She had an ingrained aversion to all professional and political groups who were obsessed with their games and causes.

She was well aware of the perversity in her nature that drove her to write for the theatre and for the films, both of which demanded teamwork, when her natural inclination demanded privacy and solitude. As she has remarked repeatedly, there was always a wall between her and the theatre, a wall which seemed to thicken with time. She never really liked the theatre, yet she knew that playwriting was what she did best. She was happiest when the play was still completely hers. She suffered the torture of rehearsals, vowing that she would not repeat the experience, yet when the curtain rose on another opening and she could again retreat, her enthusiasm for a new play returned, if sometimes slowly. She once confessed, "I'm lazy, dawdle in getting to work. I fuss. I suppose the reason I talk so much about doing research is because I like to stall. Perhaps I'm not really lazy about actually writing, but I know I don't drive myself enough."

She regarded plays as second-rate literature, compared to the novel. "I'm dying to write a novel," she once said, "but I simply haven't the guts to try it." A play was tight, unbending, unfluid, and meager, oppressed by built-in theatrical limitations, totally dependent on the acceptance of a special brand of let's-pretend, yet it offered the challenge that her writer's nature found most inviting. Like Hebbel, she was intrigued by the drama's demand for "presenting the necessary in the form of the accidental."

Miss Hellman has not spoken frequently about her own writing. "I don't really know much about the process of creation and I don't like talking about it," she once told a reporter. When she has spoken, her rules for the game have been clearly and simply expressed. Any writer must resign himself to the loneliness of writing. Anyone who tackles the theatre must be possessed of a feeling for playwriting. "He must pretend and he must represent." Writing for oneself is nonsense, a losing game. "The key thing is how you see and develop the characters—writing is the way you see something. And you must communicate this to others." A playwright must not strain to avoid clichés. "There are no new situations basically, but there are new ways to say anything, new eyes to focus on any scene. Good writing is saying old things differently." Although she habitually steeped herself in the cold facts of history to give her solid documentary truth, she drew also from the world of the half-remembered, the half-observed, the half-understood. "It is always there for you. God help you to use it right. Right? Right for what? Right to have something to say and to say it well."

In the spring of 1958, after a lecture at the University of Chicago, she talked with Richard Stern about writing and about her own writing. She tried to pinpoint when she first felt drawn to playwriting, but without success. She had gone to the theatre as a child, during her teens in New York, and regularly after she married Kober. She recalled that she was particularly impressed by the plays of Sidney Howard. There must have been some magic moment when she resolved to be a playwright, but it was now lost among all the chance circumstances that propelled her toward the theatre. Sources of inspiration for her writing were impossible to define. She did not find them in other plays. Striking performances—she recalled particularly a *Richard III* and *The Visit*—sent her back to her work with new vigor. A new play invariably began with people, not ideas. When ideas crowded out the people, she knew she was on the wrong track. When she began talking about a play while it was still in the typewriter, she sensed trouble; such talk invariably turned to ideas and that frightened her. She abhorred characters who could be labeled good, bad, funny, or heroic. She tried always to cast her characters in distinct and individualized human terms. She might be a moral writer, but she wanted no truck with moralistic types.

She claimed that audiences typed characters without encouragement from the playwright. A strange hypocrisy pervaded the public aspect of people which made them develop a set of fake morals about characters in plays, demanding that they be good or bad, instead of allowing them the complex mixture of real life. She saw the world as a human comedy. However serious she might be about the subject in hand, she always invested her characters with touches of gaiety, charm, and humor. In her own writing and that of others—she had a particular fondness for Twain and the Russians, and Donne and Blake among the poets—she delighted most in sharp satiric thrusts. When they were neatly honed, she was pleased. Miss Hellman was not self-conscious or pontifical in talking about her own writing. She knew herself, she knew her craft, and when she talked of either she spoke directly and simply.

After attempting to guide a play from inception to opening night, she recognized that total involvement was not her meat. Nothing was to be gained from fighting her own nature. The wall between her and the theatre was too strong. What's more, her plays were so precisely defined before they passed to the producer that they did not require her protective presence. She always saw the actors on stage in her mind's eye and could hear their words being spoken as she wrote, and she always tested dialogue by reading it aloud. "For many years," she once wrote, "I have been working on a theory that everybody in the theatre—playwright, director, stage designer, prop man—are actors manqué."

XI

Politics, *Montserrat*, and *Regina*

The three years between the openings of *Another Part of the Forest* and *Montserrat* were unsettled years. Postwar America and the rest of the world seemed unable to hold fast the freedoms for which the war had been fought, and anyone unwilling to retreat to the business-as-usual prewar years ran the risk of being declared unAmerican. The McCarthy witch-hunts were about to become the news of the day.

It was not a happy time with Hammett. After his return from the Aleutians his drinking had become heavier and gloomier, and Miss Hellman was unable to cope with his periods of insobriety. They still captured some glorious autumn days at the farm, days "of hunting and squirrel pies and sausage making." There were also long stretches when they went their separate ways. Once in 1948, when they had been apart for two months, she received a desperate call from his cleaning lady. Hammett needed help. At first she refused, but the pleas were too frantic to resist. That night she took him to her house and witnessed what she learned from the doctor at the hospital the next day was delirium tremens. The doctor, an old friend of Hammett, told him that if he continued drinking he would be dead in a few months. The doctor confided to Miss Hellman that he knew the warning was futile, yet he was obligated to tell the truth. Fortunately, he misjudged his patient. Hammett gave his word and stuck to it. Years later, when Miss Hellman spoke of the doctor's skepticism, Hammett was shocked. He had given his word. Whatever other human failings he might have, he did keep his word.

The postwar years were not good work years. After the return visit with the Hubbards, thoughts about a new play seemed slow in coming. No characters were hounding her to be heard, and she had been involving herself more actively in politics with speeches in support of Henry Wallace for President. Two years earlier, in 1946, she had joined the Independent Citizens Committee of the Arts, Sciences and Professions, along with Jo Davidson and Franklin D. Roosevelt, Jr. This group, allied with the Political Action Committee of the CIO, selected and supported liberal candidates for public office.

In the summer of 1948, she took a whirl at teaching a one-week course in playwriting at the Indiana University Writer's Conference. In her public appearances in Bloomington, she spoke on Wallace and on the theatre. She was ashamed of the theatre of her time; it refused to deal seriously with a serious world. Tennessee Williams was the only promising playwright on the horizon. She was more optimistic about Wallace. The charge that he was run by Communists was a bare-faced lie. She knew him as a neighbor, and he was a remarkably wise man who never put his own interests ahead of those of the United States.

Early in October, she took a flying trip to Prague, Belgrade, and Paris, her principal mission an interview with Marshall Tito. When she returned, reports of the "noted playwright and war correspondent" appeared in a series of six articles in the New York *Star* (successor to *PM*), November 4 to 10, 1948.

She visited first Zdnek Fierlinger, the vice-premier of Czechoslovakia, who told her that Americans did not really understand the Czechs. Masaryk had not welcomed a communist Czechoslovakia; he had accepted the new government and was working with it because, at that moment, it offered the only hope for the future. Americans must understand that the workers' movement in Europe was not new to the twentieth century.

Marshall Tito talked with her in his home, fifteen minutes from the center of Belgrade. At first she wished that his uniform were not so blue and not so grand, but that first impresion faded quickly. He was a strong and confident man with a good sense of humor, easy, well-bred manners, and a passion for living. Although he preferred to talk about American writers, about Wallace and the Wallace leghorns she was raising rather than about politics, he did say that the Yugoslavs were puzzled by the attacks of the Cominform and regarded them as slanders and completely unjustified. In June the Cominform (the Communist International Information Bureau) had denounced Tito's government for being nationalistic, anti-Russian, and pro-Western.

In Belgrade she also visited a home for war orphans and rehearsals and a performance of *The Little Foxes* at the National Theatre. She could not understand "why Europeans always direct American plays with actors jumping up and down, moving from chair to chair, running up stair cases, as if we were a people who spent our lives like sandpipers." Dr. Klein, the director, patiently sought her advice, but she could offer few suggestions. "I know very well," she wrote, "that when I talk about the theatre I am a disappointment; the words of art are intimate words to me, and I cannot use them with strangers: I try to solve that with advice about technicalities, as if I were talking about driving a car or cooking a stew." When she saw the play four days later, from a front box, she behaved as an author should for two acts; during the last act she yawned and had to be nudged by her companions. Looking at a play she had written years ago, she found herself "torn between wondering how you ever could have been bright enough to write that scene and shuddering with pain that you wrote the next."

When not officially engaged, she had tried, in Prague and in Belgrade, to talk with the people, to understand them. If they were not fully indoctrinated Communists, they were, she wrote, "highly moral people, sometimes too moral for comfort. (Even their standards of personal morality were more prudish and goody-goody than we are accustomed to.) And if that is true, and I think it is, then the Western world had better stop sneering and try to understand it, because national morality, its kind and degree is important in men's lives."

After the ugliness of Belgrade, Paris seemed more beautiful than ever, "all soft gray as if the buildings ran together in a fog." It was even nice "to be insulted again by Paris telephone operators who certainly must be the most neurotic and unhappy women on earth." But even in Paris the political world could not be pushed out of her mind. When she read about James Farley's happy visit with Franco, she was reminded that eleven years earlier she had boarded the train for Toulouse, bound for Spain. Now her country was "paying court to the man who allowed the German army to 'test' their guns on his countrymen and kneeling to kiss his hand, if that is the word I mean."

Before leaving New York she had talked with Norman Mailer about doing a dramatization of *The Naked and the Dead*, but she had also been advised to see *Montserrat* in Paris before she undertook a new project. The play had been exciting Parisian audiences at the *Théâtre Montparnasse* since April and had also been playing in Algiers at the *Théâtre du Colisée*. Phillipe Soupault, the poet, took her to a performance and introduced her to the author, Emmanuel Roblès. She was so moved by the play that she acquired the American rights immediately, put aside Mailer's novel, and as soon as she returned commissioned a literal translation. She worked at top speed and by the end of January had a manuscript for Bloomgarden.

When they discovered that suitable actors were not then available, they postponed production until fall.

Committed to direct the play, she could not fix her mind on another writing project. She occupied herself with farm chores, looking after poodles, cats, cows, pigs, and chickens and from time to time turning merchant to unload her overstock of eggs, chickens, asparagus, and berries, occasionally breaking her agricultural routine for quick trips to the city in her five-year-old Cadillac to attend some political assembly.

On March 25, she sat at the speaker's table at the Waldorf-Astoria for the opening dinner of the Cultural and Scientific Conference for World Peace, sponsored by the National Council of the Arts, Sciences and Professions. The 2000 guests had a noisy and confusing evening. Although the chairman, Professor Howard Shapley, the Harvard astronomer, insisted that the conference was nonpolitical, the State Department had declared the meetings "inimical to the country's interests"; many scheduled guests refused to attend; some, Bernard De-Voto, George Balanchine, and Arthur Schlesinger, Jr., among them, had formed a rival group, Americans for Intellectual Freedom, and others marched in the picket lines around the hotel. When Norman Cousins, who had at first declined the invitation to speak, announced that the sponsoring group was without standing, that Americans wanted peace but not peace at any price, he was greeted with jeers and boos and Miss Hellman replied furiously, "I would recommend, Mr. Cousins, that when you are invited out to dinner, you wait until you get home before you talk about your hosts." Shostakovich, the principal "personal-appearance" attraction, must have been perplexed by the proceedings.

Miss Hellman did not relish the hasty and flaming anger that was aroused on the public platform. She preferred to filter her rage through her stage characters. Not that she wished to shield herself; she simply wanted her sentiments to be ordered and clear. In the new play she may not, as she insisted, have sought to draw direct parallels with contemporary life, yet there was contemporary relevance in being reminded that man repeats himself in his struggle for freedom, that his enemy is heartless and brutal, that often the innocent must suffer and be sacrificed.

Montserrat signaled a change in her career. She had not before drawn on remote history; she had not done an adaptation. Of her five plays that followed, three, *The Lark*, *Candide*, and *My Mother, My Father and Me*, were adaptations, and the first two drew on history or fictionalized history.

All the action of *Montserrat* transpires in the outer room of the General's palace during the Spanish occupation of Valencia, Venezuela, in 1812. As the curtain rises on the first of the two acts, Antonanzas and Zavala are drinking and playing chess. We quickly learn that they belong to the Spanish expeditionary force, that other soldiers are with Izquierdo tracking an elusive Bolivar, that the off-stage piano is being played by His Excellency, an old soldier of seventy-seven who no longer knows or cares if he's in Valencia, Spain, or Valencia in the Americas. The soldiers talk of women, of their weariness and longing for the home they haven't seen in two years, about the "pocket rebellion of half-breeds" who refuse to be subdued by the Spanish army.

They are joined by Montserrat and then by Morales, Izquierdo, and Father Coronil. Montserrat, sickened with their adventure, spends his time in the cathedral, playing duets with His Excellency, or reading from Voltaire or from Rodalso, his present favorite: "Now Spain is a country of the dark and sad: we have only half light, half knowledge, half Christianity." Antonanzas cannot tolerate such heretical nonsense. Bolivar's head on a pole is all they need. Izquierdo reports that that prospect has faded. Bolivar has again escaped their trap. When he takes Zavala and Morales with him to report their failure to His Excellency, having been assured by Montserrat that the musical number is concluded, Father Coronil and Montserrat are left alone.

Father Coronil fears the trouble ahead. "Every time Bolivar

escapes he makes himself a greater hero and the Spanish army greater fools." Montserrat cannot understand how a priest can support this perpetual pursuit. "What have these people done to deserve such punishment?" They have not refused God; they have simply refused to accept the glory of the Spanish army. Coronil knows that Montserrat has been misled by his subversive reading. He must accept the fact that God and country are one. They are all here in the service of the king.

When Izquierdo returns from his audience with His Excellency, he has permission to pursue the traitor who must have warned Bolivar. He is certain Montserrat is his man. He orders more patrols to the Curaco road, directs Morales to bring in six people from the square, any six, and then confronts Montserrat: "Where can I find Bolivar?" Montserrat does not reply. Izquierdo believes the six innocents might persuade him to speak. His Excellency proposed this scheme, though reluctantly because of ties between his and Montserrat's family. Sensing the torture ahead, Montserrat begs leave to go to the cathedral, or at least to have Father Madaraga with him. Izquierdo refuses. He has no sympathy for a man who seeks his personal place in the world, who worries over his own salvation. He'll permit no story-book heroics.

The first hostages, Luhan, a carpenter and wood carver, and Salas Ina, a linen and textile merchant, are dragged in. Their guilt by association is painfully remote; they are simply citizens of Valencia and thus presumed to be allies of Bolivar. Before the inquisition begins, four more are added: Matilde, Salcedo, Felisa, and Ricardo. Matilde is the first to protest her innocence; she knows nothing; she doesn't even know her fellow captives. Salcedo is an actor and like actors everywhere—Miss Hellman knows them—is obsessed with his profession. He is flattered that Izquierdo had seen him perform aboard ship, though he was not at his best that night. True, acting is a strange calling, "by day yourself, by night somebody else . . . never sure which side of me is me." Izquierdo will give him a chance to discover his true identity: "If you play yourself well, you will be remembered here and your fame possibly sung at home."

Izquierdo quickly outlines his plan. He knows they are innocent; that's why they've been chosen. By evening he must know where Montserrat has hidden Bolivar. They will be given an hour alone with Captain Montserrat to discover his secret; then they will be freed. If they don't succeed, they will be killed. Montserrat, horrified by this fiendish scheme, volunteers to confess his treason, endure any torture, even death. Izquierdo rejects that bargain. Only the betrayal of Bolivar will buy their freedom.

Left alone for their fateful hour, they quickly discover that their captor is the fearful Izquierdo who had massacred a thousand prisoners, that Montserrat did indeed help Bolivar to escape. They search for the questions that will break his resistance; they bicker among themselves about whose situation is the most desperate. Montserrat pleads with them to protect Bolivar, the only man who can lead them out of their misery and give them freedom. They are only concerned with saving their own skins. They have no faith in heroes, no tolerance for fancy talk about liberty. They refuse to die for Bolivar or for him, "to make him feel fine before God." Montserrat still tries to persuade them. Every night for the past month he has been delivering guns to the partisans; he's listened only to the voice of God; he wants equality for all men. Now for the first time, Felisa speaks and then Ricardo. She pleads with her fellow hostages not to reveal what they have heard. Ricardo, the one true revolutionary, will not endanger the cause by blind allegiance to one man. Perhaps the sick and wounded Bolivar is not the man to save them. Montserrat's confidence is shaken by Ricardo's wisdom, and when Salcedo offers him a knife, he's ready to act.

He's too late. Izquierdo and Morales reenter and take the knife. His suicide will not save them. Izquierdo shifts his attention to Felisa. Perhaps she would spend a few days with him; it might save her life. Felisa knows her opinion is irrelevant; he will do as he pleases. Salas Ina urges her to cooperate and bargain for their safety. Izquierdo ignores him and moves toward Felisa as the curtain closes.

All the questions have been raised. None has been answered. Unlike previous Hellman plays, our attention is held on a single bare line of action. Will Montserrat betray Bolivar before the innocent victims are killed? Will Izquierdo carry out his threat? The chances of a melodramatic escape appear remote. The specifics of the revolution have only been sketched: It's endured for some twelve years; there's been a massacre; Bolivar has been wounded and is now a fugitive.

No time elapses between the acts. When the curtain rises, Izquierdo is still toying with his captives. If he were to release Felisa, would she return to him in the evening? She's honest; she wouldn't. Salas Ina volunteers a solution. He will find another woman; any woman in the village would be honored. Unwittingly he has taken center stage. He hates Bolivar; he's a loyal subject of the crown. When Izquierdo reminds him that Montserrat, who controls his destiny, does not admire the king, Salas Ina shifts his ground. He's a modern man; Spain must not enslave her colonies. When that turn fails, he attempts to bribe Izquierdo. He would sacrifice his wife to preserve his own life. Izquierdo delights in seeing his hysterical victim stripped of human dignity. Certainly Montserrat should want to preserve this specimen; he is "like so many of us." When Montserrat refuses, Izquierdo orders the soldiers to remove Salas Ina, and as he's being dragged out, accompanied by two monks, Montserrat's desperate plea to "take me" is ignored. We hear the death drum, the volley, the screams, and then the coup de grace. The first victim is dead; Montserrat has not broken.

Luhan, the wood carver, is next. His pleas, for the father of five children, for an artist approaching his prime, are ignored. Again, the death march and the fatal volley. During the execution Izquierdo calmly reads from Montserrat's book. If indeed Bolivar has been taken in by a dreamer "bottled on books," a date must have been set for the dream. It has been; today is the day. Montserrat, quickly realizing he's been trapped, explains that he only meant the patrols would probably find Bolivar today. Izquierdo now knows that time is short; he must turn the screws faster.

Perhaps Salcedo can persuade Montserrat. He should "say one of those large things actors say when they're dying." He tries, without conviction. He cannot return love for torture, as heroes do in plays. He hates Izquierdo. When he cries to God for forgiveness, Father Coronil reappears but admits that he's helpless. Bolivar has opposed the king, thus he is a rebel against God; a priest must not mix in military affairs. Izquierdo, impatient with the religious sparring, with Salcedo's weeping, with Montserrat's persistent silence, orders the death march for Salcedo and then pulls Montserrat to the window, forcing him to watch the execution. As Montserrat watches the actor recover his stage presence in the final moment, he wonders if it does not take the most courage to pretend courage.

Izquierdo again turns to Felisa. What has she wanted from life? Her demands are simple: "More to eat. Less filth and the death of you and all like you." Unnerved by her insolence, Izquierdo throws his glass against His Excellency's door and shouts, "Stop that goddamn music." The crash brings Zavala and a request from His Excellency that the drums be discontinued. Izquierdo refuses. And when Montserrat pleads with Zavala to persuade His Excellency to stop the slaughter, Zavala insists that he's already tried. His Excellency has retreated into a dream world, at home in his summer garden talking with Napoleon.

For the moment Felisa is spared. Ricardo, unlike the others, is ready to die for the cause, even after Izquierdo tries to undermine his faith. Did he not know that Bolivar wrote a letter begging for sanctuary? Montserrat admits there was such a letter, but it was never sent, never will be sent. Seeing Ricardo marked for execution brings Montserrat to the breaking point. He screams, "The Valencia road. . . . The road back to Valencia." Felisa restrains him from saying more, and Ricardo is led out. Again the drums, the coup de grace, and then Morales' report. Ricardo was brave to the last. He refused the blindfold, refused to face the wall. His faith never wavered. The two remaining victims, Matilde and Felisa, are dispatched together, and as they are taken out, Felisa stops and kisses Montserrat.

The ordeal is finished. For the first time Izquierdo and Montserrat face each other alone, for the first time they speak of the past. When they met a year ago, Montserrat fresh from Spain, Izquierdo sensed that he was troubled and rebellious, one of that vast silent army who read books, who plan to act but never do. Izquierdo has not been driven by theory nor by allegiance to his king. Bolivar's men once captured him, buried him up to his chin, and then marched by and urinated in his face. In two years he has never spent a night without wiping his face and hearing their laughter.

Montserrat admits that he nearly betrayed Bolivar. Without the strength Felisa gave him, he could not have endured another victim. Now nothing could make him talk. Skeptical of his fortitude, Izquierdo orders Morales to bring in six more hostages; the ordeal will be repeated. Sickened by the prospect, Montserrat mutters vague directions about the Puebla road, about a cave, about five rocks. Before Izquierdo can force sense into his mutterings, Zavala and then Morales and Antonanzas rush in to report that Bolivar has again escaped. Montserrat admits that he had planned this maneuver. Bolivar is now in Tinaco where thousands were waiting to join him.

There is no reason now to spare Montserrat. Antonanzas strikes him in the face with his gun; another officer "pulls his arm from its socket"; another smashes his face against the wall. Finally, he's dragged out and shot. As His Excellency's piano begins again, Father Coronil appears. A message must be sent to Spain. The priest cannot avoid the professional question: what did he say at the end? "Did he repent?" "Of what?" Zavala shouts, as the curtain falls. A hero can be honored even by his enemies.

Such is the stuff of revolutions. Izquierdo has slaughtered the hostages, killed Montserrat, yet he's still defeated. Montserrat has sacrificed the six innocents and himself, yet he has won, bought time for Bolivar's escape, bought a small piece of the revolution at a dreadful price. As in man's continuing battles for freedom, the struggle cannot be restricted to the committed adversaries. The Everymans, the most casual passers-by, cannot escape. Only two of the victims—there are never many—possess a touch of human nobility. Felisa is even more noble than Ricardo. She knows in her bones that Montserrat must not weaken, that the final price is not too dear, that the present must be sacrificed to the future.

The parallels with contemporary history—the Spanish Revolution, the wholesale human sacrifice to Hitler's madness, the postwar battle to preserve the freedoms World War II had won—are unmistakable, as they were in the original. Miss Hellman sharpened some parallels for her American audience. Bookish theorists and innocent bystanders could no longer be tolerated. Every man must join the battle; there were no longer any isolationist islands. His Excellency, the mysterious offstage presence, so invisible and invisibly pulling the strings, that ambiguous "they" so readily blamed for the world's ills, was her addition.

In total, her alterations and deviations from Roblès' text were minor and minimal. She divided the play into two acts rather than three, changed Elena's name to Felisa, La Mère to Matilde, and introduced the opening chess-playing scene. Her greatest change was in reducing the discursive passages, the extended philosophical speculations on the nature of freedom. She knew that Americans had a lower tolerance than the French for such disputations. At the same time, her Montserrat became less an activist and more a tortured and skeptical intellectual whose revolutionary ideas have been nurtured by books. Her Izquierdo, villainous as he is, has been stripped of his most vicious racist sentiments. In the original he proposed to exterminate all Indian young men to make the future safe for Spain. Roblès' ghost of Hitler is more visible.

Miss Hellman sought a stronger base in believable reality by tempering the melodramatic commitments of the principals. She focused more strongly on what is done, Roblès on what is said about what is done. She heightened the theatrical effect of the executions with a longer death march, with the accompaniment of His Excellency's piano in the background. Still her play is talky; our heads are engaged more strongly than our hearts. We appreciate the plight of the pathetic hostages; we never know them well enough to be moved by their destruction. We admire Montserrat's heroic resistance, yet we are not magnetized by him and his cause, partly because—and this is the major weakness of the play—we never know Bolivar. Unless well tutored in advance on Bolivar and the Spanish invasion, our hearts are not warmed to the spiritual importance of the revolution, and thus the effects appear mechanical and the carnage gratuitous.

The play does not meet Miss Hellman's usual standard. The writing seems barren and uninspired. In the single line of action, the underdeveloped characters, the laborious repetition of the impasse between Izquierdo and Montserrat, we miss the lifelike richness of the earlier plays. The deficiencies can, of course, be charged only partly to her. They belong as well to Roblès, though one critic thought she misinterpreted Roblès. Harold Clurman, writing in the *New Republic* (December 5, 1949), insisted that she missed the existentialist point of the original. She tried to make a revolutionary document out of a play that was primarily concerned with moral issues and with an existentialist hero who knew exactly why he must die. Montserrat sacrifices himself in the clear knowledge that he is fulfilling his necessary moral duty in behalf of millions of others.

Miss Hellman had missed the research that customarily preceded a play, the historical facts having been supplied by Roblès. In the late summer when she began preparations for the staging, she filled that void with extended sessions at the Spanish American Museum in New York. If nothing else, her production must be authentic. She had thought the Paris production too stagey, too much like a Franz Lehar or Victor Herbert operetta.

After the initial rehearsals in September, the production

moved to Princeton, Philadelphia, and then Detroit for trial runs prior to the scheduled opening at the Fulton Theatre on October 26, 1949. The rehearsals and tryout performances had not gone well. Miss Hellman could not understand why actors could not respond to straight plain English and do what they were told. The communication block was particularly severe with the Actors' Studio actor who was playing Montserrat. One night after rehearsal she asked Bloomgarden to explain this mysterious improvisation business that so fascinated these "method" people. Bloomgarden, with occasional assists from Howard Bay, did his best. An actor invented exercises and acted out portions of a character's life not supplied by the playwright. He might even improvise the life of a cat or of an orange. That ended the first lesson. Miss Hellman said, "Let's go home." Before the next day's rehearsal she cornered Bloomgarden. No, she didn't want the second lesson. She was bleary-eyed because she'd sat on the edge of the bed all night thinking of oranges. Would he please get on the phone and get another actor from New York, a straight, honest, human actor who didn't mix with animals and fruit? That night William Redfield, a quick study, went on as a replacement in the part of Montserrat.

When the play opened in New York on October 29, three days behind schedule, the critics praised its sincerity and pertinence but found it ponderous and monotonous, "one of those Gallic seminars in which a moral question is talked to death." Often it was so repetitious and static that one couldn't wait to have the victims shot. Bolivar's heroic resistance was too remote and unknown, and the director and actors had not charged the performances with enough fire. William Redfield, as Montserrat, hit one note of suffering torment and held it throughout the evening. Only Emlyn Williams, as Izquierdo, and Julie Harris, as Felisa, received uniform commendation. Williams' cold and calculating villain was so impressive and so completely dominated the stage that against such odds it became futile to root for the hero. Julie Harris alerted the audiences and the profession to her great talent, and when *Mont-*

serrat closed on December 24, after sixty-five performances,* Harold Clurman, now as director, engaged her for the role of Frankie in Carson McCuller's *Member of the Wedding,* which was to open on January 5, 1950.

If the reviews on Monday morning, October 31, 1949, did not make pleasant reading, Miss Hellman could contemplate a kind of second chance. *Regina,* the musical version of *The Little Foxes,* was to open at the Forty-Sixth Street Theatre that evening. For the first time she would have two productions running simultaneously, though each in its way was second-hand Hellman. The music and the libretto for the opera, or "musical drama" as it was billed, had been done by Marc Blitzstein. Although essentially a literal copy of the original set to music, it had been embellished with production numbers. For example, Horace was given a festive homecoming party with singing, dancing, and a noisy Negro jazz band.

Miss Hellman had seen the script of *Regina* only once prior to opening night, when Blitzstein had solicited her opinion. Her comments, in a letter to him (June 27, 1949), indicate her sensitivity to the right word, right for sound and sense, right for place, period and character: ". . . 'key to Southland'—Southland is a Northland word . . . 'pinch' and 'cram'—very unSouthern. . . . 'For your sweet tooth to crave'—bad line, very unlike Regina. . . . 'And I'll tell you why you hate it so'—an uneuphonious line. . . . I don't think Regina is a flirt. She would flirt with Marshall for a reason; she would flirt with anybody for a reason, but I don't for a second believe she would flirt with the men in this town . . . no talk about another

* Although the revolutionary message of *Montserrat* failed to attract a following in its initial run, the play held a persistent appeal for Off-Broadway groups. In the spring of 1954, the Equity Library Theatre's production was opened to the public at the Barbizon-Plaza Theatre. Another production had a month's run at the Gate Theatre in January, 1961. In each instance the critics were not convinced that the passage of time and the more suitable environment of an intimate showcase had improved the play. It was revived again by the Hollywood Television Theatre and shown on educational television stations throughout the country in March, 1971.

woman getting fat. I think she is long past such small feminine pleasantries. . . . Regina must never, never, never answer the question, 'Are you afraid, Mama?' . . . I think the whole approach to the Negro in the play is too sentimental. I think the original play had too much of such sentimentality and it was an artistic mistake. But I don't think we should increase the mistake."

Although Blitzstein's music was highly praised—one critic labeled it "the most exciting musical theatre since *Rosenkavalier*"—and most reviews spoke well of Robert Lewis' staging and Jane Pickens' Regina, the total judgment was not favorable. The bite and belligerence of the original had been lost. Arias did not become Miss Hellman's avaracious Hubbards; too frequently the songs slipped over the border into burlesque, particularly when Ben finally turned on his evil sister and sang, "Greedy Girl." If music could not add dramatic force but instead dissipated the relentless menace of the original, why make the attempt? Having characters sing quite casual things and speak quite emotional lines was, according to George Jean Nathan, "a hell of a way to go about writing anything even approximating opera."

Regina also suffered by comparison with the Weil-Anderson *Lost in the Stars* which had opened the night before. Though it too had been adapted—from Alan Paton's novel, *Cry, the Beloved Country*—it could stand as an original work, having had no previous stage life. *Regina* closed on December 16 after fifty-six performances, nine less than *Montserrat.*

Her directing chores concluded and resigned now to the lack of enthusiasm for her two new ventures, Miss Hellman began contemplating a new play, thinking it might even be ready for a late season opening. Unfortunately, as she confessed in an interview, it was difficult for her to realize that she was no longer twenty, that words reached the page more slowly. *The Autumn Garden* would not be ready for another year.

XII

The Autumn Garden

Before settling down to work, Lillian Hellman visited for a month with her aunts in New Orleans to press the memories of them and their boardinghouse freshly into her mind. They were to form the basis of her new play. When she returned to Hardscrabble Farm in February, eager to begin, she was struck with a six-week siege of headaches and stomach sickness that kept her from the typewriter. Hammett wrote from Hollywood suggesting that she would probably feel better if she stopped "playing around with the Iowa yogi [Henry Wallace] and his fringe of impracticals." Whether or not his therapy supplied the cure, starting in April she wrote with uncommon speed, as if to make up for lost time, and by early June, when Hammett returned, she had a completed script.

Hammett was a severe and uncompromising critic, yet usually more gentle and kind than he was now: "You started as a serious writer," he told her. "That's what I liked, that's what I worked for. I don't know what's happened, but tear this up and throw it away. It's worse than bad—it's half good." Crushed by his disapproval she left the farm and went to New York for a week. When she returned, she deposited the scraps of the manuscript in a brief case outside Hammett's door and started a fresh page. By the end of the year, after some five or six drafts, or partial drafts—none of which were discussed with him—she had a new version. His criticism and her industry had paid off. He now thought it was "the best play anybody's written in a long time. Maybe longer." Only one speech in the last act troubled him. She should rework it. When she refused, he said he'd try. He did, and General Griggs' summing up his life belongs to Hammett, the only such passage in any of the plays. She acknowledged her debt on the dedication page of the printed version. It reads, "For Dash."

As usual the text of *The Autumn Garden* at the opening performance on March 7, 1951, at the Coronet Theatre was almost identical with the text delivered to Kermit Bloomgarden and Harold Clurman, the director. And although it achieved only a moderate success with 101 performances, it now appears regularly, along with *The Little Foxes*, on those lists of American plays people would like to see again, and for many people and in many ways it is her most fascinating play. Miss Hellman, though frightened by absolute judgments, once declared that it was probably her best play.

As if to compensate for her own political activism, ulterior and political overtones were excluded. No background canvas of world events is required; the context is supplied by Miss Hellman's own text. If Ibsen had guided her hand in weaving the strands and tightening the knots in the past, here she has turned to Chekhov. One critic was sure he could hear the echo of the woodsman's axe slashing at the cherry trees at the final curtain. The portraits are drawn with subtle, impressionistic strokes. The characters wander aimlessly, following their inclinations rather than hers, seeking in their October years to fathom the mysteries of their past lives, to discover solace in the present. As in the two plays about the Hubbards, she has drawn from her family memory book but from later pages. She has abandoned the old South and jumped to the present—the Tuckerman summer resort on the Gulf of Mexico, 100 miles from New Orleans, in September, 1949. And instead of crowding the play with tense, touch-and-go crises, with tormenting questions about how, when, and who will win, she has gently enfolded us and the characters in a Chekhovian spell. Some critics thought that Chekhov served her even better than Ibsen, regretted that she had not called on him earlier, that she did not call on him again.

Fascinating as the new Hellman was in the theatre and is on the printed page, the behind-the-scenes evolution of the play is equally fascinating. After she had destroyed the first manuscript, the play underwent a radical transformation from the first to the final draft. Initially the characters, and there were more of them, resembled the characters of *The Little Foxes* and *Another Part of the Forest*, their aggressive impulses driving them into sharp and unyielding confrontations. Only as the play developed were these impulses suppressed, and their gentle, introspective natures took command. The alterations from first to final draft can, of course, be appreciated more fully after looking at the play in its final form.

Again Miss Hellman chose an expansive living room, with a side porch, hall, and staircase partially in view. She remembered such a public room in a resort hotel she had visited as a child, and Howard Bay, the designer, captured the frowsy elegance she recalled. Again the action is compressed in time, covering a single week in September, 1949. And again her characters are, for the most part, a handsome lot and reasonably well-fixed. As the curtain rises, each in his way is wasting away the afterdinner evening. General Ben Griggs is seeking isolation in his newspaper; his wife Rose, soft-looking, forty-three, ten years his junior and in an evening dress ten years her junior, is chattering across the room with Carrie Ellis. Carrie, attractive and distinguished, is near her son Frederick, a pleasant-looking young man of twenty-five, and her mother-in-law, Mrs. Mary

Ellis, whose sprightly manner and quick tongue belies her seventy-plus years. Like Moses Taney and Mrs. Farrelly, she belongs to the outspoken older generation. Edward (Ned) Crossman, in his late forties and looking more tired than the others, has retreated to the side porch, though still in view.

Frederick is correcting a manuscript, while his grandmother tries to read over his shoulder. Rose is the first to speak, about wanting "it" right after dinner, about going to see "him." Mrs. Ellis cannot abide her giggling and ridiculous ambiguities. "There's nothing particularly genteel about pronouns, my dear. Coffee is coffee and not it. Robert Taylor is Robert Taylor and not him." Rose will not be silenced, and her loose tongue furnishes the necessary introductions. Ben, her husband, is from Boston and his mother disliked Southerners. She urges Crossman to join them; he might just "get to like being alone—and that's dangerous." Old Mrs. Ellis does not share her fear of loneliness. Her happiest years date from the death of her husband. She wonders if Frederick might not like to write her biography when he's "finished with regional poetry."

Place and situation are only partly defined when the telephone rings and someone answers in the hall, informing the caller that they take only permanent guests. When Sophie hangs up and enters, reporting that Aunt Constance is most sorry for the delay with the coffee, we wonder about her accent, about why this plain-looking girl of seventeen with a hesitant over-polite manner is wearing a party dress under her kitchen apron. And who is Constance? Some answers come immediately. Sophie, though not in the social league with the Ellises, has become Frederick's intended; the word sounds like "indentured." Fred had supposed their plan was secret, but apparently secrets are not easily suppressed with so many idle women about. According to Griggs, women have no honor with secrets about marriage or cancer.

Frederick is relieved when his grandmother shifts to another awkward subject, the manuscript by his friend Payson. She is perplexed by the new out-of-doors sex relations, and not between men and women as in her day. (In one of the early drafts Miss Hellman used Payson's manuscript as an excuse for some literary observations. Mrs. Ellis thought the writing sounded like imitation Faulkner: "The only difference is that Faulkner is good." Mrs. Griggs disagreed about Faulkner: "A dreadful man. He's done more to give the South a bad name. I've been very grateful that Frances Parkin [sic] Keyes moved down." The excursion into criticism did not survive.)

Fred's mother, undisturbed by the quality of the manuscript, only hopes it will sell, unlike Payson's earlier books. The three generations of Ellises do not see eye to eye on literature, or on money. They're troubled about living on unearned income. Grandmother clips the coupons, Carrie Ellis cashes them, and apparently Fred spends more than his share.

Impatient with the money talk, Rose again takes command. If Ben doesn't want to accompany her to the party, he can check the Robert Taylor war picture to see if it's accurate, though on second thought she might prefer to wait to meet the Denerys, who are about to arrive. Does Carrie think that he's "absolutely fascinating?" Carrie doesn't know; she hasn't seen him for twenty years. But didn't they all grow up together: Carrie, Constance, Denery, and Crossman? Crossman is on the porch buried in his own dreams of the past; he can't recall that Denery was fascinating. Our curiosity is whetted, but we must wait for more details on the Denerys.

Sophie is back with a tray of brandy, accompanied by Leon, the Negro servant, with coffee. Fred helps her with the tray, and Rose begins prettying Sophie's hair. The attention is again on Sophie. Apparently she's from Europe, does not mind being fussed over, has become accustomed to have the others talk about her as if she were not in the room, and all summer Crossman has heard her say nothing but "thank you." If they cannot manage their own lives, they delight in managing hers.

Again the scene is interrupted by the phone and the introduction of Constance Tuckerman, who answers. The telephone may have lost its novelty; it's still handy for the playwright.

Constance is a handsome woman in her early forties. As she comes in to announce that the call is from Payson and for Frederick, we learn that she runs the establishment, that she'll not be going to the party, and as she disappears Rose explains her nervousness. She'd be excited too if she were "seeing an old beau for the first time."

When Frederick returns from the phone, Crossman and Griggs have retreated to the porch, having captured the bottle of brandy for themselves, and Rose goes to her room to fix her face for the evening. Payson has apparently had a wire from his publisher demanding that the manuscript be mailed the next morning. Fred cannot escort his mother; he'll have to spend the evening proofreading. Carrie is offended and jealous that her son has no sense of obligation to her or to Sophie. Sophie tries unsuccessfully to escape the crossfire between mother and son. Apparently Payson has been sponging on the family for the past year. Mrs. Ellis tries to break the tension; she's been worried all day about the disappearance of tapeworm in the South. Everyone used to be afflicted and talk about it constantly. Now she's not heard the word for years. As she exits, she persuades mother and son to kiss and make up. This scene must have been enacted before. Carrie cannot suffer the intrusion of an outsider, and Frederick has learned to bend to her will when necessary. With her authority restored, Carrie exits, and Sophie and Frederick are alone for the first time.

Sophie cannot understand that Carrie's anger could be dissipated so easily. Perhaps it's the language difference. "Everything in English sounds so important." In their brief moment together we sense that they're both resigned to their engagement and willing to proceed as scheduled. Frederick and his mother are going to Europe for the summer, and presumably sometime after they return, he and Sophie will be married. He gives her a gentle, if perfunctory, goodnight, and leaves to join Payson.

Rose has now returned, ready for the party and distressed that the others have gone without her. She summons her husband from the porch. Sophie apparently knows what will follow and disappears into the hall. Will Ben escort her, even if he doesn't go in? Griggs refuses. Will he then call for her at twelve or meet her at the tavern so they can talk? He still refuses. There's nothing more to say; they've repeated the same things every night and every day. Rose quickly satisfies our curiosity about their burden: "Do people get divorces after twenty-five years, by just saying they want them and that's all and walking off?" Is there another woman? What will their children say? Has he written to them? He knows their sons better than she. They wouldn't even finish reading the letter. Yes, they did love each other once, but that time has passed. His sons think of him only when they find his name useful. (In an early draft Miss Hellman made more of the Griggses. Two grandchildren, aged five and seven, were with them for the summer and appeared as characters in the play.) Rose has lost interest in the argument; she simply had to repeat the routine. He can spend the evening with his Chinese grammar, while she goes to the party and tries to have a good time. Before she goes, however, he reminds her that he's not playing a game. When she returns to town next week, he'll not be going with her. Rose has not waited to hear his ultimatum.

As he goes to get his book on the porch, he realizes that Crossman has heard their quarrel. Crossman has also thought of beginning a new life, though he fears that he would simply duplicate what he's done. Griggs wonders if the starting point really matters. He went to West Point because he was fascinated with mathematics. What he got was two wars and Rose. "All professional soldiers marry Rose. It's in the Army Manual. She is as she always was. It is my fault, not hers." Crossman accepts things as they are. Hasn't Griggs lived in the South long enough to know that "nothing is ever anybody's fault?" We begin to sense the current that will be flowing through the play. These people are captured in their own pasts, obsessed with their dreams of what might have been, yet bound to the present and the small comforts that provide an illusion of escape.

When Griggs departs with his Chinese grammar, Constance comes down the stairs. Everything is prepared in the bedrooms. Nick is to have Sophie's room—Sophie will sleep in the living room—and his wife the yellow room. She's perplexed, yet pleased, that they wanted two rooms. Crossman assures her the request is not unusual. "Fashionable people don't sleep together. It's not sanitary." There's an easy intimacy between these two. Constance is eager to see Nick again. She's never forgotten the day he left for Paris to paint, twenty-three years ago, the eighteenth of next month. His heart cooled after he left, everyone's privilege, and he married another woman. She's certain—more certain than Crossman—that it's been a happy marriage, yet she's nervous about meeting his wife. She's changed her dress three times since dinner; everything looks too cheap to withstand the inspection of another woman. Clearly the reunion with Nick is a big moment in her life, and that moment is rapidly approaching. Just after Sophie returns with her bedding, the sound of a car is heard and Constance races for the stairway, perhaps to change her dress again. Crossman hastily explains to Sophie that her aunt was in love with Nick and even after all these years the flame is still burning. The past hangs heavily over all of them. Sophie not only understands; her wisdom outstrips her years. "It always happens that way with ladies. For them it is once and not again." As we hear the voices outside, Sophie also disappears, and Ned is left alone to greet Nick and Nina.

They, like the others, are handsome people. Nick has dreamed of his return to this summer mansion, though his memory is not as sharp as he imagined. He does not recognize Crossman at first, and when he does, he's forgotten his name and introduces him as Willy. Nick has not kept in touch. Ned must tell him, and us, that old man Tuckerman died unexpectedly and broke. Constance was obliged to sell their New Orleans home and take in boarders to retain the summer house. Mrs. Tuckerman died shortly after her husband, "just to show him anybody could do it." Ned, like Mrs. Ellis and General Griggs, has a sense of humor. Constance carries other burdens.

Her brother Sam went to Europe in the thirties, married, and died there during the war. Five years ago she brought over his child, Sophie. Miss Hellman has not abandoned the Ibsen manner completely. We profit from Nick's demand for background information.

We may wish to know more, but the reunion cannot be delayed. Constance has not recovered her composure; she trips as she enters and pretends that she was reading and did not hear the car. Nick does his best to fulfill his anticipation. He kisses her, then, holding her at arm's length, recites his prepared speech: "This is a good hour of my life, Constance." He had expected she'd be standing in the drive with the sun in her face, in the kind of lovely pink thing she used to wear. Nina, the realist, cannot endure his palaver. The sun would not shine at night, even for him. They're off to a bad start and must find some pedestrian refuge. Constance has food ready, if they're hungry. Nick wonders if she still has the portrait he did before he left. She does, and she's tried to follow his career by subscribing to the Sunday *Times*. His activities have not been reported there; he's been exhibiting in Europe.

Again Nick tries to recapture the past, when they all loved each other. And though Crossman does not recall all "that much love," Nick's rapture cannot be restrained: "I think as one grows older it is more and more necessary to reach out your hand for the sturdy old vines you knew when you were young and let them lead you back to the roots of things that matter." Nick has sounded the sad melody of *The Autumn Garden*. When no one echoes the theme song, he resorts to routine, if awkward, questions. Two years ago in Paris an old friend told him that Crossman and Constance had never married, that Crossman had sought solace in drink. If that's the game Nick wants to play, Crossman can match him: "I want to know about you, too. Ever had syphilis, Nick? Kind of thing one has to know right off, if you understand me." He doesn't wait for an answer; he'll see them in the morning and show Nick around "all the old places."

Undisturbed by Crossman's brusque retreat, Nick returns to the portrait. He would like to do another, after he's seen the first one. Constance finally agrees to bring the painting down from upstairs. Left alone, Nina quickly strips off Nick's romantic mask. She hasn't heard him speak of Constance in years until last week, and then he remembered only that she was rather silly. He's probably proposed this sentimental journey simply to find a new arena for his fancies. He's said nothing about a painting, about doing a new portrait. He admits that he just thought of that on the way. But Nina does not hold the upper hand. When he suggests arranging for her early departure, she's frightened and backs off. She is tired and wants to go to bed, and as she starts for the stairs, Constance returns with the painting. The full revelation about Nick and Nina must wait. Again Miss Hellman has called time before the scene has run its course.

Nick is proud of the painting. He recalls the day it was finished and he said, "Damn good work for a boy of eighteen." Constance's memory is better. He was twenty-two that day and he also asked her to marry him. He does remember that they were in love, but now he's more concerned about the portraits. The old and the new could hang side-by-side in his retrospective in London. Constance can't bear to risk the comparison. Hurt by her refusal, he starts to go, but he's caught by Carrie and Rose returning from the party. Rose has become faint from too much dancing, though she revives when she sees Nick. She's been looking forward to meeting such a famous man and hopes he'll be staying with them to brighten their days. The prospect is inviting, but he'll probably have to leave the next day. He does, however, volunteer to help her upstairs. Carrie refuses his assistance and leads Rose into the hall.

Troubled by the threat of Nick's departure, Constance agrees to sit for the portrait. They'll have to work early in the morning before the daily chores begin. Reluctantly she confesses that her life has not been easy. She's brought Sam's daughter from Europe and tried to send her to the best schools.

She doesn't really know why she's not married Ned Crossman; they just never did. Nick is quickly bored by the recital of her past; he's more intrigued by Sophie when she enters. The pretty face awakens the old Nick: "I've been looking forward to meeting you for many years." Sophie is lost in this league; her tongue can't make a word. Fortunately, General Griggs, coming from the porch, rescues her. Nick has read about him, almost met him when the General marched his troops into Paris. Yes, it was an awkward time during the German occupation. Still one must not be unjust to the Germans: "They acted like gentlemen." Nick has another strike against him in Miss Hellman's book and ours. The rogue is becoming less beloved.

And even less beloved when Nina's maid, Hilda, brings a message from Mrs. Denery. She would like Nick to come upstairs; she has a gift for him that she bought in New Orleans. He goes upstairs, but not to her. Hilda can tell Mrs. Denery to take a sleeping pill; he'll see her in the morning. Hilda and Nick have spoken in German, and Sophie translates as she and Constance make up her bed on the couch. Constance tries not to believe Nick's rudeness. Sophie is not surprised. She knows how such people live: "Down at the beach there is the frankfurter concession. I think I will get the sleeping-pill concession and grow very rich."

Try as she will, Constance cannot understand this new generation. Why didn't Sophie and Fred go to the party? Why is there no romance with their approaching marriage? How could another appointment be more important? Reminded of the party, she tells Griggs that Rose has returned, that he'd better tend to her. Griggs, as if by habit, dutifully obeys. The household is closing down for the day. Constance kisses Sophie goodnight, Sophie finishes her bed and goes out, and Crossman comes down the stairs, crossing to the porch to retrieve his brandy bottle.

As he returns, Sophie is back with her robe and pajamas. He wants some end-of-the-day wisdom from Sophie, now that "the Royalty" has gone to bed: "Does anybody improve with age? Just tell me that, Sophie, and I'll have something to lie awake and think about." He begs her to risk an opinion about something: "Try it, and see what comes out." She tries: "Some people improve with age, some do not." Crossman is delighted. She's beginning to sound like an advertisement, "which is the very highest form of American talk." He fears that Sophie has lost her spirit: "What the hell is this marriage business between you and Fred Ellis?" She should "beat it quick." That's her only way out. Sophie is too practical to rebel; Constance has done too much for her. She must stay and do the best she can; life must be lived as it is, not as one would like it to be. "Maybe you've never tried to do that, Mr. Ned. Maybe none of you have tried." Sophie sees them more clearly than they see themselves. Ned has had enough truth for one night: "Sophie, lonely people talking to each other can make each other lonelier. They should be careful because maybe lonely people are the only people who can't afford to cry. I'm sorry." He's on his way upstairs as the curtain falls.

The lost souls wandering in Miss Hellman's autumn garden are trapped in the lives they have made, and though they have not yet abandoned their dreams, final resignation seems pitifully near. Miss Hellman is reciting the universal human experience. Sometime in the middle years every man is awakened to what might have been and struggles to give his dreams a last chance.

Hope seems revived in the bright light of an early Sunday morning a week later. The portrait is in progress on the porch. Sophie is making her bed and running the sweeper. Leon is transporting breakfast dishes to the porch. Mrs. Ellis is complaining about breakfast getting later every day, about the dampness, about her lack of sleep. She doesn't like the portrait. Nick is making Constance look "right mean and ten years older." Her tongue shifts rapidly from one subject to another. When Sophie brings her coffee, she proposes that Sophie come to New Orleans with her while Carrie and Frederick go to Europe. When Crossman enters, she asks his advice about a wedding present for the young couple. He advises her to betray her class. Instead of giving something old and precious, something that doesn't cost her anything, she could give Sophie a nice new check.

As in earlier plays mealtime becomes talktime for Miss Hellman's characters. The Tuckerman breakfast group brings us up to date on their activities. Nick has been busily trying to turn their lives in new directions. He's been whispering to Sophie, telling her she's pretty. Before he leaves he must paint her portrait. Last night he shared a bottle with Crossman and prodded him into his "juke-box song called Constance." He could talk of nothing but his love, of how often he had asked her to marry him. Even if she has no vanity, Constance should be flattered. She'd be more flattered if Nick had considered her vanity when he bought the dowdiest dress in the cheapest store in town for the portrait. Nick's wife understands him better than the others. She's worried when he embarks on a "rampage of good will," trying to manipulate other lives. She hopes they'll be leaving soon.

When Rose enters, wanting Nick's assurance that she's doing the right thing in going to her brother's and asking her doctor to check her heart, Nina tells her that she'll need to jog his memory. He's probably forgotten his advice of yesterday; he has "so many ladies to attend to." Rose is worried about the effect of her divorce on her boys, particularly the one who works on the atom bomb and is so religious. The breakup will be traumatic for him. Apparently his religious conscience is not disturbed by the bomb, an observation Miss Hellman could not resist.

Nina has lost patience with Nick's flirtations. He's always charmed women, men, children, and animals, but "nowadays it seems to me you include books-in-vellum and sirloin steaks, red squirrels and lamp shades." Nick is a persistent meddler like Teck in *Watch on the Rhine* and the yet-to-be-created Julian in *Toys in the Attic*, though he's not so evil as Teck or so flamboyant as Julian. Miss Hellman's characters learn their ways from each other. Carrie is the next to suffer from Nick's meddling when he tells her that he was in the travel agency when Fred was booking passage for his friend Payson. She should know about Payson's reputation in Europe; he's just escaped from a "filthy little scandal in Rome." Miss Hellman and Nick know the evil power of suggestion. There's no need to say that Payson is a homosexual on the make.

When Carrie retreats to the dining room, Nina's anger explodes: "Have you ever tried leaving things alone?" She detects the smoldering brimstone: "It's all around us. The flower-like odor right before it becomes troublesome and heavy. It travels ahead of you, Nick, whenever you get most helpful, most loving and most lovable. Down through the years it runs ahead of us—I smell it—and I want to leave." She can leave if she wishes; he intends to stay until Friday. He kisses her and goes to the dining room. If no one else enjoys his meddling, he does.

As Sophie comes onto the porch to remove the dishes, Nina starts for the stairs, meeting Frederick on the way. When Sophie tells him what she's overheard about buying the ticket for Payson, he's untroubled; he planned to inform his mother this morning. While they're abroad they'll visit Sophie's mother. Sophie thinks that unwise; she's not informed her mother about the marriage because no date has been set and "every act of life should not be of such importance." She manages a smile as she exits, and Fred calls his mother from the dining room.

Carrie has been planning the trip with him for three years, and now Payson has been invited and with Fred paying for his ticket. She's decided they won't go. Fred thinks otherwise. He's going on the sixteenth; he deserves to see the things he's always wanted to see. "We're lucky to have somebody who knows about them and who is willing to have *us* tag along." Carrie realizes her power is slipping. She begs him to think about it until tomorrow morning. Mrs. Ellis, who has been listening in the hallway, at first sides with Carrie, then finally urges Fred either to go or stay without any bargaining. He accepts her advice and leaves.

Mrs. Ellis suggests an escape for Carrie. She can cut off his

$10,000-a-year allowance and tell him she's "decided young people have a happier time in Europe without American money." When Carrie rebels at such severity, Mrs. Ellis volunteers to cut Carrie's allowance. "Yes, old people are often harsh, Carrie, when they control the purse. One should have power or give it over. But if one keeps it, it might as well be used, with as little mealymouthness as possible. Go up now, and press him hard, and do it straight." Mrs. Ellis is bound for church; Carrie can skip it for today. She has "God's work to do."

With breakfast on the porch and in the dining room and coffee in the living room, the characters move in and out at will. Rose Griggs is now back from the table, planting herself for one last attempt to persuade Ben to forget the divorce. How will she explain to her brother Henry? There must be another woman; that's probably why he stayed in Europe so long. Griggs assures her that he didn't arrange World War II, and she shouldn't listen to the rumors that he did. Has he thought of his mother? The news would kill her. When he reminds Rose that his mother's been dead for sixteen years, she tries another tack. Isn't he curious about the man who sent her flowers from Teheran? She's going to break her silence and tell who it was—his cousin Ralph Sommers. When that news fails to shock him, she gives up and departs.

Exhausted by Rose as he has been repeatedly, Ben settles into a chair as Crossman enters to share the Sunday paper. He admits he has no clear reason for the divorce; he's simply weary of living with a foolish woman and dreams of the peace he might find by himself. The men are joined by Nina and then by Constance. Constance, on her way to church, asks Crossman to go with her. He's stunned by the proposal and more stunned when she says, "Goodbye, darling," and kisses him. She's taken his drunken confession too seriously.

Nina has a plan of escape from the heartbreak house. She's packed a picnic lunch with a bottle of wine. Would they come with her? Crossman is willing, if there's enough for lunch *and* dinner, and Griggs, if the wine supply can be enlarged. For a brief moment they recapture the summer gaiety that must have permeated the Tuckerman house in earlier years. The picnickers depart and Sophie is back to clear the dishes as the curtain falls.

When the curtain rises on the second scene of Act II, it's nine-thirty in the evening. Neither the picnickers nor Rose have returned. Carrie and Fred are not in sight. Constance is playing solitaire and listening to the phonograph; Sophie is on the porch reading to Mrs. Ellis; Nick, though busy with a bottle of champagne, is restless with the lack of activity. He tries some verbal sparring with Mrs. Ellis, but loses. She advises him to sit down with the champagne he's been "chewing since early afternoon and try to make a paper hat out of the newspaper" or get himself a nice long piece of string. She does not appreciate his friendly pats on her shoulder, his "little moments of sensuality. One should have sensuality whole or not at all. Don't you find pecking at it ungratifying? There are many of you: the touchers and the leaners. All since the depression, is my theory."

Subdued by Mrs. Ellis and unsuccessful in persuading Constance to dance with him, he returns to meddling. Why hasn't Constance married Ned instead of dangling him around, even if she didn't love him? Love and marriage are not all that inseparable. He loved her, yet he married Nina. Marriage with her would not have worked because "you're a good woman and I am not a good man." He has his moments of truth. When Constance begs to know what Ned really said about her, Nick returns to the hyperbole he enjoys: "He said he loved you and wanted you and had wasted his life loving you and wanting you. And that he wasn't coming here any more. This is his last summer in this house." Constance is crushed by the thought of Ned not returning; she would like to hear more, but the chance has passed. Carrie rushes in to report that she can't find Fred; she's even swallowed her pride and gone to Payson. Only one person has seen him, down by the water. Should she call the police? Nick is aroused by the new adventure. He'll get a boat and she can tell the police to follow. Sophie, angered by Nick's interference, shouts at him in French: "Do not enjoy the excitement so much. Stop being a fool. Mind your business." She tells them that Fred has hidden himself in the cove down by the dock. Carrie is shocked that Sophie would know about Fred and let her suffer. Nick is annoyed with Sophie's outburst and demands an apology. When it doesn't come, Mrs. Ellis suggests that he wait outside. Nick goes, pouting like a small boy: "I don't think I like it around here. No, I don't like it."

Mrs. Ellis is certain that Fred no longer wants to go to Europe. Perhaps the marriage should be arranged immediately. Sophie does not object. "If Frederick is willing for an early marriage, then I am also willing." Constance is astonished at her tone: "Is this the way it's been? *Willing* to marry, *willing* to *marry*—" Perhaps it would be better if she were sent home. Sophie knows it's too late to go home, knows what's best for her: "Frederick and I'll have a nice life, we will make it so." She's gone before Constance can say more.

Carrie does not approve of the hasty marriage. Frederick is going abroad as planned. She's spoken too soon. Fred returns to announce that he's not going. As Mrs. Ellis suspected, he has new troubles. "Payson made it clear to me that I was not wanted and never had been unless I supplied the money." Carrie is unwilling to give up, even if Fred is. She'll talk to Payson. Mrs. Ellis knows that would be futile. People like them must pay for the interest of people like him. Fred should "take next week to be sad: a week's long enough to be sad in." With that advice and a final command to Carrie not to interfere, she departs. Mrs. Ellis, unlike the others, has learned to take the world as it comes and make the best of it.

Sophie has returned to take Fred to dinner, and Constance and Carrie are left struggling to fathom the young and the old. To Constance it all sounds like "the sale of a shore-front property." Perhaps Carrie understands; she was always so clear and strong about everything, even when they were girls.

She doesn't; she doesn't even know why she wanted them to marry. And like the others, she has her own sadness, her own dreams of what might have been: "I wish I could tell you what I've missed and what I've wanted." She exits toward the stairway, meeting Nick in the hall.

Nick's spirits have been restored with the help of more champagne. He wishes he wanted to take Constance to bed but he doesn't, and he doesn't know why. He's lonely though and wants her to stay with him. As she's urging him to go to bed, the telephone rings. It's Rose, wanting to talk with Nick. He's too drunk to take seriously her doctor's report about her heart. Yes, he's willing to paint her niece's picture, though he refuses to paint out her braces. Rose's call has restored his confidence, and when the picnickers return, he insists that Ned and Griggs join him in a drink. He won't accept their refusal; he grabs Crossman's arm and presses the glass to his lips. When Ned crashes the glass to the floor, Nick still persists. Crossman must pour himself a drink and apologize. Ned refuses and leaves. Nick is exactly as he remembered him, "and that I wouldn't have believed of any man." General Griggs also refuses to drink with Nick, but he can't escape Nick's advice: "I think you're doing the wrong thing, wanting to leave Rose. You're going to be lonely at your age without—" Griggs does not wait to listen. If his wife wishes to consult Mr. Denery, he doesn't.

Nina understands her husband: "You know it's a nasty business hating yourself." They must leave before Constance finds him out; her dreams should not be disturbed. Nick agrees to be ready on Friday. They'll go to New Orleans where they'll spend a month with Rose's brother, painting his daughter's portrait for $5000. Nina is frightened at that prospect. He hasn't finished a portrait in twelve years. What's more, she believes his real reason for going to New Orleans is to carry on a flirtation with Mrs. Griggs. Nina has gone too far: "No man can bear to live with a woman who feels that way about his work." She'd better leave tomorrow; and this time she mustn't return filled with self-humiliation and self-hate, begging to be reinstated. As he follows her up the stairs, Constance comes into the hall, overhearing Nick's final angry words.

When Sophie joins her, they empty the ashtrays, make Sophie's bed on the couch, and turn off the lights. Constance tries to make her understand her loneliness, how lonely she'll be after Sophie's marriage, how she's wasted her life in rejecting Ned's love. After she's gone, Sophie removes her robe and climbs into bed.

In a moment we hear footsteps in the hall and then Nick's voice, as he trips over a chair. He turns on a lamp; he wants to talk to Constance. When he sees Sophie, he gets other ideas. Why doesn't she throw on a coat and come with him; they could be happy together for a few days. He stumbles toward the bed and lies down beside her, his head on her knees. As he clumsily tries to embrace her, she pushes him away, spilling his drink on the bed. He's angry-drunk as he retreats across the room: "Poor little girls always turn rude when they're about to marry rich little boys." He ignores Sophie's pleading, refuses to leave, and comes back to her. If she'll be kind to him for a moment, he'll go away. When she raises her cheek to be kissed, he pulls her down beside him. Again she struggles away, threatening to call his wife. That suggestion delights him. He snuggles into the bed, urging her to return. They'll just tell the concierge that he's her brother. His words are beginning to fade away; the liquor has finally subdued him. She tries to shake him from his stupor, without success. Breathing heavily he mutters, "I'll go away in a few minutes. Don't be so young. Have a little pity. I am old and sick." Sophie gives up and crosses away as the curtain falls.

Mrs. Ellis is the first one down in the morning to discover Nick still asleep on the couch and Sophie across the room drinking coffee. She takes command, trying to force coffee into Nick's throat. He continues to call for Julie, as he has all night according to Sophie. Mrs. Ellis proposes to wake his wife and see if she can locate Julie for him, "or would you rather be cremated here?" He may not know where he is, but she does. "You are in Sophie's bed, in the living room of a house in a small Southern town where for a hundred-and-fifty years it has been impossible to take a daily bath without everybody in town advising you not to dry out your skin." He must get up and "get the hell out of here." She does not succeed before the others begin to arrive. Leon comes with the morning coffee

The Autumn Garden GRAPHIC HOUSE

urn. He's already got the word in the kitchen. Then Rose, who is returning with her overnight bag, enters. Constance is next. The neighbors are already alerted. The Carters have three extra guests on their breakfast porch. Sophie finally explains what happened; alcohol has the same effect in every country. Nick has now begun to recover. They should understand that "the kid didn't want to make any fuss and thought I'd wake up and go any minute." It was damn nice of Sophie and he's grateful. Constance cannot tolerate such "niceness." Rose is certain that Sophie is not as innocent as she pretends. Any nice girl would have screamed.

As Rose leaves, she meets Crossman. He's more philosophical than the others. Not all situations can be remedied and this is one of them. Nick must not make too much of what's happened, nor too little; Sophie must be protected. As Crossman heads for the dining room, Nina appears. She is in no mood to forgive; he can forego his customary excuses. She's going to New York, and he can get their lawyer to handle the legal stuff. Nick doesn't want her to leave; he was talking drunken nonsense last night. They've had too many good times together, "wild times." She's always hated herself for loving him; she must come back and "without shame in wanting to." He'll book the bridal suite on the *Ile de France*. Nick's old magic is working; Nina is weakening. She can even laugh when he insists that this business with Constance and Sophie never happened before: "No, it never happened in this house before. Cora had a husband and Sylvia wanted one. And this isn't a hotel in Antibes, and Sophie is not a rich Egyptian." They've worked their way through to a reconciliation, the first of the troubled Tuckerman guests to recognize that old dreams cannot be revived.

As Nick goes and Nina rings for breakfast, Constance appears and then Carrie and Frederick, ready for traveling and looking for Sophie. Constance will send her in. As Nina goes to the porch, she offers what comfort she can. She should "be carrying a sign that says my husband is deeply sorry and so am I." When Sophie enters, Fred tells her to forget Nick, and Carrie urges her to come with them to New Orleans. Sophie knows that any change of plans would be taken as a confession of guilt. Fred kisses her goodbye and promises that they'll meet again in a few days. Mrs. Ellis has heard their farewells but waits until Carrie and Fred are gone before she speaks. In a few weeks Frederick will go abroad with his mother. Carrie, though she may not know it herself, does not want her son to marry. Sorry as Sophie may feel for Fred, she must not waste herself on defeat.

Sophie is not inclined to weep in defeat; she moves to the porch where Nina is having breakfast. She must speak to her and to Mr. Denery. Unfortunately Nick has already departed, but Nina will do whatever she can. Sophie knows exactly what she can do. "You can give me five thousand dollars. . . . I have been subjected to the most degrading experience from which no young girl easily recovers." She reinforces the demand in French. Somehow talk of sex and money are simpler in French. She's lost her fiancé; she cannot return to school; her aunt is going to be burdened with her. "I am utterly, utterly miserable, Mrs. Denery, I am ruined." When Nina laughs at her histrionics, Sophie reminds her that she's serious; such incidents are not regarded lightly in this neighborhood. Nina is happy to give her the money; she deserves that much help from them. But Sophie wants no charity: "We will call it a loan, come by through blackmail. One does not have to be grateful for blackmail money, nor think of oneself as a charity girl." If Nina refuses, she'll spread the word that Mr. Denery seduced her. Sophie is a tough young lady under her facade of innocence. Mrs. Denery must realize she's profiting from the bargain: "How would you and Mr. Denery go on living without such incidents as me? I have been able to give you a second, or a twentieth honeymoon." Fortunately Crossman appears at the convenient moment; he can assist in concluding the transaction by identifying Nina at the bank, though Nina thinks it unwise for Sophie to accompany them. "You and I in a bank, cashing a check this morning, could well be interpreted as a payoff, or blackmail."

As they depart for the bank, Rose returns complaining that no one has brought her breakfast. Sophie goes for it, as Griggs enters from the porch. He's already heard the news about Nick and Sophie. Now he wants to hear about Rose's consultation with the doctor. She has bad heart trouble, even worse than she's pretended. She knows there's no one but him to help her, knows as well as he that their sons would not life a finger: "I've got nobody and I'm not young and I'm scared. Awful scared." Ben is softening, and when she begs him to give her another year before the divorce, he agrees. Like the Denerys, the Griggses have accepted the inevitable. Rose returns to her room, still hoping for breakfast.

Griggs is alone, his hands shaking as he tries to light a cigarette, when Crossman returns. He's suffering from the "worst disease of all. I'm all gone. I've just looked and there's no Benjamin Griggs." He's speaking for himself and for the others:

> So at any given moment you're only the sum of your life up to then. There are no big moments you can reach unless you've a pile of small moments to stand on. That big hour of decision, the turning point in your life, the someday you've counted on when you'd suddenly wipe out your past mistakes, do the work you'd never done, think the way you'd never thought, have what you'd never had—it just doesn't come suddenly. You've trained yourself for it while you waited—or you've let it all run past you and frittered yourself away. I've frittered myself away, Crossman.

This was the speech that troubled Hammett and which he rewrote. He had even had a hand with an earlier version that read:

> And so there are no minutes of big decisions. No time when you can suddenly turn around. All those years when you promised yourself the day would come when you would wipe out the mistakes, or do the work you'd never done, or think the way you'd never thought, or

> have what you'd never had. No. That's not for people like me. I guess it has to be the sum of it all, of a whole life, and none can be thrown out as you tell yourself you can wait for the great day. Can't do it that way. Well, I let it all run past me, all the waste time, sure that when I knew the way to go, nothing could stop me. Then suddenly it gets too late.

Griggs finds little consolation in knowing that he's as useless as the rest of them. He wonders if he didn't welcome the medical opinion that made it easier for him to give up.

As he moves toward the door, Constance appears with the breakfast tray for Rose and gives it to Ben. Constance too is troubled by not knowing what she thought she knew. Perhaps she'd been wrong in bringing Sophie here. She can't bear the thought of Ned not returning every summer, or was that one of Nick's lies? Nick has gone again, as he did the first time, without saying goodbye. How could she have made "a shabby man into the kind of hero who would come back some day all happy and shining"? She makes one last stab at capturing the happiness she missed. After all these years of not knowing how she felt or not wanting to know, would Ned marry her now? Before Ned can reply, we see Sophie in the hall going up the stairs. She's carrying an envelope and "singing a cheerful French song." At least she is happy.

Ned knows they have long since passed the moment when they might have found happiness together. He's reconciled to his aimless life: "I live in a room and I go to work and I play a game called getting through the day while you wait for the night." If he made her think he was still in love, he's sorry: "Sorry I fooled you and sorry I fooled myself." Constance can no longer resist the inevitable and as the curtain closes, she, like the others, buries her dream: "Never mind. Most of us lie to ourselves, darling, most of us."

The Autumn Garden is certainly Miss Hellman's most original, most probing, most mature, and many would say, her best play. She has captured the universal human experience of the middle years: the last desperate grasp at the dreams of what might have been, the sad and inexorable discovery that time and habit have fixed a mold that cannot be broken. As Miss Hellman once said, "Here is what I think happens to many people at this time of life." She was exploring her own time of life, "a time when one has had a chance to try all one's capacities, felt the emotions of life, known love. One has the power to enjoy life in any way that is preferred. At the same time, one can always have the additional pleasure of being reflective about experiences. . . . I suppose the point I had in mind is this—you come to a place in your life when what you've been is going to form what you will be. If you've wasted what you have in you, it's too late to do much about it. If you've invested yourself in life, you're pretty certain to get a return. If you are inwardly a serious person, in the middle years it will pay off."

More than in any of her other plays, the characters follow their own inclinations, discover their own destinies, seemingly undirected by her. Preoccupied as they are with their hidden worlds, they are extraordinarily verbose, fonder of talking than listening. And as they expose their private realities, their frustrations, their defeats, we become more intrigued by their inner crises than by their surface perplexities. Yet they are not literary creations. All are vividly dramatic with "blood, not ink, in their veins," as John Mason Brown put it, and their complex personal narratives give the play the "density of a big novel." She admitted no villain to her summer house, though the tinny charmer Nick Denery knows the ways of Mephistopheles. Without his machinations, the ghosts of the past would have slept through another summer. The pace, though leisurely, is never dull; the inner tensions are never lost in the casual atmosphere; and much as the characters enjoy their tart and entertaining frivolities, their serious natures are not obscured. It is not a cheerless play, and when the characters are compelled to abandon their dreams, they retire gracefully into their old habits, accepting the stalemate that faces them.

Most critics, even in the morning-after reviews, caught sight of Chekhov in the new play. These shallow people trapped in the slow confusion of their lives would have been at home in one of Chekhov's country houses. Yet had Chekhov commanded the Tuckerman house, they would have been more poetically endowed, their heartbeats would have been more distinct, and a more lyrical mood would have pervaded the atmosphere.

One day after rehearsals Miss Hellman had pressed Harold Clurman, the director, for some comments on the play. Pleased as he seemed to be, certainly he must have spotted some deficiencies. Reluctantly he spoke as a critic, not as the director. The play was rich in Chekhovian qualities, yet she had missed a Chekhov essential. In his plays, no matter how stupid, silly, and petty the characters might be, they were invariably lovable people because Chekhov loved them. In her play the glow of love was missing; Clurman could not believe that she loved her summer guests. She agreed that he was probably right. When he said the same thing in print, he angered Kermit Bloomgarden but not Miss Hellman. Clurman wrote in the *New Republic* (March 26, 1951) that she refuses "to be metaphysical, poetic, or soft. She will not embrace her people; she does not believe they deserve her (or our) love. Love is present only through the ache of its absence. Miss Hellman is a fine artist; she will be a finer one when she melts."

She had not been reading Chekhov prior to writing *The Autumn Garden* and had not tried to duplicate his style, though she was, in a way, attempting to reverse his theory. She wrote in a recent letter, "I said to myself, suppose there are lost people, beyond recovery, in a civilization that *isn't* failing, or isn't failing for their kind as in other places." Perhaps her moralistic compulsion prevented her from adopting the Chekhov line. Thoroughgoing realist that he was, Chekhov rarely endowed his characters with the strength to face the truth about themselves. Hellman felt compelled to make her people confront their weaknesses and suffer from what they saw.

That she had some reservations about Chekhov and his dramatis personae is apparent in her edition of the Chekhov letters, published four years after *The Autumn Garden.* For example, she found the characters in *The Cherry Orchard* shallow people who had a desperate need "for emotional fancy dress, a desire to deck out ordinary trouble in gaudy colors, and to teeter around life like children in their mother's high-heeled shoes . . . these lovable fools are not even worth the trees that are the symbol of their end." For her Chekhov lacked passion and power. He was "without that final spiritual violence which the very great creative genius has always had. And he knew it as he knew most things about himself." In forcing her characters into a showdown with themselves, Miss Hellman supplied some of the power that she missed in Chekhov.

Although most critics thought that *The Autumn Garden* showed Miss Hellman at the peak of her talents—the writing stimulating and assured, the characters the most truthful she had portrayed, the flow of action easy and lucid—some found her philosophizing platitudinous and pedestrian, her coincidental duplication of middle-aged malaise in the Tuckerman guests a strain on credibility. Some would have sacrificed the quiet intensity of inner turmoil and frustration for a larger portion of the bite and vigor of the old Hellman. Many came close to calling it a great play, and only George Jean Nathan dismissed it. He saw only "a room full of men and women suffering from nothing but the calendar."

If *The Autumn Garden* revealed a new Hellman, the early manuscripts again reveal her extraordinarily meticulous workmanship. She began, as she has said, with her memories of a Gulf Coast resort she had visited as a child. When she assembled her middle-aged vacationers, many bits and pieces of characters she had observed in her adult days came together to flesh out her creations. As she progressed through the successive drafts, she abandoned characters, reordered incidents, and above all, minimized the action, blue-pencilled the literal and explicit, softened the characters, and gradually cast an autumnal haze over the Tuckerman resort.

In the beginning the "Tuckerman girls," Constance and Amelia, Sophie's aunts, managed the establishment. In sacrificing their lives for their brother, who had gone abroad and married Anna Marie, they had been obliged to sell their New Orleans house, which had been converted into "a club for Jewish people." They had imported Sophie and her mother, both of whom now help with the household duties. Anna Marie and General Griggs have fallen in love and propose to escape together even without a divorce from Rose. Ben has also agreed to provide for Sophie, to forestall her disastrous marriage with Fred. Sophie does not accept this plan; she'll take care of herself and her mother without tears and sighs. She's cold and calculating, never helpless and pathetic. At one point she orders her mother "to come in and we will drink to Fred and me. And then I order you not to order me again." In the seduction scene, though Nick is less drunk and the lovemaking more explicit, she holds her own against Nick. She is not traumatized by the attack, and when the gossipers' tongues start wagging, she shouts, "Oh shut up. You all talk too much." She confronts Nick's wife immediately: "Mr. Denery seduced me last night and I would like five thousand dollars for the—for the inconvenience." And when her mother accuses her of being foul-mouthed, she snaps, "You talk like a ladies' maid. You be still. If you do not stay still and act like yourself I will go out of here today, and I will not come back with you." The original Sophie would have felt at home with the Hubbards. If her nature had not sweetened in the succeeding drafts as she became less pivotal and the other characters gained prominence, we might have been better prepared for Sophie's blackmailing, but we would have missed the new Hellman.

Several characters disappeared as the play evolved. A superfluous guest, Mrs. Vouloir, and two Griggs grandchildren were the first to go. Aunt Amelia was next. The story of two maiden aunts who sacrificed themselves for their brother—partly the record of Miss Hellman's aunts, Hannah and Jenny, and their devotion to her father—would be told in *Toys in the Attic*, nine years later. Sophie's mother, Anna Marie Tuckerman, relinquished her place in the third draft. Her affair with General Griggs and her struggles with her daughter were too strong for the new play.

Only one major change was made in the ordering of events, similar to the change in *The Little Foxes*. In the first draft Nina and Nick had arrived prior to the opening curtain. Miss Hellman quickly recognized the dramatic advantage of a delayed entrance. Other changes were more telling. The language became less literal and specific, more aimless and elusive, as the characters became mesmerized by the autumnal spell that hung over the final version.

If the critics qualified their praise, none had reservations about the production and the performances. Few plays of the period could boast such an all-star cast:

Rose Griggs .... Florence Eldridge
Mrs. Mary Ellis .... Ethel Griffies
General Griggs .... Colin Keith-Johnston
Edward Crossman .... Kent Smith
Frederick Ellis .... James Lipton
Carrie Ellis .... Margaret Barker
Constance Tuckerman ..... Carol Goodner
Nina Denery .... Jane Wyatt
Nicholas Denery .... Frederic March

And Joan Lorring, a newcomer who played Sophie, often drew the highest tribute for holding her ground against the old pro's. Florence Eldridge was invariably singled out for her "brilliant, unforgettable performance." Clurman's direction caught the casual atmosphere without losing the inner tensions, and Howard Bay's setting provided the proper decaying atmosphere for the Tuckerman mansion. Yet after its first showing in Philadelphia on February 21, 1951, and its opening at the Coronet in New York on March 7, the play held on only until June 2, with 101 performances, barely squeaking by the magic 100 mark that Broadway folklore calls a success. In a showdown at the box office audiences apparently preferred the old Hellman. Some associated with the production thought that the play suffered from too many star players who were more concerned with burnishing their own images than submerging themselves in their roles. The play needed a strong repertory company with players freed from the necessity of marketing themselves as they performed. The American theatrical system could not provide such a company.

XIII

HUAC, McCarthy, and Chekhov

The early fifties were unsettling times for Miss Hellman, as they were for many Americans. Hammett was sent to jail in 1951 and after his release was interrogated by the McCarthy committee. Miss Hellman was called before the House Un-American Activities Committee and, with that stigma, was blacklisted by Hollywood. She struck back with a revival of *The Children's Hour*, alerting a new public to the fearful dangers of the big lie.

In April, 1951, a month after *The Autumn Garden* opening, Federal Judge Sylvester Ryan held Hammett in contempt of court and sentenced him to six months in jail. Hammett had refused to name the persons who contributed to the bail-bond fund of the Civil Rights Congress; presumably this fund had been tapped to secure the release of four Communist leaders who had jumped bail. During the trial Hammett pleaded the Fifth Amendment, refusing even to admit or deny that the documents in evidence carried his handwriting or his initials. The court was convinced that he was one of the chairmen of the bail fund and that the Civil Rights Congress deserved its place on the Attorney General's list of Communist-front organizations. Throughout the summer and fall, while Hammett was confined in the Federal House of Detention on West Street in New York and then in the Federal Correctional Institute near Ashland, Kentucky, the case was repeatedly back in court. First bail was set at $10,000, but when Muriel Alexander, Hammett's secretary, arrived with the money and refused to say where she got it, the bail was denied. In September, the Court of Appeals for the Second Circuit in New Haven denied the motion to reverse the original decision, and the Supreme Court refused to review the case on December 4, 1951, just a week before Hammett completed his jail term. It appears now hardly coincidental that while he was imprisoned the government discovered that he owed more than $100,000 in back taxes.

Hammett had insisted that while he was discharging his debt to society, Lillian should not stay in New York grieving over his incarceration. She respected his wish and went to Europe, returning just in time to welcome him home. Their torment had not, however, been concluded. In May, 1952, she was called to testify before HUAC.

The invitation was not unexpected. She first sensed that she had gained the disfavor of the frightened postwar Hollywood establishment in 1948, when she and William Wyler proposed to do a motion picture based on Dreiser's *Sister Carrie*. Wyler was told by someone—some said Barney Balaban—that she could not be hired, that her name appeared on Hollywood's secret blacklist. Her name apparently became more deeply etched in June, 1949, when Jack Tenney, the state senator from Los Angeles and his California committee listed her, along with Chaplin, Pearl Buck, Katherine Hepburn, Dorothy Parker, Danny Kaye, Hammett, et al., as "having followed or appeased some of the Communist party-line programs." Then, in September, 1951, the screenwriter Martin Berkeley told HUAC, on tour in Los Angeles, that she along with a hundred other prominent Hollywood personalities had been members of the Party and that she had attended a meeting in his home in 1937. Her permanent place on the blacklist was assured when she appeared before HUAC in Washington in May, 1952, and not until the sixties, when the list lost its sanctity, was she again able to work in Hollywood.

In her Washington ordeal she was not honored by the full committee. At eleven o'clock on Wednesday morning, May 21, 1952, she and her counsel, Joseph L. Rauh, Jr., met with a subcommittee, Representatives John S. Wood and Francis E. Walter and their counsel, Frank S. Tavenner, Jr., in Room 226 of the Old House Office Building. The initial questions were easily answered. She was a playwright; most of her activity centered in New York; her Hollywood sojourns never lasted more than a few months; her last assignment was only for two weeks in 1948, when she prepared a ten-page treatment of *Streetcar Named Desire* for submission to the Breen Office; her longest stay had been for six or seven months in the winter and spring of 1937. With the critical dates fixed, Mr. Tavenner asked if she had ever known Martin Berkeley. She replied, "I must refuse to answer, Mr. Tavenner, on the grounds it might incriminate me." He then read from Berkeley's 1951 testimony, describing the Communist organizational meeting that had been held in his home in June, 1937. Among those present were Dorothy Parker and her husband Alan Campbell, "my old friend Dashiell Hammett who is now in jail in New York for his activities, and that very excellent playwright, Lillian Hellman." When asked if this account were true, Miss Hellman requested the chairman to reconsider what she had said in her letter to him. Chairman Wood then suggested that his correspondence with Miss Hellman be entered in the record, and Mr. Rauh circulated copies to the press while Mr. Tavenner read aloud. In her letter, dated May 19, 1952, she spoke for many Americans who had been called to the stand under similar circumstances:

> Dear Mr. Wood: As you know, I am under subpoena to appear before your committee on May 21, 1952.
>
> I am most willing to answer all questions about myself. I have nothing to hide from your committee and there is nothing in my life of which I am ashamed. I have been advised by counsel that under the Fifth Amendment I have a constitutional privilege to decline to answer any questions about my political opinions, activities, and assocations, on the grounds of self-incrimination. I do not wish to claim this privilege. I am ready and willing to testify before the representatives of our Government as to my own opinions and my own actions, regardless of any risks or consequences to myself.
>
> But I am advised by counsel that if I answer the committee's questions about myself, I must also answer questions about other people and that if I refuse to do so, I can be cited for contempt. My counsel tells me that if I answer questions about myself, I will have waived my rights under the Fifth Amendment and could be forced legally to answer questions about others. This is very difficult for a layman to understand. But there is one principle that I do understand: I am not willing, now or in the future, to bring bad trouble to people who, in my past association with them, were completely innocent of any talk or any action that was disloyal or subversive. I do not like subversion or disloyalty in any form and if I had ever seen any I would have considered it my duty to have reported it to the proper authorities. But to hurt innocent people whom I knew many years ago in order to save myself is, to me, inhuman and indecent and dishonorable. I cannot and will not cut my conscience to fit this year's fashions, even though I long ago came to the

conclusion that I was not a political person and could have no comfortable place in any political group.

I was raised in an old-fashioned American tradition and there were certain homely things that were taught to me: To try to tell the truth, not to bear false witness, not to harm my neighbor, to be loyal to my country, and so on. In general, I respected these ideals of Christian honor and did as well with them as I knew how. It is my belief that you will agree with these simple rules of human decency and will not expect me to violate the good American tradition from which they spring. I would, therefore, like to come before you and speak of myself.

I am prepared to waive the privilege against self-incrimination and to tell you everything you wish to know about my views or actions if your committee will agree to refrain from asking me to name other people. If the committee is unwilling to give me this assurance, I will be forced to plead the privilege of the Fifth Amendment at the hearing.

A reply to this letter would be appreciated.

Sincerely yours,
Lillian Hellman

In his May 20 reply, Representative Wood advised her that "the committee cannot permit witnesses to set forth the terms under which they will testify." She should understand that the committee has gained invaluable information from former members of the Communist Party who had honestly felt it was not a subversive organization, that she could be assured that "any persons identified by you during the course of committee hearings will be afforded the opportunity of appearing before the committee."

With these letters in the record, Tavenner returned to the critical issue. Had she attended the meeting? Again she claimed her constitutional privilege. More of the Berkeley testimony was repeated: She and the others had not become members of the Hollywood group; they had been designated as members-at-large, receiving their instructions from V. J. Jerome in New York or John Howard Lawson in Hollywood. Had she been a member-at-large? Again, the same reply. But when Tavenner asked, "Are you now a member of the Communist Party?" she replied firmly, "No sir." With this opening, Wood pursued her. Was she a member yesterday, last year, or two years ago? To each she replied, "No." When he jumped to five years and three years, she refused to answer on the grounds of self-incrimination. Was she a member on February 12, 1948, when the National Institute of Arts and Letters addressed a letter—one of the signatures was hers—to the Speaker of the House of Representatives protesting the investigation of Communist infiltration of the motion-picture industry as a subversion of the traditional American sense of fair play and human decency? Again she refused on the same grounds. And to the final question, had she ever paid dues to the Communist Party, she also claimed her constitutional right.

Although the ordeal had lasted only thirty-seven minutes and her revelations were far from sensational, the devastating aftereffects endured for years. Some of the immediate consequences were only annoying—the innuendoes in the press accounts of her testimony. For example, *Time* (June 2, 1952) described her as "the greatest meeting-goer in the country." Her sympathies for the world's downtrodden, the article continued, had led her twice to visit Russia, once as the Soviet's honored guest, and also to attend "countless Red-inspired rallies and to lend her name to various Communist-front crusades."

Other effects were more permanent. The Hollywood blacklisting cut off half her professional life and reduced her potential income by much more than half. And like Hammett she was exposed to double jeopardy. Uncharacteristically, one arm of Washington's bureaucracy knew what the other arm was doing. The tax detectives discovered that she owed a monumental tax bill. Her accountants and others involved had miscalculated her obligation, and she had been too ignorant of, and bored by, such matters to check them. With inadequate cash on hand, with Hollywood's riches out of reach indefinitely, she was obliged to sell her Pleasantville farm. Because she had to sell quickly she received only $67,000 for her houses and 130 acres. Anyone who has canvassed real estate in that region today will shudder at the thought.

Selling the farm was a devastating blow to her and to Hammett; their happiest hours together had been spent at Hardscrabble. For years afterwards she was to recall those long country days when she had begun working at seven in the morning, often continuing until two or three the next morning, when they learned to trap turtles and to convert them to soup, to make sausage and to cure ham. She often wondered in later years about the forest of twelve-inch pines they had planted, about the 100 French lilac bushes that were still in the nursery the last day she had visited the farm in May, 1952. The rich memories of Pleasantville could not quickly be erased.

When she was unable to put her mind to a new play, in need of some income and desperate to raise her voice against the outrages of HUAC and McCarthy, Bloomgarden persuaded her to revive *The Children's Hour*. The script required no updating. The avalanche power of a well-propagated lie struck with more force in 1952 than it had in 1934. Miss Hellman's minor readjustments in the text were simply designed to improve the play, not to make it more timely.

The principal changes were aimed at making the characters and actions more credible. Mrs. Tilford is disposed to believe Mary's lies not only because Mary's father had been her favorite son, but also because he had committed suicide and she refuses to accept that fact. Dr. Cardin has delayed his marriage to Karen because he has not paid off his medical-school bills. And after the trial, Cardin proposes that they find their new life, not in Vienna, but in the hometown of an old college friend. Some of the fortuitous entrances are manipulated more reasonably. Mary sneaks into the school room, sees the class in progress, disappears, and then returns in a few minutes with the flowers. In the final act, the grocery boy and Mrs. Mortar have seen Mrs. Tilford's car waiting in front of the house, thus making her entrance, immediately after the suicide, more believable.

In eighteen years none of the play's lacerating power had been lost, and audiences and critics recognized the immediacy of its message. Henry Hewes in the *Saturday Review* (January 10, 1953) suggested that it should be titled "The McCarthyites' Hour." Some now found it harder to believe that Martha could have suppressed her Lesbian impulses for fifteen years, that intelligent, cultured people could have been taken in by the lie, that Mrs. Tilford could have condemned the girl whom her favorite nephew was about to marry, but these questions seem not to have disturbed the audiences who kept the play running for 189 performances. Eric Bentley, echoing Krutch's earlier reactions, insisted that Miss Hellman's third-act shift weakened the play even more in the new context; our sympathy and indignation is diminished when we learn that Martha did harbor Lesbian (Communist!) impulses.

The critics who remembered the 1934 production thought that Miss Hellman, as director, did not achieve the frightening reality that Shumlin had injected into the earlier version. She paced the first two acts too rapidly and let the third proceed "with abominable slowness and exaggerated histrionics." Kim Hunter (Karen) and Patricia Neal (Martha) did not match Katherine Emery and Anne Revere. Miss Neal appeared too markedly mannish, giving a disturbing truth to the lie before Mary began her campaign. Many thought that Iris Mann, playing her own age as Mary, created a more fearful child. Katherine Emmet (Mrs. Amelia Tilford), the only holdover from the original, added eighteen years of maturity to the solid performance she had given in 1934.

In March, 1953, while the new *Children's Hour* was still drawing crowds into the Coronet Theatre where it had opened on December 18, 1952, Hammett was called before the Permanent Subcommittee on Investigations of the Committee on Government Operations, better known as the McCarthy committee. On his day, March 26, only Senator John L. McClellan joined Senator McCarthy and his peripatetic investigators, Roy Cohn and David Schine. Senators Mundt, Dirksen, Potter, and Symington were absent. McCarthy had assumed the role of superlibrarian for the government, scouting the shelves of the State Department's foreign libraries for books by Communist sympathizers. Langston Hughes (poet and playwright), Edwin Seaver (author of *The Company* and *Between the Hammer and the Anvil*), and Helen Goldfrank (author of children's books under the name of Helen Kay) were on the same morning's program. Their names, along with others, had been supplied to the committee by Louis Budenz, former editor of the *Daily Worker*.

Goldfrank took the Fifth Amendment. Hughes and Seaver admitted that they were former Communist sympathizers, had now changed their views, and were shocked that their books were in the information centers. Hammett resorted to the Fifth Amendment in response to the direct questions: Had he been a Communist? Had he contributed money to the cause? Had he been a trustee of the bail fund of the Civil Rights Congress? When asked if he had engaged in espionage or sabotage, he replied with a firm, "No." When McCarthy asked if he would favor the adoption of Communism in the United States, he was equally firm. He thought it impractical, and most people didn't want it. When McClellan wondered if he were not in effect committing an act of self-incrimination before the bar of public opinion by taking the Fifth Amendment, Hammett reminded him that it was not the bar of public opinion that had sent him to jail for six months. McCarthy had one final question: "Mr. Hammett, if you were spending, as we are, over a hundred million dollars a year on an information program, allegedly for the purpose of fighting Communism, would you purchase the works of some seventy-five Communist authors and distribute their works through the world, placing our official stamp of approval upon those works?" In the official record, Hammett's reply read, "Well, I think, of course I don't know, if I were fighting Communism I don't think I would do it by giving people any books at all." On television, Hammett was reported to have told McCarthy, "If I were you, Senator, I don't think I would allow any libraries."

McCarthy quickly forgot Hammett; Representative Wood had already forgotten Miss Hellman. Their nets had snagged new victims. However, for Hammett and Hellman the memory was kept alive. Hollywood was out-of-bounds, Hardscrabble was sold, and when their names appeared in the press the public was repeatedly reminded of their shadowy past. As late as 1967, Miss Hellman told a reporter that she had never forgotten "the aimless spit-ball malice of the times and the men who had deprived her of her farm."

During the next three years, while she worked in her New York home and Hammett lived alone in a house he had rented at Katonah, she soon observed, on their weekly visits back and forth and when they talked daily on the telephone, that his health was deteriorating. One day he announced that he had been falling, that he couldn't live alone any longer, that he was going to a veterans' hospital. After two tearful days, she persuaded him to come to New York and live with her.

In the summers they deserted the city for Martha's Vineyard, where she had rented a cottage from time to time since 1948. She needed a retreat from the New York scene and, with Pleasantville gone, a place that was her own. In 1955, she found a yellow-shingled house within sight of the water at Vineyard Haven and bought it. At the far east wing was a tower formed by the shell of an old Cape Cod windmill. This house became her summer home, and the windmill tower Hammett's room until his death in 1961.

While she had been busy with *The Autumn Garden*, no ideas for a new play had been loitering in the back of her head, ready to be sparked into life. Fortunately, her old friend Louis

Kronenberger rescued her from inactivity. As general editor of a "Great Letters Series" for Farrar, Strauss and Company, he invited her to edit the Chekhov letters. Happily she discovered in Chekhov reflections of her own views about herself, about writing, and about the theatre.

Chekhov was a pleasant and witty man, tolerant and kind, though never "wishywashy in his kindness nor self-righteous in his tolerance." Seemingly he saw through everybody, yet he was too compassionate to brutalize his victims. Most of all he was a man of balance, of common sense: "He tried to see things as they were and to deal with them as he saw them." The highest glory for man was to lead a reasoned life with a clear outlook. Undirected reason was "a burden and a horror." She shared Chekhov's view that ideals are "proved in action not in fireplace chit-chat." She saw something of herself in his relationship with his family. He accepted "his family without any of that romanticism that makes so many creative people either hate their background with a hate that is destructive, or cling to their parents and their past with a love so little different from hate that its destructiveness is only of another naure." He discovered himself in his years alone, separated from his family. He learned to face a tough world without being frightened by it. She had learned the same lesson in much the same way. As he developed as a creative artist, he found no conflict between imagination and scientific fact. A writer must know the "color of the eye, the marrow and the blood" of his characters. He was impatient with metaphysical or religious generalizations, with "four A.M. philosophy," contemptuous of self-deception and hypocrisy. He believed in intelligence, and "intelligence for Chekhov meant that you called a spade a spade." Laziness was simply not working. He had to work, determined to see life as it was. Miss Hellman was blessed and hounded by a similar built-in compulsion.

At some moments, Chekhov appeared to be a political radical eager to overthrow the system, at other times apolitical, documenting social problems without offering solutions. In some places, he seemed saddened "by a world that destroyed the delicate and punished the finely made." Whatever particular line he pursued, he was always a man of "deep social ideals and an uncommon sense of social responsibility." She shared his sense of social responsibility and hoped that it was apparent in her work. He was generous and tolerant, eager to give pity where it was due. At the same time, "he was a tough unsentimental man with a tough mind, and thus he had tough tools to write with." Miss Hellman possessed comparable "tough tools."

When she wrote admiringly of Chekhov as a playwright, she must have hoped that others saw these qualities in her work. The audience knew five minutes after the curtain was up that they were in the hands of a playwright who knew his business. "Neatness in design and execution is, after all, only the proper use of material, but it has a beauty of its own. It is exhilarating to watch a good workman at work, to see each detail fall into useful place, to know that the shortest line, the smallest stage movement, has an end in view and is not being used to trick or deceive or pull fashionable wool over our eyes. It is then that we say to ourselves, this writer knows what he is doing, he has paid us the compliment of learning his trade. To such writers, in whatever field they be, we give our full attention."

XIV

The Lark

After her editorial work on the Chekhov letters was finished in the spring of 1954 and an advance selection was published in *Partisan Review* in July, Miss Hellman was at loose ends. Again an old friend, this time Kermit Bloomgarden, put her to work. He had seen Anouilh's new play, *L'Alouette*, which had opened in Paris in October, 1953, had acquired the American rights, and wanted her to do the adaptation for Broadway. At first she volunteered a half-way yes, then troubled by her better judgment—"You know, you keep thinking that you can do these things in a month or so, while gamboling on the grass with ribbons in your hair"—she said no. She felt no strong affinity with Anouilh, no particular fascination for the play; but after reading the play she could not resist St. Joan, the feminist for all ages.

Once she began, she dug in with her usual intensity. She had three literal translations made for her, studied the accounts and meticulously outlined the chronology of Joan's life, and copied quotations from the original trial testimony. She was determined, with due respect for Anouilh, to be faithful to Joan in her own way, to write the story of Joan for an American audience. She was not going to repeat the mistakes she had made with *Montserrat.* After four months of feverish concentration, she had a manuscript satisfactory to Bloomgarden but not yet to her.

She tinkered and doctored for three more months, still unwilling to release the script. Before Bloomgarden took over, she wanted an outside opinion; she also wanted to see Christopher Fry's adaptation directed by Peter Brook, which was opening in London on May 12. Anouilh might even have some suggestions. Before she departed for London, she sent a copy to her friend Professor Harry Levin, the specialist in comparative literature at Harvard. After seeing the London production, which was closer to the original than hers, she was convinced that she had taken the right track. She was also encouraged by Anouilh's reaction. She had sent her script to him via his agent, Jon van Loewen. On May 21, while she was still in London, van Loewen wrote to her from Paris:

> I am just back from a long conversation with Anouilh who is most grateful for all the trouble you are taking over the play. Unfortunately, and as I predicted, he himself has no constructive ideas how to enlarge on the end of the play in order to make it more acceptable for American audiences. On the other hand he would be delighted if you find more suitable lines to make the gap between the scene on the stake and the coronation finale less abrupt and leaves any reasonable changes entirely in your capable hands.
>
> I am sorry about this scanty outcome, which however is by no means prompted by any lack of cooperation on his part. He simply is not and has never been able to rewrite.
>
> He is, also, of my opinion that the second part of the

play in your version reads well indeed and doesn't need any amplification.

I am very pleased to have met you in London. Hope you will have a pleasant trip back home.

With this encouragement, with an approving letter from Professor Levin waiting for her when she returned, and with some minor readjustments in the script, she turned it over to Bloomgarden.

Bloomgarden was now less sanguine about the prospects for a Broadway success, though he had not lost his enthusiasm for her adaptation. Brooks Atkinson had reviewed the London production in the *Times* (May 13, 1955). Although he admired Fry's text, he found that the "long, subtle, intricate arguments grow increasingly undramatic." It had neither the "size nor passion of Shaw's *St. Joan*." And if some had thought Shaw too cerebral, he was "wonderfully electric" compared with Anouilh. Bloomgarden knew that Broadway audiences took their cues from Atkinson, and he painfully discovered that some potential backers had been frightened by the *Times* and closed their checkbooks. When Miss Hellman volunteered to withdraw from the project, he insisted on battling the odds and going ahead. He told Atkinson that he had been unfair in undermining his chances, that he would prove him wrong, at least wrong about Anouilh adapted by Hellman.

Intimidation would not work with Atkinson; an exciting experience in the theatre would. When *The Lark* opened at the Longacre Theatre on November 17, 1955, Atkinson gladly sang a new tune in both his morning-after review and in his Sunday piece (November 27). In London the play had seemed "pale and trifling"; in New York it was "sublime." Julie Harris's Joan glowed with an "incandescence that illuminates the theatre and touches the hearts of everybody in the audience." In fairness to Dorothy Tutin, it must be reported that Harris had the advantage of a sturdier foundation in the text. Hellman was a keener theatrical technician than Fry, "a forceful person in her own right," with "an instinct for the forthright statement." And although he still missed Shaw's "blazing spirit as a crusader," Hellman's rendering possessed a solid strength that was missing in London. Any damage that had been inflicted by his earlier review had been repaired, and with Atkinson's blessing the play settled into a substantial run.

Miss Hellman retained the basic pattern of the original; her alterations and deviations were not radical but they were incisive. She reduced the discursive arguments, dramatized rather than reasoned her way through the sacred mystery, changed the ending, added a biting briskness, and energized the proceedings with an emotional charge that was absent in Anouilh and in Fry. She also maintained a constant reminder of the religious overtones, with incidental music composed by Leonard Bernstein and sung by seven men and women, without instruments and with solos by a countertenor.

Before the characters assemble in the playing arena—assorted bare platforms enclosed by a cyclorama—we hear the chorus singing a psalm, "Exaudi orationem meam, domine." As the lights come up, the singers shift to a motet on the words "Qui tollis" from the Mass. Joan is alone on a stool downstage center, at the side Cauchon and the Promoter, and on the Judges' bench priests are taking their places. The Inquisitor sits on a stool near them. In separate groups upstage are Joan's family and the royal family. English soldiers and guards assume positions as village women cross the stage with bundles of faggots. Beaudricourt and La Hire take their places upstage. Warwick is the last to appear and the first to speak as he moves through the crowd: "Everybody here? Good. Let the trial begin at once. The quicker the judgment and the burning, the better for all of us." The fatal decision has been made even before the trial.

Warwick prefers not to hear the whole story again, though he knows someday they'll probably erect a monument to Joan in London: "The politics of my government may well require it and what's required Englishmen supply." The girl has been an expensive nuisance, "this dirty virgin witch girl tucked away on a litter of straw. . . . So put her on trial, and burn her, and be finished." Hellman's Warwick is a no-nonsense warrior, remarkably more addicted to straight talk than he was in Fry's more faithful rendering of Anouilh. If Cauchon insists, he'll hear the story, though he hopes they won't act out all the old battles. "Nobody wishes to remember defeat." The recollection of past defeats is Hellman's addition. She grasps every opportunity to intensify the drama.

As Joan rises to begin her story, her family joins her. She was alone in the meadow watching her sheep when the vision first appeared "in this little corner of the earth near Domremy," the one little piece of French earth not yet destroyed by the English. She wasn't thinking of anything when "someone behind me touched my shoulder. I know very well that no one is behind me. I turn and there is a great blinding light in the shadow of me. The voice is very grave and sweet and I was frightened." The vision appeared again at the noon Angelus: "A light came over the sun and was stronger than the sun. There he was. I saw him. An angel in a beautiful clean robe that must have been ironed by somebody very carefully. He had two great white wings. He didn't tell me his name that day, but later I found out he was Monseigneur the Blessed Saint Michael." Hellman's Joan knows how to dramatize her story. How unlike Fry: ". . . in the quiet countryside of Domremy, while the English soldiers are looting and burning villages up and down the land . . . a great light was filling the shadows behind me. The voice was gentle and grave. . . . A man in a white robe, with two white wings reaching from the sky to the ground." Miss Hellman's peasant girl does not talk like a book.

Nor could Miss Hellman allow her Joan to impersonate the deep voice of the archangel as she acted out her conversation with him. Instead of Joan's Archangel's voice intoning, "You will go and search out Robert de Beaudricourt, the Governor of Vaucouleurs. He will give you a suit of clothes to dress you like a man, and he will take you to the Dauphin," she described her mission simply and directly in her own voice: "To you people the Sire de Beaudricourt is only a country squire, but to us he is master here. He would never take me to the Dauphin, I've never even bowed to him—(*Turns to the Court*). Then the Blessed Saint Michael said Saint Catherine would come along with me, and if that wasn't enough Saint Marguerite would go, too."

In the original and in Fry, Joan's speech is twice as long, with an extended plea to St. Michael to spare her. Here Joan simply announces to the court that her saint refused to pity her. "And that was the day I was saddled with France. *And* my work on the farm." How much stronger than Fry: "And there I was with France on my shoulders. Not to mention the work on the farm, and my father, who wasn't easy."

As her father steps forward we see immediately that he was not easy. He can't understand what Joan would be doing out in the fields at six o'clock, dreaming under a lady tree. Miss Hellman does not risk "fairy tree," and she eliminates a half-page of extraneous discussion between the Promoter and Cauchon on a young girl's right to keep her fairies. She comes quickly to the point. No matter what her mother says in defense, her father is certain she's waiting for a lover. Joan's lover had "two great white wings and through the rain he came so close to me that I thought I could touch his wings." She was sure there was a mistake until Saint Michael assured her that God doesn't make mistakes. Could she have contradicted him?

Miss Hellman's Promoter now speaks for the first time, "Why didn't you make the Sign of the Cross?" Joan's replies are more legalistic than in the original: the Promoter's question was not written in the charges against her. She had not said, "Vado retro Satanas," not only because she didn't know Latin but because that too was not in the charges. Anouilh and Fry say nothing of "written charges." If Hellman's Promoter acts more like a prosecuting attorney, he also possesses a more colloquial tongue. Joan should have told her visitor, "Go away, you filthy, stinking devil." In Fry the speech read, "Get thee behind me, foul Satan, and don't tempt me again."

Talk of the devil tempts Anouilh's Promoter into an extended theological discussion. Here the trial cannot be delayed for arguments between the Promoter and Cauchon. When the Promoter asks if her saints were naked, Hellman's Joan is robust and direct. She laughs and replies, "Oh, Messire! Don't you think our Lord can afford to buy clothing for His Saints?" In Fry: "Oh, my lord! Do you imagine that God can't afford clothes for the saints in heaven?"

Cauchon admonishes the Promoter for sidetracking Joan "with the suggestion that good and evil is a question of what clothes are worn," and reminds Joan that they are her priests, her masters, and her judges. When Joan insists that the voices were God's invention, not hers, the Promoter explodes: Could God wish to damn a human soul? The Court should see in her insistence "the germ of a frightful heresy that could tear the Church." Now for the first time Miss Hellman introduces pantomimic action not in the original. As the Inquisitor rises, a young priest, Ladvenu, comes to him. The Inquisitor whispers to him, Ladvenu whispers to Cauchon and Cauchon speaks: "Joan, listen well to what I must ask you. At this moment, are you in a State of Grace?" In the original the speech is given to the Inquisitor. The significance of the question is further underlined when Ladvenu tells them that they must not hold her answer against her. Joan is perplexed by the question. Do they mean at the beginning when she heard the voices, at the end of the trial when the king and her friends abandoned her, when she lost faith, when she recanted, or at the very last minute? If she is not in Grace, God will help her. If she is, God will keep her so. The Inquisitor is angered by her reply: "And the Devil would have the same clever answer."

Again Miss Hellman introduces a brief sequence not in the original, heightening the drama by suggesting that the lines of authority are not clear. Warwick wants to know who the

Promoter is and when he arrived. Cauchon assures him that he is a member of their contingent, that the Church does not acknowledge Warwick's authority in the present proceedings. Warwick is impatient with their religious legalism. He's almost as bewildered as the girl. These questions may be fascinating to the Church, "but if we continue at this speed we'll never get to the trial and the girl will be dead of old age." Warwick cannot forget that she took France away from them, that the coronation of the idiot Charles was managed by a sorceress. Everyone knows God is on the side of the English. "God and my right" is inscribed on their armor, and they are not going to change the armor. "So get on with her story. The world will forget her soon enough. Where were we?" In Fry the speech reads, "Earlier on I was joking. I give it ten years, and this whole incident will have been forgotten." Again Miss Hellman's Warwick is a hard-hitting, straight talker who cannot tolerate ecclesiastical doubletalk.

Joan's father now comes forward. What was she doing under the tree? He heard her crying out to someone when he arrived, "but the bastard fled before I could catch him." The "bastard" is Hellman's addition, also the blow he lands on his daughter. He'll teach her not to "start whoring like the others." If he catches her again with her Blessed Saint Michael, he'll plunge "his pitchfork into his belly and strangle you with my bare hands for the filthy rutting cat you are." Anouilh's father is by no means gentle with his daughter, but he's more loquacious. Miss Hellman makes him a rough irate peasant who sticks to the point and whose patience is quickly exhausted. When Joan insists that her voices told her to go to Beaudricourt and ask him to give her an armed escort to the Dauphin at Chinon and then take the army to Orleans and push the English into the sea, her father knows she's crazy. This is his reward for working himself to death for forty years, trying to raise his children like Christians. Finally he loses his temper completely and beats her until she screams. Ladvenu shouts to have the beating stopped, but Cauchon reminds him that they cannot yet participate in the story; this ugly family quarrel is simply being enacted as it happened. Warwick is less distressed than the others; any Englishman knows that punishment makes character.

Now for the first time Miss Hellman uses a passage from Anouilh which Fry omitted, though she compresses it radically. Warwick insists that if they had known about the girl at the beginning, they could have struck a deal with her father: "We tell people that our intelligence service is remarkable and say it so often that everybody believes us." In this instance it broke down. No doubt Miss Hellman intended the contemporary allusion.

Joan's mother tries to comfort her and get her mind off the nonsense of putting on men's clothes. She'll buy her a broidered kerchief at the next fair. Joan has no interest in female finery; she knows she'll never be pretty. This is Hellman's addition to Joan's character. When Joan insists that she needs men's clothes to ride her horse with her soldiers, her mother breaks into tears: "What have I done to deserve a daughter like this? You will kill me." Joan, again transfixed, ignores her: "Saint Michael's voice grew soft, the way it does when he is angry. . . . He said that God trusted me and if a mountain of ice did rise ahead of me it was only because God was busy and trusted me to climb the mountain even if I tore my hands and broke my legs, and my face might run with blood— Then I said that I would go."

Her brother makes a final attempt to restrain her. He knows she doesn't have the sense she was born with, but next time, if she rewards him, he'll not tell that he saw her with her lover. Joan slaps him. That's for this time. She slaps him again; that's for the next time. As she runs after him, her voice changes and her pace slows: she has returned to her story: ". . . I walked a long way west and a little way south and there was the night I was shivering with rain—or with fear—and the day I was shivering with sun—or with fear—and then I walked to the west again and east. I was on my way to the first fool I had to deal with." As she finishes, Beaudricourt comes forward to meet her.

In Hellman, this sequence is more direct and concise. She omits Joan's cute bantering with her brother, their playful fighting "like urchins," Joan bumping into Beaudricourt as she races after her brother. Her Joan could not utter such childish prattle as, "Sneak, sneak, I'll give you a tweak! Tell tales out of school, duck him in a muddy pool! There's your halfpenny, lardy-head. Tell-tale-tit, your tongue shall be split, and all the children in the town shall have a little bit!" Fry carries the passage considerably beyond the original.

Beaudricourt has heard about her, "standing outside the doors raging at the sentries until they fall asleep." What does she want? She wants a horse; she's been sent by the Blessed Saint Michael. Beaudricourt crosses himself quickly. He doesn't want to mix with saints. Such talk might have fooled the sentries; it will not get her a horse, a horse is an expensive item. Is she a virgin? She is. Perhaps then he's willing to talk about a small horse, particularly since she has lovely eyes. But Joan also wants an armed escort to Chinon to find Monseigneur the Dauphin. Beaudricourt wonders why she didn't go to the Duke of Burgundy: "He's more powerful, and he likes the girls." (Hellman's version of Fry's ". . . you might have a sporting chance with him; the Duke's as hot as a buck rabbit.") The Dauphin "runs from war and women. An hour with either would kill him." Why should she want to see such a fellow? She must see him to get an army to march on Orleans. Beaudricourt orders his men to douse her in water and send her home to her father, but Joan will not be dismissed. She tries flattery. He must be a kind man not to have her beaten and he's intelligent; it shows on his handsome face. Many people may say that handsome men are stupid; she knows better. Beaudricourt is weakening. He knows he's not ugly, not really stupid, though he does sometimes have trouble when he's asked to "decide something, a tactical or administrative point." Yet he makes decisions and roars out his commands. Usually things will turn out the same no matter what he does. He may be an awesome figure in this small village, but he hoped for more, to be brilliant and remarkable, "to shake a nation."

Now that he's opening up, she quickly grasps her advantage. Robert must listen to her, and he will "shake a nation." She'll see that he gets noticed and talked about by the higher-ups. He's fascinated, even has his arm around her, though he pretends shock at hearing his Christian name. She outlines the situation. The English are everywhere, the Dauphin is "shaking and jibbering" with his court in Bourges, the army has lost heart, and Dunois, bastard that he is, drinks and tells stories of his past battles to his camp whores. Robert knows as well as she that war can't be treated like a gentleman's tournament: "You must be smart to win a war." They're lucky that Robert has had such a tremendous idea. He's astounded by this news; he can't quite spot the idea. She assures him that it's coming, and she helps it along. The Dauphin, Dunois, and the Archbishop are simple men, much less intelligent than he. Can't he hear himself saying that if the troops believe the girl comes from God that's all that matters? He'll send her to Bourges tomorrow on a white horse with the courier and a half-dozen of his best men. If he doesn't believe she can stay on a horse, why doesn't he bring two horses now? She'll bet him a man's dress that she can; Saint Michael will keep her in the saddle. Beaudricourt is exhausted with all his thinking; perhaps a ride would relax him. As he goes, she attempts to follow, but one of the guards stops her. The lights fade and she returns to the trial. Again Miss Hellman has compressed and sharpened; the speeches are shorter and stronger, always in the active voice and focused on Joan's manipulation of Beaudricourt.

Warwick has been impressed by Joan's skill: "She made the idiot believe that he wasn't an idiot." Cauchon thought it was all a bit coarse. Warwick can't resist a brutal question. Does Cauchon really "have the faith?" Of course he does, and his judges will do everything they can to save Joan. Warwick may think they're "collaborators," but they had to collaborate with the English; they lived in occupied territory; they had no choice. Miss Hellman has retained Anouilh's contemporary allusion to French collaborators, though much abbreviated.

Cauchon reminds Warwick that for nine months they protected the girl. They may not have understood her, turned away from her anguished cries in the final moment, yet he recalls how beautiful the old priests were who tried to save her from what "can never now be mended." The interlude is concluded with a forecast from Cauchon not in the original. The time will come "when our names will be known only for what we did to her; when men, forgiving their own sins, but angry with ours, will speak our names in a curse—" The original concludes with a scene-changing speech from Warwick. It's time for them to observe the action at Chinon: "I've got a profound disrespect for that lounging little idler, Charles, but he's a character who never fails to amuse me." Hellman accomplished the transition simply by dimming the lights and bringing them up on the Dauphin's court.

Charles is playing at bilboquet, desperately trying to get the ball in the cup, Agnes and the little queen are practicing a new dance, Yolande is moving about, while four courtiers are playing cards. Throughout the scene Miss Hellman retains the details of the original, though her version is more completely dramatized and less talky. She gives Charles an action, not in the original, to make him even more ludicrous. He tosses a coin in the air, misses it, crawls on the floor searching for the sou and is cowering in fright when La Tremouille and the Archbishop enter. They insist that he's getting more like his father every day, though his father had the decency to take to his bed. When Charles wonders, "Which father?" La Tremouille assures him he's legitimate; his ridiculous behavior proves it.

After they're gone, Yolande urges him to get up. He shouldn't be so frightened. She's done what she could to increase his virility. Although she is his mother-in-law, she's supplied him with a mistress, and certainly Agnes has done her best to make him a man. Miss Hellman gives a stronger comedy edge to the compassionate mother-in-law who knows that love is not the proper business for her daughter. Of the Dauphin's extended observations on the history of his kingdom, his difficulties with the Treasury, with his ministers, with himself, only the bare essentials are retained. Charles is sick of hearing people say that France will be victorious, that he'll be a great king. He knows that he's a poor frightened nobody with a lost kingdom and a broken army.

Yolande pleads with him to admit the peasant girl. She's strange and remarkable, and it's time that his council hear some common sense from humble people. Charles is more fascinated with his ball and cup. What's more, La Tremouille would not allow him to see the girl. Charles is still playing his game, sitting up straight on his throne so he won't miss, when La Tremouille and the Archbishop enter again, to report the latest intelligence on the girl. He insists that if she's admitted, the door will be open "to every charlatan, every bone setter, every faith healer." In the original Charles listens to pages of arguments from his two advisors. Here his patience is quickly exhausted: "Bring her in and have it ended. Maybe she has a little money and can play cards."

Joan appears, small and frightened, and bows before him. Try as he will to act like a ruler, Charles still appears ridiculous: "What do you want? I'm a very busy man. It's time for my milk." (These sentences are not in the original.) Joan's reply is firm and direct, more direct than in Fry. The "King of Heaven" has sent her. She'll take him to Reims, have him anointed and crowned King of France. She has no patience with La Tremouille's skepticism. His armies may well have been trying to take Orleans, but she's been sent by God to push the English into the sea. When the Archbishop assures her that if God wished to save France he would not need armies, she tells him that God does not want a lazy kingdom and if they put up a good fight, they'll win.

The Archbishop tries another tack. He'll have Joan examined by learned doctors; Charles won't be disturbed by her again today. Their maneuver gives Charles new courage, particularly when he's holding Joan's hand. He orders them to leave her alone with him: "Your King commands you." His giggles burst into a laugh, as they depart: "It's the first time they ever obeyed me." All this is in the original, though again tightening and compression have given it greater vigor.

From her honest face Charles knows that she hasn't come to kill him, though in his surroundings he's almost forgotten what an honest face looks like. He's prepared to be bored, to be told that he ought to be a great king. She must stay for at least an hour to give a proper impression. Perhaps she knows how to play cards. He's pitifully confused. If he's a bastard, he doesn't need to worry about going crazy, but if he's not, then he'd know he was meant to be king. Most days he'd rather escape to some foreign land and live on whatever he had left. Joan will not let him escape. He must have courage every day, beginning now. If she's offering some secret charm, Charles will buy it. When she tells him it's free, he doesn't want it: "What you get free costs too much." (Fry's translation: "Disinterested people are too rare, at any price.") Charles is not as silly as he pretends; he's had to use his head. It's been his only protection against the cutthroats around him. Joan can help him; she'll teach him how not to be too smart and not to be afraid.

If she wants that lifetime job, Charles will teach her to play cards. Does she know which of the cards is the most powerful? It's not the king; it's the single heart, the ace, and it's not called God. Why must she talk of God every minute, as if she had dined with him last night? Doesn't she know that the English pray to God, that every man thinks God is on his side, that the rich and powerful know he's on theirs? Unfortunately he's not rich and France is not rich. Joan insists he's wrong about God. God's angry because "we have no courage left." Even with his legs Charles could have tried to do better. He's not surprised that she's noticed his legs. Even Agnes makes fun of them. Joan tells him not to worry about inconsequentials. His head may also be ugly but not what's inside of it. Sure he's frightened; she is too. She's vanquished fear by acting as if she weren't afraid. You simply say to yourself that you're afraid, that it's nobody else's business, and then you go on. When he sees the English cannons and archers outside Orleans and knows that he's outnumbered, he'll be frightened. Then he'll march right through because he "had sense enough to get frightened first." She knew a boy in her village who was once trapped by a killer dog. (The story is Hellman's invention.) The boy used his head, threw a stone at the dog and when the dog turned away, he strangled him: "That was courage. That was victory." Charles must become as frightened as that boy, get sicker and sicker, then the worst will be over. As payment for her witch's secret he must give her his army, and when he's convinced he's as sick as he'll get, she calls for the Archbishop and La Tremouille. Though panicked by his bravery, Charles announces, "I have made a decision. The Royal Army is now under the command of Joan the Virgin Maid, here present. (*Roars out*) I wish to hear no word from you. None." (In Anouilh and Fry, Charles is not so feverish: "Yes, I've come to a decision, my lord, and it also concerns you, M. de La Tremouille. I am giving the command of my royal army to this Maid here. [*He suddenly shouts.*] If you don't agree, M. de La Tremouille, I must ask you to surrender your sword to me. You are under arrest.")

The concluding moments of the first act become more theatrical than in the original. Everyone kneels to the Dauphin, the Archbishop pronounces his blessing, the chorus sings the Benedictus, a page gives a sword to Charles which he transfers to Joan, and Warwick comes forward to inform the audience that in real life Joan's command was not achieved so simply. There were long discussions and council meetings before they agreed to dress her in battle flags. It was true, of course, that "a simple girl inspired simple people to get themselves killed for simple ideals." Joan is moving away from the Dauphin, her head lowered in prayer, as the lights dim out. In the original, Joan, Charles, and La Tremouille simply drop to their knees as the Archbishop pronounces his blessing.

The opening of the second act is also more spectacular. Soldiers are singing of Joan and her victories, Joan in full armor marches across the stage, her sword stretched above her head, the Court assembles, and Warwick moves forward to take up where he left off. There is no pageantry in the original; Warwick simply begins with the story of Joan's assumption of power that Miss Hellman had transferred to the close of Act I.

Warwick has been enchanted by Joan's magic: "The girl was a lark in the skies of France. . . . Singing a crazy song of courage . . . outlined against the sky, a target for everybody to shoot at. . . . To Frenchmen, she was the soul of France." But the trial must be resumed. The lark has been captured. The king she crowned and his court are about to abandon her. As Joan calls for Charles, he turns and moves away. Cauchon tells her that Henry of England has become their king, because he will put an end to the terrible war: "We are here only to return a lost girl to the bosom of the Sainted Mother Church." The extensive history-book details about France and England are sacrificed to keep the attention on Joan.

Cauchon is left alone to reason with Joan. She's not stupid. Does she think she's the only girl who ever heard voices? When she was commanding her men, what would she have done if one of her soldiers heard voices ordering him not to follow? Joan's laugh is echoed by loud laughter from her soldiers offstage (Hellman's invention). Obviously Cauchon doesn't understand soldiers: "A good army fights, drinks, rapes—but they don't hear voices." He's offended by her ridicule; she must know that a disobedient soldier must be silenced in any army. "The Church militant is also an army of the earth and we, its priests, do not believe in the Divine origin of *your* disobedience." Because the common people, who will follow any leader, believe in her, because she is stubborn, does not mean that God is on her side. (A lengthy disquisition on obedience, on pride, on the power of the Holy Father the Pope and on the devil is omitted.)

The Promoter now joins the attack. What spell did she cast

on the man she calls her king? "By what means did you force him to give his armies to you?" Some say she gave him a piece of mandrake. Her secret was simpler. She gave Charles courage by speaking good sense. When people listened, that proved that God was present. Miracles are not tricks performed by gypsies: "True miracles are created by men when they use the courage and intelligence God gave them." Cauchon is shocked. Is she telling them that man, who is nothing but sin and error, is God's real miracle on this earth? Only Ladvenu among the priests believes her wild fancies. The Promoter is shouting, "You blaspheme. Man is impurity and lust. The dark acts of his nights are the acts of a beast—" Joan admits he's right, but that's not the full report. That beast can "rise from a brothel bed and throw himself before a blade to save the soldier who walks beside him. That makes God happy because God made him for just this contradiction."

Joan has pushed her good sense too far. The judges are muttering angrily. The Inquisitor rises, signals for silence, and speaks for the first time. He's from Spain, isn't concerned with who rules France, with the "temporal integrity of the church," nor does he see evil everywhere as the Promoter does. The Holy Inquisition occupies itself with matters unknown to temporal kings: "Our enemy is a great enemy and has a great name." Is the girl a Christian? She is. The Inquisitor knows she is a pious girl. She prayed regularly in her village church, she cried for the wounded in every battle, even for the English. Yet the Holy Inquisition alone is "qualified to distinguish between theological virtues and that troubled brew that man so boastfully calls the milk of human kindness." Like the others, he speaks more directly than in Fry. He is distressed that her judges have been so overwhelmed by the kind eyes of a young girl. Ladvenu must not attempt to defend her. If he wishes to remain in the trial, he must be silent. (The original contains an extended theological argument between the Inquisitor and Ladvenu which becomes so intense that Cauchon orders Ladvenu to leave. This diversion is omitted. Miss Hellman holds to the main business, the Inquisitor's questioning of Joan.) Didn't she think it strange that her voices would instruct an ignorant peasant girl to save France? Not so strange, she insists, when it turned out to be the truth. Wouldn't it have been better for a pious girl to spend her life in penitence and prayer? She has not stopped praying, but God wanted her to strike first and then pray. She admits that she was excited "in the dawn, riding boot to boot with friends," yet she did not like the killing; she wept at night for the dead. God must absolve her if she seemed to love the war; she was obeying his command to rid France of the English. Her judges' heads are so filled with celestial science that they cannot understand the simplest things. Even the dullest soldier understood, La Hire understood! She moves away as the lights dim on the trial. The soldiers are whistling their song as La Hire comes forward to join her.

It's been a cold night in the field. La Hire has been sleeping nearby, watching over her. As he comes to awaken her, he's peeling his breakfast onion. She mustn't come too close; he stinks badly of wine and onions. He admits he's a hazard for the army. If the wind is right, the English will know where they are. Joan does not object; he smells as a man should. With all his sins, he's a "bright new coin in the hand of God," and though she's shocked by his battle prayer (Hellman's invention)—"God, I hope you'll help me as I would help you if you faced those God damned—"—she's sure he won't be kept waiting at the gates of Heaven. Mention of gates reminds her that this is the day they will ride to the gates of Orleans. She climbs on her stool and La Hire on the one beside her, riding imaginary horses. The stools are Hellman's addition, and she's brought Joan and La Hire to horse in half the time required by Anouilh.

Joan is exhilarated riding into battle with a good soldier by her side. Suddenly she stops her horse and whispers, "There are three English soldiers. We've outridden the others. We are alone." La Hire jumps from his stool, draws his sword and charges out of sight. In the original he charges into the tribunal, scattering them with his sword, violating the theatrical fence that had separated the scenes. Here Joan simply kneels in prayer after La Hire's exit and then turns to the judges as the lights come up again on the trial.

She is sure that La Hire will rescue her from prison. Cauchon tells her he tried, but his soldiers were outnumbered. And when La Hire discovered that Charles was tired of war and ready to sign any peace, he marched his men toward Germany. The priests she sees before her are the only men who now care for her soul and for her life. Again extensive historical detail about Charles and La Hire has been omitted.

Joan accepts her fate and, after a long silence, speaks, "For that which is of the Faith, I turn to the Church, as I have always done. But what I am, I will not denounce. What I have done, I will not deny." Her announcement creates "a great movement in the courtroom," which is finally subdued by the Inquisitor as he walks among the priests, peering into their frightened faces.

None of them seems to know "on whom you sit in judgment, nor the issues of the judgment. I have told you that the Holy Inquisition is not concerned with royal rank or merchant gold or peasant birth. . . . Because *we* know the name of our enemy. His name is natural man." The girl is the symbol of all that is to be feared: "She raises her eyes, not to God, but to man's image of himself." Unlike Anouilh's Inquisitor, Hellman's does not indulge in ecclesiastical circumlocutions. His meaning is unmistakable, even to the layman. When Ladvenu reminds him that even Jesus became a man, the Inquisitor expells him from the court. And when Joan again asserts that she will not deny what she has done, he pronounces the fearful sentence. She must be excommunicated from the Church and returned to the secular authority to receive her punishment. He makes only one concession. He asks the secular arm "to limit her sentence to this side of death and the mutilation of her members." Warwick does not relish the prospect; the dirty work is being passed to him; Charles should have done the job. Charles insists he could not have done it; he doesn't like killings. The involvement of Warwick and Charles is Hellman's invention. Knowing their sentiments, she could not leave them standing silent in the background.

The Executioner appears, assuring Cauchon that everything is ready, though he'll have to abandon his usual act of mercy, strangling the victim before the flames reach her. He's been instructed to make the fire too high for that. Joan screams in pain, remembering a fearful childhood dream. (Joan's premonition is Hellman's addition.) Cauchon makes a final desperate attempt to offer her the saving hand of the Mother Church. The time is short; the crowds are already gathering. Joan, still in her dream, forgives them, as she also forgives Cauchon. The Promoter is enraged. Cauchon is trying to save her miserable soul, and she answers by forgiving him. Cauchon does not give up. If she confesses her sins, they can still save her. He speaks simply and directly, omitting the laborious talk about their responsibility as apostles of Peter: "I am an old man. I have killed people in the defense of my beliefs . . . I do not wish to kill again. . . . Help me to save you."

Joan's spirit is broken: "What do you want me to say? Please tell me in simple words." Cauchon has three questions. Will she humbly entrust herself to the Holy Roman and Apostolic Church and rely on the Holy Father the Pope and his bishops to be her judges? Will she make the complete and total act of submission? Will she ask to be returned to the bosom of the Church? As she answers, "Yes, but—," the Inquisitor rises, Cauchon is visibly shaken, and she continues: She can't deny her voices. She doesn't want to turn on Charles after she fought so hard for the glory of his consecration. Charles prefers not to think that his crowning was a miracle; she could save him a lot of trouble if she'd forget about him and go her own way.

Cauchon is angry but he persists. She must not "quibble like a peasant at a village fair"; she should be on her knees.

Joan obeys. If the Lord wishes her to submit to the judgment, she's willing. Will she renounce forever the bearing of arms? She hesitates, knowing there's more to be done, but she will. Will she renounce forever "the wearing of that brazen uniform"? Her voices told her that when she was riding with soldiers they must see her as a soldier like themselves. And she's worn the clothes in prison to protect herself against her two English guards. Warwick is shocked. English soldiers must have been corrupted since they came to France; it will not happen again. With that assurance and Cauchon's promise that the Church will protect her, she agrees to put on a dress.

Cauchon summons Brother Ladvenu, who has drawn up and now reads the "Act of Renunciation" ("Abjuration" in the original). She confesses having sinned through pride and malice pretending a Divine revelation, having incited men to kill through witchcraft, having blasphemed by wearing an immodest costume. She foreswears the heretic dress and the bearing of arms. She will submit to the judgment of the Church. When Ladvenu hands her the pen, she waves it in the air, not knowing what to do. He helps her, guiding her hand to make her mark. (The pantomime carries the meaning. No need for Joan to say, "Do I make a circle or a cross? I can't write my name.")

Cauchon is overjoyed. She will now spend the remainder of her days in prison until she repents; she has been delivered from excommunication. He makes the Sign of the Cross and orders her taken away. The judges rise and slowly move off. As Cauchon passes him, Warwick commends his wisdom: "The making of a martyr is dangerous business." Cauchon is not honored by his praise.

As the lights dim, four soldiers raise their spears, simulating the bars of Joan's cell. In the original, Agnes, Yolande, and Charles come to comfort her with such inanities as Agnes's "Joan, my dear, we're so very happy it has all turned out well for you. Congratulations!" Here Charles has come alone to say goodbye. He hadn't wanted her to sacrifice herself, though he knew she loved him. Left alone she calls on Saint Michael to find her: Does he want her to live? When he doesn't respond, she's sure he must have some good reason.

Warwick also comes to comfort her. He was proud of her in court. She behaved "damned well," particularly in handling the Inquisitor. He detests such intellectual idealists. He's glad it worked out so well: "Martyrs are likely to stir the blood of simple people and set up too grand a monument to themselves." He was sure it would work out well because of the way she rode and the way she talked like a boy, like his fiancée in England. He's as simple and direct as he's been throughout. In the original he's a talker like the others, even at this point babbling about the future Lady Warwick, about the entertaining they'll do at Warwick Castle, about fox hunting.

Joan can bear her inner torment no longer. She committed a great sin against God when she swore against herself. True, this way she'll survive, wear cast-off brocades and grow old, be remembered as that crazy girl who rode into battle. Warwick tries to reassure her. Everyone tries to preserve a little honor, "but the main thing is to be here—" Joan can no longer submit. She calls to her voices. No doubt they're silent because they see her frightened and for what? "A few years of unworthy life." She orders Warwick to call the soldiers; she denies her confession. Her warrior's clothes must be returned; the priests must be called back. She's kneeling in prayer as the music of the "Sanctus" begins and the court returns. Two soldiers bring a crude stake and lash her to it. Again Miss Hellman has kept the action pacing rapidly toward the final moment, making us share Joan's agony. Warwick's participation has been radically reduced, depriving him of such ill-considered observations as, "How out of place this all is. What bad form. It's impossible to get on well with these French for long." Hellman also eliminates the shouts from the crowd, Cauchon sending Ladvenu to the chapel for a cross, the English soldiers insulting the Promoter, and Beaudricourt rushing in to stop the burning, insisting that they had agreed to play all the events of her life, including the coronation.

Here Joan is led offstage, as an English soldier gives her two sticks to make a cross. The light dims and the flames rise, projected on the cyclorama. The Inquisitor orders the Executioner to make it quick. Cauchon falls to his knees praying, "May God forgive us all." The chorus chants a Requiem. The Inquisitor turns away, refusing to watch. Ladvenu shouts in triumph, "It is a terrible and noble sight, messire."

The lights dim, and as they come up, La Hire appears in full armor. They were fools to burn Joan of Arc. Cauchon knows they have committed a monstrous sin, and Warwick regrets their unforgivable error. "We made a lark into a giant bird who will travel the skies of the world long after our names are forgotten, or confused, or cursed down." The summing-up speech is Hellman's.

La Hire insists that they cannot conclude with the burning: "The true story of Joan is the story of her happiest day. Anybody with any sense knows that. Go back and act it out." The lights dim again and come up on the coronation of Charles in Reims Cathedral, a glorious spectacle with candles, a stained glass window projected on the cyclorama, and Joan in a fine white robe ornamented with a fleur-de-lis. Warwick cannot believe this was her happiest day, watching "Holy Oil being poured on the mean, sly little head!" Joan is smiling happily: "Oh, Warwick, I wasn't paying any attention to Charlie. I knew what Charles was like. I wanted him crowned because I wanted my country back. And God gave it to us on the Coronation Day. Let's end with it, please, if nobody would mind." As the curtain falls, the chorus is singing the "Gloria" of the Mass.

Miss Hellman gives a vibrating theatrical crescendo to the final moment. Just as we have suffered Joan's agony, we glory in reliving her happiest day. Compared to the original, it may seem unduly loaded with cheerful sentimentality, but it rings true for a Joan who is to be declared a saint for all the world. Anouilh's ironic description of the final tableau, as Fry translates it—"The curtain falls slowly on this beautiful illustration from a school prize"—would be inappropriate here.

As closely as Miss Hellman followed the characters and pattern of Anouilh, her idiom makes the play her own. Her characters speak in action and in words of action; they never talk like books. She deprives them of their voluminous excursions into theology. Fascinating as these may be for classes in the seminary or monastery, they impede the story of Joan in the theatre. Her country girl with all her gamin vitality and her earthy shrewdness must stand in the forefront battling against the priests who futilely attempt to vanquish her soul. That action must command the center of the arena. Anouilh devotees may protest that she's altered his text too radically. The point need not be argued. She labeled her version an adaptation; Fry calls his a translation.

Her Inquisitor is not Anouilh's Inquisitor. "Natural man" may be his enemy, but he does not pursue him so persistently and feverishly as he does in the original. In Anouilh he's driven by his obsession: "The hunting down of Man will go on endlessly. However powerful we become one day in one shape or another, however inexorably the Idea shall dominate the world, however rigorous, precise, and subtle its organization and its police, there will always be a man who has escaped, a man to hunt, who will presently be caught, presently be killed: a man who, even so, will humiliate the Idea at the highest point of its power, simply because he will say 'No' without lowering his eyes." Some French Communists boycotted the play, contending that Anouilh's Inquisitor was a caricature of Vishinsky. Anouilh insisted that the charge was ridiculous.

Miss Hellman maintains a bold, sincere, and often solemn sense of reality throughout, the fictive reality of the theatre that welcomes involvement, that establishes its own terms of credibility. Anouilh alternates between the long discursive passages, more his than his characters', and the scenes from

Joan's life which he maintained were "truer than the real thing" because he laced them with skepticism and irony. Miss Hellman makes the shifts from the trial to the flashback episodes sharper and more precise, employing the powers of the theatre's lighting artists. And each flashback has its own illusionistic reality. Anouilh wanders in and out of the trial much more casually.

Anouilh's Joan was less endowed with magic and mystery, depending more on her powers as a woman to rally the soldiers, and certainly was more arrogant and vain as she faced her final torment. "For me," Miss Hellman once commented, "Joan was too big to be concerned with vanity. Death is the most dramatic choice a person can make. Very few have made it. I just couldn't see Joan going to the stake out of arrogance." She could not retract her confession because she feared the humiliation of growing old in prison, dowdy, and forgotten. Nor is her Joan exclusively a French nationalist. She belongs to the world and her sacred mystery belongs to the world.

When the cheers broke at the final curtain on the opening night at the Longacre Theatre on November 17, 1955, it was clear that the audience had been moved. And the critics unanimously added their endorsement the next day. Not only had she drawn a Joan to their tastes and for their time, she had been magnificently served by Bloomgarden, by Joseph Anthony (the director), by Jo Mielziner (the designer), by all the actors, particularly Boris Karloff as Cauchon, Christopher Plummer as Warwick, and Julie Harris as Joan. Karloff's Cauchon was filled with compassion, and Miss Harris not only captured an irresistible combination of naivete, boisterousness, hard-headed courage and candor, she played as if Joan's voices and Joan's voice were really speaking to her from the past.

With the solemn sense of truth that pervaded the play, the absence of theatrical guile, Miss Hellman had enlisted the theatre's special genius for exploring sacred mysteries, for dramatizing the relationship between man and God. The steam-roller power drawn up against Joan could not vanquish her soul. Most critics approved her weeding out of the intellectual asides and centering her attention on Joan's story. Many commented on its contemporary pertinence. The trial was a classic example of political expediency, "as shameless and corrupt a frame-up as anything in Soviet annals." With the critics' enthusiastic send-off, *The Lark* was gloriously embarked on a run of 229 performances.

In an interview in the New York *Times*, on the Sunday before the play opened, Miss Hellman insisted that she would never again attempt an adaptation. "I'll have to be terribly hungry before I do, and I don't ever expect to get that hungry." Her appetite must have increased more than she anticipated, or she may have meant she never intended to adapt another play. A year later her dramatization of Voltaire's *Candide* was ready to open.

XV

Candide

Voltaire had dashed off his philosophical tale in four July days of 1758, locked in his room at the palace of his old friend the Elector Palatine in Schwetzingen. Miss Hellman, blessed and burdened with the help of Leonard Bernstein, Richard Wilbur, John Latouche, Dorothy Parker, Tyrone Guthrie (the director), and Oliver Smith (the designer), took the better part of a year to complete her operetta. Of course, Voltaire was not obliged to respect the demands of the American musical theatre, making everything palatable and pertinent, nor did he need to satisfy a committee of collaborators. Voltaire alone guided his sarcastic pen in attacking the pronouncement of the German philosopher and mathematician Gottfried Wilhelm von Leibnitz that "all is for the best in this best of all possible worlds." Many times that spring and fall, Miss Hellman envied his solitude and independence. She did not enjoy "writing by democratic majority vote with the director, producer, friends, cast and all relatives on the Board of Directors." For the first and only time she "listened to an army of people," and as she recalled later, it was the only time she "went to pieces."

The mass of *Candide* manuscripts at the University of Texas—a dozen complete versions, some twenty-five folders of various scenes, some discarded, others rewritten, another half-dozen miscellaneous notes—indicates the extensive rewriting. More man-hours of artistic endeavor, hers and her collaborators, went into *Candide* than into any of her other efforts and with doubtful rewards for her. By the final version, about three-fourths of her original book had dwindled away until little more than the connective tissue between songs and production numbers could be called her own.

During rehearsals, chaos alternated with frenzy and frenzy with panic, and somehow the frenzy set in sooner than with a straight play. Even before a full working script was ready, she and her collaborators were commandeered to loosen the purses of prospective investors with a capsule audition version, the prologue of which announced that this "musical circus," based on the greatest satire ever written, was to have a roaring-river quality, "hitting out in all directions, enclosing all human nonsense in a never halting rush to the end."

It was, of course, the demand for a swift pace and a hitting in all directions that gave the production its eventual sparkle, but it created problems in the process. The collaborators were all strong hitters with fast reflexes. The chief lyricist, Richard Wilbur, and the composer, Leonard Bernstein, were also her close friends. Oscar Levant once commented that Lenny Bernstein never missed an opportunity at parties to climb up on Lillian's lap. It was Bernstein who had urged her to attempt a musical, though *Candide* was her idea, not his. If her collaborators had been less expert, if she had been less fond of them and their work, she might have salvaged more of her book. Or perhaps if Bloomgarden, instead of Ethel Linder Reiner, had been in command, the book, lyrics, and music might have been more evenly balanced and the production drawn together more tightly. Miss Reiner was a novice and so overwhelmed by her array of artists that she gave them carte blanche to make their own compromises with each other. As a result the *Candide* that reached the stage on December 1, 1956, had not achieved a collective coherence. Even with all the cutting, revising, reordering, pushing songs in and out, the give-and-take among the participants was amicable and the temperamental clashes infrequent. Only once did Wilbur apparently anticipate trouble. He wrote to Miss Hellman, "If you catch L. [Bernstein] rewriting my lyrics, clip his piano wires."

The director and the designer entered the proceedings in the spring, long before rehearsals began. Tyrone Guthrie proposed that Candide's wanderings be held together by Pangloss, acting as if he were director of a vagabond opera company. Although the suggestion was not explicitly adopted, the ubiquitous Pangloss did assume a kind of stagemanager's role. And Oliver Smith suggested the traveling scenery to transport the action from country to country.

All the whirlpools and eddies in Voltaire's roaring river could not find a place in Miss Hellman's book, though some were in and then out, supplanted by lyrics and music. A few characters were slightly altered, some contemporary satirical thrusts were added, but essentially, people, places, and episodes were drawn from Voltaire. Hellman's naive Candide may be more a disillusioned hero and less a blithering idiot; but as in the original, he gradually emerges from his pious illusions as he encounters the viciousness of the ordinary world. Her Cunegonde, though not thoroughly virtuous, is certainly more ladylike than Voltaire's ready opportunist. And though the evils of the world are more fully documented in Voltaire, his assault on optimism is faithfully preserved, if with less irony and less bite.

The operetta begins, as does Voltaire's satire, at the castle of Baron Thunder-Ten-Tronch in Westphalia. Dr. Pangloss introduces himself and sets the scene. The Westphalians are preparing a wedding; they've just concluded a bloody war and have taken their hereditary enemy, the King of Hesse, as prisoner. At one point Miss Hellman proposed a pantomimic introduction of all the characters and a long soliloquy by Dr. Pangloss. He was to warn the audience that instead of a "jolly potpourri of songs, jokes, and dances," they would "witness War, Death, Famine, Disease, Petty and Grand Larceny, Hate, Greed, and a small amount of Rape. . . . There will also be plague, earthquake, and tragedies at sea. Therefore, if there are children in the audience I advise responsible adults to sit beside them and hold their tiny hands. We found that children rather enjoy these things and they can be a tremendous comfort when the going gets rough."

In the final version only a quarter of the original introduction was retained, and the music began almost immediately with Pangloss' song announcing the wedding in "this best of all possible worlds." In traditional operatic fashion the chorus joined to "hail the groom/ And bride, of whom/ Our hearts could not be fonder." And then Cunegonde and Candide appeared to vocalize their questions. First Cunegonde: "Dear master, I am sure you're right/ That married life is splendid./ But why do married people fight?/ I cannot comprehend it." The chorus echoes, "She cannot comprehend it." Then Pangloss answers, "The private strife/ Of Man and wife/ Is useful to the nation:/ It is a harmless outlet for/ Emotions which could lead to war/ Or social agitation." He also answers Candide's question about divorce. "Why, marriage, boy,/ Is such a joy,/ So lovely a condition,/ That many ask no better than/ To wed as often as they can/ In happy repetition." These sprightly thrusts at marriage and at the conventions of operetta belong to Wilbur and Bernstein, not to Hellman and Voltaire.

After the opening song, in the quick telegraphic style of the Broadway musical, we meet the Baron, Cunegonde's father, and her aristocratic brother Maximillian, who disapproves of her marriage to a commoner even if he is their stepbrother. We also get a hasty glimpse of Paquette, one of Pangloss' favorites. Those who remembered Voltaire delighted in her presence. She was the young lady, in Voltaire, whom Cunegonde saw in the bushes receiving a lesson in experimental physics from Dr. Pangloss, and whose example led Cunegonde to try the experiment with Candide. This bit of Voltarian naughtiness is omitted, though in earlier versions, Cunegonde observed that "when Professor Pangloss gives us our lessons we sit upright on hard benches. Whereas Paquette is now in a far more comfortable position, and learns, it seems to me, with greater ease and speed." In another draft, Pangloss sang a "Syphilis Song." One stanza of Wilbur's lyrics ran:

Dear boy, you will not hear me speak
With sorrow or with rancor
Of what has paled my rosy cheek
And blasted it with canker.
'Twas love, great love, that did the deed,
Through Nature's gentle laws,
And how should ill effects proceed
From so divine a cause?

Apparently the collaborators decided that the Broadway audience would be more offended than delighted and these passages were cut.

The Candide-Cunegonde love story belongs more to Broadway and operetta than to Voltaire. When Pangloss suggests that Candide, in some daring moment, might have learned about women, the puritanical Candide doesn't even grasp the question. Broadway is also present when the couple pledge their undying love—"I will give my life for you. . . . I want nothing, absolutely nothing but you"—and sing their nuptial duet, "Oh, Happy We!" Other parts of the opening scene belong to Hellman rather than to Voltaire. Candide invites the captured King of Hesse to the wedding, not knowing that a Hessian army is hiding on the grounds. The Hessians strike just as Pangloss is conducting the wedding company in the St. Stanislaus version of the wedding chorale. The battle, in the best operetta style, is speedy and noisy. The Baron, Maximillian, and Cunegonde are presumably killed, and Candide escapes with Pangloss' assurance that there is some sweetness in every woe, that the world will be good to him.

As Candide sings Pangloss' parting words, "There is a sweetness in every woe!/ It must be so. It must be so," the scene moves from Westphalia to Lisbon. Candide has arrived in Lisbon at carnival time, the day of the great earthquake. He kicks at an old bag of rags which turns out to be Pangloss. He too has escaped from Westphalia after the others had been slaughtered. Candide is grieved that he has injured his old master; what a horrible world where the weak kick the weak. Pangloss reminds him that that's better than the strong kicking the weak. Furthermore they should not regret their hunger: Hunger stimulates the brain.

The crowd gathers in the marketplace to hear the alchemist, the junkman, and the fortuneteller hawk their wares in Bernstein's "Lisbon Sequence." The number concludes with the Infant Casmira predicting that the towers of Lisbon are about to tremble. Two old Inquisitors, aware of the forecast, are wheeled on in thronelike chairs, accompanied by their legal adviser. In McCarthy fashion they're searching for wizards and witches. The Infant Casmira, a drunken old-lady fortuneteller dressed as a child, points the finger at Pangloss and Candide. Pangloss is a foreigner and Candide carries earthquake germs in his sack. One old Inquisitor admits that they may be innocent, but that's the hardest way to die; the guilty are rewarded with a sense of accomplishment. The other Inquisitor solicits gold to support their witch-hunts, assuring them that all contributions are tax-deductible. Pangloss, on the gibbet with a rope around his neck as the earth begins to shake, urges Candide to continue his journey: "There is some sweetness in every woe."

The carnival sequence is Hellman's invention. In Voltaire the earthquake has already occurred and the Inquisitors, trying to prevent another quake, hang Pangloss and flog Candide, Pangloss for pretending to speak wisdom and Candide for listening. At one point the Inquisitors and the crowd had another song,

"What a Day, What a Day for an Auto-da-fé." This was cut during the rehearsals.

A short travel scene with Candide singing, "There must be sunlight I cannot see./ It must be me. It must be me," takes him from Lisbon to Paris. As he arrives at the ballroom of a fine Paris house, he encounters a painted old Lady (daughter of Pope Urban X and the Princess of Palestrina in Voltaire) whom he addresses as "sir." She corrects him: "I am not a sir. I am a madame." When she urges him to stay until six when her lover will arrive, Candide knows he's in Paris. A Marquis and Sultan (Don Issacher and the Grand Inquisitor in the original) are in the ballroom waiting for their lady love, whose favors they share and who is dressing in the next room.

The lights dim on the ballroom and come up on Cunegonde in the boudoir, singing Wilbur's "Glitter and Be Gay." She's been "victimized by bitter, bitter circumstance," but she's retained her spirit: "Observe how bravely I conceal/ The dreadful, dreadful shame I feel." As she enters the ballroom to waltz with the Sultan, she sees Candide in the garden and screams. As she's about to faint, all the guests disappear and Candide joins her for a duet (lyrics by Wilbur and Latouche), "You were dead, you know./ You were shot and bayonetted, too." Cunegonde admits "That is very true./ Ah, but love will find a way." Their reunion is interrupted by the Marquis and Sultan, who volunteer to dispose of the beggar. Candide stabs the Marquis and when the Old Lady trips the Sultan, he stumbles onto Candide's sword. Candide has killed two important men and must escape, but first he wants to know where Cunegonde acquired all the jewels, why she is in this house. She assures him that the jewels were her mother's and that she had simply sought refuge here when she was starving. Candide has no time to register his skepticism. A procession of pilgrims arrives in the garden, welcoming all sisters and brothers in faith to join them on their journey to the New World. Cunegonde doesn't want to mix with the pious congregation, doesn't want to go to the New World, but she has no choice. A police whistle sounds and a drop with a ship painted on it is lowered behind them, and they join the procession. (The pilgrims were Miss Hellman's invention.) As they and their followers board the vessel, they sing of their joy to "leave France's wicked sod," to be on their way to "dwell where Satan's hoof has never trod." (The lyrics are Wilbur's.)

Miss Hellman's Captain sails to South America via Mississippi, though he never seems to have passengers who wish to disembark there. When they arrive at the wharf in front of the Governor's Palace in Buenos Aires, the pilgrims, who had expected to land in Canada, are now in chains and are to be sold as slaves, their "welcome to the land of opportunity." The Captain is disgruntled with his unprofitable cargo, a load of those white slaves who show the dirt, as he explains to the streetcleaner Martin. All of this is Hellman, not Voltaire, as is the notion of having Martin, the pessimist, impersonated by the same actor who played Dr. Pangloss. Voltaire's Martin, who enters the story at a later point, is not Dr. Pangloss in disguise.

After Martin has stolen the Captain's keys and released Candide, Cunegonde, the Old Lady, and the pilgrims, who run off, the Governor appears with his aides. He's had a wakeful night working on his book on the ugliness of C flat, analyzing every note in the scale. (No doubt an inside joke for Bernstein and his friends!) One of the Governor's aides turns out to be Maximillian, who is delighted to be reunited with his sister and with Candide, though he's enraged when he discovers that the "low-born climber" still wants to marry Cunegonde. As he's about to strike Candide with his glove, Candide takes it and Maximillian conveniently drops dead. Miss Hellman enjoys the special privileges of the operetta. As Martin drags the body off, the Governor serenades Cunegonde with "My Love" (lyrics by Wilbur and Latouche); he wants to marry her. That's impossible because she's in love with Candide. Not all that impossible, the Old Lady assures her: "Marrying another man is no more unfaithful than sleeping with another man." Cunegonde recognizes her point and joins the company in singing and dancing Bernstein's tango, "I Am Easily Assimilated." Candide is reluctant to leave Cunegonde, but having killed three men and still believing that he'll find the place where men are "honest and kind and good and noble," he accepts Martin's emerald compass which will point him up the Andes on the way to Eldorado. Before departing he joins Cunegonde, the Old Lady, and the Governor in a farewell quartette by Wilbur. As the curtain falls, Candide sets his compass and runs off.

Candide's next adventures in Voltaire are relegated to the intermission in Miss Hellman's version. We never meet his valet Cacambo with whom he visits Paraguay, where he kills Cunegonde's brother; we miss their frightening encounter with the Oreillons, the monkeys who chase two naked young ladies and bite at their buttocks. They shoot them, not knowing that the monkeys are their lovers. We miss the magnificence of Eldorado, "the marketplace ornamented with thousands of columns, the fountains of rosewater and of liquors distilled from sugarcane, which played continually in the public squares paved with precious stones which emitted a perfume like that of cloves and cinnamon." Originally Miss Hellman had included an Eldorado scene and a Dorothy Parker song in which Candide sang, "Anchors aweigh and set our courses/ Back to the folk who invented divorces," and the Eldoradians replied, "Leave us in our streets of gold,/ Sail to the countries of the common cold!/ Sail to the world you're longing for—/ And be sure to land where they're having a war!"

When the second act opens, again on the dock at Buenos Aires with a view of a room in the palace, Cunegonde and the Governor are playing a dreary game of chess. The Old Lady is slumped on the steps singing: She's been starved in a ditch, burned for a witch, been beaten and whipped and repeatedly stripped, "But I'm finding of late/ That the very worst fate/ Is to perish of comfort and BOREDOM." One needn't consult the program to know that these are Wilbur lyrics. Cunegonde can match her distress, if for other reasons. For three years the Governor has promised a wedding: "Every day you forget/

What you promised, and yet/ You continue to rumple my bedding." The Governor joins the trio at intervals, speaking the song's title, "Quiet." When Cunegonde threatens to depart by the next boat, he's delighted to help. His officers throw sacks over Cunegonde and the Old Lady and carry them off, just at the moment when Candide and Martin return, loaded with gold and jewels, and Candide sings of the wonders of Eldorado: "They have no words for fear and greed,/ For lies and war, revenge and rage./ They sing and dance and think and read./ They live in peace and die of age." In her only song, Miss Hellman's lyrics cannot match Wilbur's lilting verbal twists.

When the Governor informs Candide that Cunegonde has gone, presumably to follow him to Europe, Candide must buy a ship to pursue her. An outright purchase, Martin insists, is impossible; the rich don't deal with each other so crassly. He must contribute to the Governor's favorite charity. Candide agrees to endow two insane asylums in exchange for the boat. As Candide and Martin sail on an old vessel that has not been to sea in years, the Governor and his retinue sing Wilbur's "Bon Voyage," and as he watches the boat sink he concludes, "But I never would swindle the humble poor,/ For you can't get a turnip to bleed./ When you swindle the rich you get so much more,/ Which is why I have swindled Candide."

In an early version of this scene, the citizens of Buenos Aires are waiting for the return of their army, the third army that has tried to plunder Eldorado. Instead, Candide and Martin ride in on the back of a giant dove loaded with their Eldorado treasures. They have seen the army as they flew over the jungle, all of them dead, because, as Martin says, they went "with cannon in their hands and conquest in their hearts." Candide found Eldorado because he was poor and hungry and needed love: "I came to them: they took me as I was."

In the traveling scene from Buenos Aires to Venice, Candide is rowing a raft, while Martin fishes. Candide is trying to keep his faith in the Pangloss doctrine, though it's become increasingly difficult with most of his Eldorado riches at the bottom of the ocean and Martin constantly reminding him of the evil "in a world where men march across continents to kill each other without even asking why. Where the scientist strives to prolong life and at the same minute invents weapons to wipe it out. Where children are taught the rules of charity and kindness until they grow to the age where they would be considered insane if they put the rules into practice. Where half the world starves and the other half diets." The contemporary social comment belongs to Hellman, as does Martin's transformation. Just as Martin is insisting that the human heart is more vicious than the monsters of the sea, a shark yanks him out of the boat. When Candide discovers he's gone, Dr. Pangloss (Martin) appears in the water and climbs aboard the raft. A doctor's wife saved him in Lisbon and he's just now escaped from the pirates who had made him a galley slave.

As the raft moves off, a Venice gambling house comes into view. In Voltaire, Candide travels from Bordeaux to Paris, where he's cheated out of most of his remaining wealth, goes to Venice by boat via England in search of Cunegonde, and then on another boat to Constantinople, where he finally finds her. In the original it's not until this last leg of his journey that he's reunited with Dr. Pangloss. Much of the Venice scene is Hellman's invention, though sparked by Voltaire.

The gambling table, surrounded by masked guests, is doing a lively business as the scene opens, though apparently without substantial rewards for Perone, the manager, his associate Sofronia (the Old Lady), or for the Prefect of Police. They sing of their unhappiness in Wilbur's "What's the Use." Everyone shares his profits with someone else, even the Prefect of Police: "It's a very fine thing to be Prefect,/ Shaking down all the gamblers in town./ My position has only one defect:/ That there's somebody shaking me down." Perone spots Pangloss and Candide as likely prospects. They're still carrying gold in their jeweled bags. Pangloss is enticed to the table and Sofronia and her maid (Cunegonde) pursue Candide. To the music of a gavotte, lyrics by Dorothy Parker (her only song), Sofronia bemoans her sad fate: "I've got troubles, as I said./ Though our name, I say again is,/ Quite the proudest name in Venice,/ Our afflictions are so many,/ And we haven't got a penny." Candide's heart is moved: "I shall look them up tomorrow/ And alleviate their sorrow/ With a check made out to bearer./ In the meantime, buona sera." Pangloss, to the same tune, extolls gambling and the pretty ladies who surround the table: "Millions of rubles and lire and francs!/ Broke the bank, broke the bank./ Broke the best of all possible banks./ Pieces of gold to the ladies I throw./ Easy come, easy go./ Shining gold to the ladies I throw." His beginner's luck does not hold, and as Pangloss is wiped out, even the table disappears. Candide is pinned into a corner by the Old Lady and Cunegonde. When their masks are torn off in the scuffle and Candide discovers Cunegonde, he throws his bags of gold at her feet: "This is what you want, I give it to you." Completely disillusioned, Candide rushes out. Pangloss, the eternal optimist, stays behind, certain that if he waits long enough the table and his money will return.

The lights dim on Venice and come up on the ruins of Westphalia. Although the place doesn't look very nice, according to Pangloss, "there's always something homey about coming home." The return to Westphalia is Hellman's concession to operetta. Voltaire sets his reunion on a farm in Transylvania. The wanderers are not happy at the sight of each other; they're weary of life and ready to die. Candide cannot endure their presence and drives them all away: Pangloss can tell his lies to the trees; Maximillian had better escape before Candide kills him again; the Old Lady's stories have lost their charm; no more men will be killed in defense of Cunegonde's dubious honor. They all depart, but only for a moment.

As Candide builds a fire, Pangloss returns with a small fish. He once took a short course in oceanography at Leipzig, and he cannot abandon the notion that this is the best of all possible worlds: "It's most difficult to get rid of what you once thought, isn't it?" The Old Lady brings a bundle of twigs and branches. Maximillian contributes a homemade broom. Cunegonde carries a giant mushroom. Unfortunately it's poisonous and has to be retrieved from the stew, and when Cunegonde tries to demonstrate her usefulness by stirring the stew, she knocks over the pot. Stupid as she is, Candide still wants to marry her: "We will not live in beautiful harmony because there is no such thing in this world, nor should there be. We promise only to do our best and live out our lives."

The entire company slips in from the wings to join Candide in the final song, "Make Our Garden Grow." "We're neither pure nor wise nor good./ We'll do the best we know./ We'll build our house, and chop our wood,/ And make our garden grow./ And make our garden grow." The glorious finale is truer to operetta than to Voltaire. We miss Martin's observations that man was "born to live in the convulsions of distress or in the lethargy of boredom." We miss the ironic edge of Pangloss' final pronouncement: "All events are linked up in this best of all possible worlds." If Candide had not endured all the calamities of his journey, he would not now "be eating citrons and pistachios." Candide accepts the argument: "Tis well said, but we must cultivate our gardens." Wilbur has inflated Voltaire's final admonition into a radiant affirmation of man's hope.

The Broadway *Candide* suffered from an abundance of riches. It also suffered from the inescapable comparison with Voltaire. Although John Chapman (the *Daily News*, December 3, 1956) called it an artistic triumph, "the best light opera since *Der Rosenkavalier*," it was more commonly labeled "a spectacular disaster," "a beautiful bore," "more like a high school pageant than a social satire." It was inevitable, if unjust, that the deficiencies would be attributed to Miss Hellman and the theatrical delights to her collaborators. She alone was speaking for Voltaire. No one expected Wilbur's witty lyrics to be restrained by the original, and Bernstein's brilliant score went its own gay way. Even before the critics' reports were in, Miss

Hellman confessed that she had "botched it." The idea had been hers, and she should have battled more fiercely to protect her book and cajole the others into conforming. Later Wilbur insisted that everyone had fallen down: "Lenny's music got more and more pretentious. The audience forgot what was happening to the characters. Lillian's book got to be mere connective tissue. And I was inclined to be too literary and stubborn."

Miss Hellman was not trained for the brisk telegraphic style demanded by the musical theatre. With her text radically reduced, her satiric thrusts seemed too dull, cumbersome, and serious for the mocking lyricism of Bernstein's score and the verbal playfulness of Wilbur's lyrics. As one critic remarked, she had blunted Voltaire's cutting edge. Where he had been ironic and bland, she became explicit and vigorous. Instead of lightning thrusts, she employed body blows. Where he had been diabolical, she became humanitarian. She had been trapped into making Candide a romantic hero rather than the absurd and gullible victim of his philosophical miseducation. Without sufficient support from the lyrics and the score, her acceptance of war, greed, treachery, venery, snobbishness, and mendacity as staples of civilization—true as they were to the twentieth century—seemed too cynical. And her timely attacks on such traditional enemies as aristocracy, puritanical snobbery, phony moralism, inquisitorial investigations, and brave-new-world optimism appeared heavy-handed.

Uninhibited by Voltaire, Wilbur winged his verbal delights at the absurdities Candide encountered, giving them a contemporary pertinence and parodying operatic convention. Bernstein's exhilarating score "played hopscotch," as he described it, "with the traditional musical forms: the serenade, tango, ballad, waltz, and gavotte."

The other collaborators added to the brightness and gaiety. Tyrone Guthrie kept Candide's adventures moving at a sprightly pace, and Oliver Smith's gorgeous and dazzling scenic effects made *Candide* one of the most sumptuous productions ever seen on the Broadway stage. With all its elegance and even if it was "the most imaginative and sophisticated product of the American musical stage," it did not command an audience. While *Li'l Abner* and *Bells Are Ringing* were playing to capacity, *Candide* could only muster half a house at the Martin Beck. It closed on February 2, 1957, after seventy-three performances. As Miss Hellman once remarked, "Failure in the theatre is more dramatic and uglier than in any other form of writing. It costs so much and you feel so guilty." She suffered this guilt about *Candide*.

In spite of her unhappiness, when *Candide* was produced in London two years later (April 30, 1959), she participated actively in its preparation. She changed the Venice scene back to Paris and insisted that strong actors be hired. In New York they had been misled into casting singers rather than actors. Her second chance with *Candide* was not rewarding. The London *Times* (May 3, 1959), after giving Bernstein a few kind words, castigated Miss Hellman for missing the irony of the original and devising an "ignoble entertainment."

XVI

Toys in the Attic

After each adaptation Miss Hellman vowed not to try another. After *Candide* her resolution became firmer. She told a reporter, "I don't want to do another adaptation—ever!" Not since 1951 had she worked on a new play of her own. It was time she became her own master again. During the summer and fall of 1957 the pieces began to fall into place: the story would be about a modern beloved rogue who has been raised by his devoted maiden sisters and whose neurotic childbride desperately tries to discover the womanly wiles that will hold him. They all love him and want him to succeed, but when success comes they are frightened that they'll lose him.

She was intrigued with the notion of writing about love. "There's too damn much loose talk about love these days," she told a reporter, "a lot of bunk going around about how we must all find love, we all need love. . . . We live in a time of junky words, junky ideas." Contrary to the accepted fiction, not all kinds of love were good and noble. "There's much in love that's destructive, including the love that holds up false notions of success, of the acquisition of money." These thoughts would find a place, and as she began mulling over the new play, remembered realities began to appear. She recalled a friend of her father's who was obsessed with a love of horses and who was forced by his sister and his wife's sister to abandon his true love and cultivate a love of success and money. When he failed in business, he also failed as a man. On a visit to New Orleans she was reminded again of her aunts' great love for her father, of their sacrifices for him, of their patience with her mother's whimsicalities. In her first drafts of *The Autumn Garden* she had portrayed two sisters who resembled her aunts. They had lost out in that play. Now was the time to give them another chance.

The composition moved rapidly and easily. By mid-fall she had completed half of a first draft, and then suddenly everything stopped on dead center. Rather than try to force her characters against their wills, she put the manuscript aside and went abroad. Off and on since spring she had been talking with Lester Osterman, Jr., who had been an associate producer on *Candide*, about joining forces in a new producing organization. While she was waiting for a second wind to propel her own play, she would canvass the London and Paris scenes for scripts that might be suitable for New York. She had given the novelist Saul Bellow an advance on a new comedy he was writing. When she returned to New York in February, she had acquired the rights to Albert Camus' stage version of Dostoevski's *The Possessed*. If they could find someone to adapt it—she refused to do it herself—they hoped to schedule a Broadway opening in the fall to coincide with the Paris first night. She also held an option on a new play by Roger Vailland. With four properties, including her own play, the Hellman-Osterman partnership seemed off to a good start. Like so many Broadway enterprises, it never progressed beyond that point. No play was ever produced under their banner, though Osterman independently sponsored several unsuccessful productions during the next few years.

In the spring, while *Toys in the Attic* still resisted her efforts to complete it, she accepted an invitation to lecture at the University of Chicago and on May 21, 1958, in Chicago, she talked about her new play in an interview with Richard G. Stern. She told Stern that she was worried. It was her first play to revolve around a man, and she feared that the idea was almost too good. "It sounds whacky to say, but somewhere it's a little too neat." The two sisters and his wife "find that this man whom they thought they wanted to be independent—they haven't wanted him that way at all. They loved him for being the *schlemiel* that they brought him up to be, and they don't like the new independence." It was a bad sign that she was worrying about how the money was going to be taken away from him, worrying that she had not made him interesting enough. She knew that by the end of the play she wanted to show that the two sisters had been in competition for their brother, that one of them was really in love with him, that none of them had really seen the truth of their relationship. She knew that the wife must inflict some damage on her husband, perhaps shooting him, but that didn't seem right. Somehow she'd become too interested in the wife's mother, a mother who wanted to get rid of her daughter. Attention on her had to be reduced. Above all she worried because she was talking about the play. She'd always had a horror of such talk, probably a sure sign that she'd tear it up in a month.

Fortunately she misjudged her own temperament. She returned to work and within a month had a full first draft. Writing "Curtain" did not, of course, finish her task. It was more than a year later, with a fourth full draft, before she was ready to put the play into production. "There's one virtue in taking as long as I take," she once explained, "you get so worn out you can't do much more." Then too she was still terrified of hotel-room rewriting and wanted to forestall that necessity.

As she had moved through the succeeding drafts, she had dimmed the spotlight on the brother and on his mother-in-law and focused more attention on his sisters and on his wife. Three characters had been eliminated and some names had been changed. In the beginning Miss Hellman had used the names of her two aunts, Hannah and Jenny. As dramatic fiction was imposed on remembered reality, they became Anna and Carrie. She did, however, retain her own nickname, Lily, for the young bride. Her long and private hours with the play were ended in December, 1959, and her old friends Kermit Bloomgarden and Howard Bay and her new director, Arthur Penn, who had just achieved a notable success with *The Miracle Worker*, began preparing it for the public.

Before the first performance at the Hudson Theatre on February 25, 1960, her first-nighter audience was alerted to the theatrical event, the first original Hellman play in nine years. And not long after the curtain was up they sensed that the Hellman of *Foxes* and *Autumn Garden* had returned, yet with a new voice somewhere in the middle range between Ibsen and Chekhov, with occasional overtones of Freud.

Again we're welcomed to a living room and a porch that have been home to more than one generation, yet not the usual elegant and expansive public area of an old mansion. In its best days this room provided no more than middle-class comfort. Now it has become seedy and shabby, the porch and garden furniture heavy with the paint that was meant to refresh them. The profusion of potted plants provides the only evidence of new life. With his usual expertise Howard Bay's setting captured the appropriate decaying atmosphere.

The Berniers sisters, Anna (forty-two) and Carrie (thirty-eight), are just returning from their daily tasks, hot and tired, happy to shed their respectable hats, gloves, and purses, and to open the blinds, water the plants, and recite the events of the day. Carrie is annoyed that her boss quit early because of the heat. Anna has had to haul out every coat in the store for two lonely rich old ladies. On the way home Carrie went to the cemetery. Anna wonders if everybody was still there. Miss Hellman's sense of humor thrives anywhere. Perhaps it was not right to bury Mama and Papa at Mount Olive with the rich people; when they die they should go to Mount Great Hope. Anna will settle for any place that's cool. Talk of death reminds them of how they cling to life, and to each other. They exchange their weekly presents—this week, cologne and candied oranges. Carrie wonders, as she has often, how Anna can like their old house. She never did even when she was a child and ate supper on the porch with Julian while Anna sat with Mama and Papa in "that awful oak tomb" (a bit of remembered reality from Miss Hellman's Aunt Hannah). Now Anna confesses that she did resent Carrie's private suppers with Julian. Carrie never suspected that she minded: "Funny how you can live so close and long and not know things." The line could have come from Chekhov.

There is more that Carrie doesn't know. Anna has talked again to their real estate man about selling the house. She's also been to the post office to inquire if a letter could be lost. They haven't heard from Julian in two weeks. She had concealed her anxiety, asking for letters from Rome and Paris about their "forthcoming tour." With her usual skill, Miss Hellman is gradually building the mosaic. Anna has even telephoned the hotel in Chicago, only to discover that Julian and Lily have moved. Two of her letters have been returned, "address unknown." Of course she understands that now that Julian's married and has a business to take care of he's probably busy.

As Gus, the "colored man," comes with ice for the icebox, more of their life unfolds. Now that they no longer have to worry about Julian, he thinks they should treat themselves to a refrigerator and a new house. Carrie has bigger plans. They'll sell the house and go on a big long trip, for a year, perhaps for five. Gus goes about his business; he's heard this story, seven years ago, when Julian went on his first business trip. The pathetic sisters have been trapped in their dreary routine longer than we might have guessed. When Julian married, he'd promised they'd all go to Europe together, but they had to buy sterling for the bride to match the $10,000 gift from Lily's mother. With only $2800 left in the bank, Anna thinks they should postpone their trip. She wants to speak more French than "C'est trop cher, M'sieur." Carrie has further depleted their savings; she wired $1000 to Julian in Chicago and wonders now if she did wrong. Anna thinks she did, not because of the money, because they should not be interfering. Neither will pursue the argument; frustration has become a way of life.

As Anna goes to the kitchen, Albertine Prine, Lily's mother, and Henry Simpson appear in the garden. Henry, a Negro of about forty-five, wears a chauffeur's cap. Albertine, a handsome woman of the same age, is "dressed with elegance, but in no current fashion." She hesitates; she hardly knew the sisters before the marriage, doubts that she'd know which was which. When Henry refuses to ring the bell for her, we quickly sense that Henry is more than servant.

She goes to the porch alone and does confuse their names, but the sisters, though flustered, are rescued by their automatic Southern hospitality. They're relatives now and should be better acquainted; Mrs. Prine must join them for supper. She refuses. Her supper's at midnight: "It's my bad habit to live at night and sleep the days away." Albertine is a strange lady from another world. She only wants to know when they expect Lily and Julian; she's had a message that they are to arrive tonight. Carrie and Anna are overwhelmed by the news; they've heard nothing in seventeen days; they must prepare to meet the Chicago train. That won't be necessary. Henry got the message in a local call, and two nights ago Albertine saw Lily walking back and forth in front of her house, "as if she wished to come in and didn't wish to come in." If Albertine seems strange, her strangeness must have rubbed off on Lily. She only wants to invite the couple to stay with her, though she's sure Julian will want to be with his sisters. She'll visit Lily in the morning. As she leaves, she introduces the sisters to Henry.

After they've gone, Carrie echoes our perplexity. She remembers that Henry was wearing a white coat when they were there for dinner, and now Albertine introduces him. "I never heard anybody introduce a nigger before." (Times have changed. The line would have been less offensive even in 1960 than it is now!) Anna wonders if perhaps Lily is pregnant and has come to see a doctor, or more likely, "It's happened again, and he feels bad and doesn't want to tell us."

Anna brings in their supper as they continue to worry about Julian. Carrie is sure he'll make a fortune some day; she recalls the money he won at poker to pay for Anna's operation. A fortune is not necessary, a job is. Anna doubts that they'll ever find "a prescription put up fresh each time Julian fails." Their speculations are halted by the sound of a car. Carrie runs to the porch; she's like a child at the sound of Julian's voice. She calls, "Shall I jump and you will catch me?" A taxi driver appears first with luggage, then Julian and Lily. He is tall and handsome, in his mid-thirties. Lily is pretty and frail, just past twenty. (Originally she'd been twelve to fourteen, even more "a child who wants to be a woman.") Julian is loaded with packages and bubbling with enthusiasm, certainly not the failure we've expected. He drops his packages and sweeps Carrie into his arms. His embrace of Anna is warm, though less exuberant. When the driver has brought in all the baggage, Julian overpays him in bills. He deserves them: "No porters at the station because the train came in early." When Anna tries to ask about the train, Carrie quickly shifts the subject to rooms and food. Finally Lily has a chance to speak. She's tired and Julian doesn't like her to be tired. Julian reminds her that she's tired from the long train trip. Lily says whatever Julian tells her to say. Her own mind wanders in a curious dream world. Of her wedding day, when Anna recalls it was raining, Lily remembers: "I was on a high hill running down with the top of me, and flying with the left of me, and singing with the right of me—" We're not unprepared for Lily after seeing her mother.

Unwilling to luxuriate in their reunion, Anna wants to know what's happened. What about the shoe factory in Chicago?

At first Julian doesn't recall the factory, but then admits that it's gone, a bad investment of Lily's money. The man who sold it faked the books. Julian knows that they expected him to come home with Chicago over his shoulder, "dressed in pure gold, bringing candied oranges to hang in your hair." He has. Anna won't be sidetracked. Lily's mother has been there; they know that he didn't just arrive. Julian admits that they've been at a hotel in town for a week. In fact, he walked by the window one night and saw them playing casino. Anna has heard all she can endure and retreats to the kitchen. For a moment Carrie fingers idly at the piano, trying not to listen to Lily and Julian, and then joins Anna.

Lily is frightened. She wanted to see her mother; she didn't mean to do wrong by sending a message. She wants to know about the lady on the train, why he kept leaving the hotel after they arrived. One day she followed him and saw him talking with the lady on a bench in Audubon Park. Julian ignores her questions as he carries in the parcels from the porch. He only wants to be sure she's not told anyone and that she'll stop following him: "That's no way to be married." He sends her to her room and calls Anna and Carrie to come for their presents.

Carrie has walked around the house and onto the porch. She wants him to have their savings bankbook, and Anna, returning from the kitchen, agrees. Julian is overcome by their generosity: "God bless you. All my life it's been this way." Anna assures him this is the way it should be: "You are our life. It is we who should thank you."

Warmed by their affection, the prodigal opens the valises and unwraps the packages: first, two fancy evening dresses. His commentary matches their elegance: "I don't think dresses like these should be worn twice in the same city, do you? Everybody in Paris will talk, and we can't have that." Next, two fur pieces for the drafts in the opera house and two fur-trimmed opera coats to go with the gowns. Then there are suits for traveling and dresses for informal evenings, "for flirtations on Italian terraces." He drapes the clothes over them and digs deeper in his Santa Claus bag. For Carrie he has a large necklace; for Anna a gold-mesh bag: "Remember when old lady Senlis used to come along swinging her gold-mesh bag, and your eyes would pop out wondering what was in it? Look and see what's in this one." Julian opens the envelope for them: two passages for Europe.

Anna finally regains her voice. She wants to know where all this has come from. Julian answers literally; it's come from all over town. Anna and Carrie are frightened and bewildered, but before they can repack the gifts Lily returns, in her slip, with the delivery men who wheel in a refrigerator and a spinet with a big sign lettered "Carrie." Carrie touches the piano and puts her hand over her face. Anna again tries to force him back to reality: "What is all this? Answer me, please, Julian." They mustn't worry. It's not from poker; he's only sold some real estate and he's not finished. Inside the refrigerator they'll find the paid-up mortgage. Certainly Anna must remember when he was a child and she took him to Mr. Shine and "made me tell how I wouldn't have any place to live unless—Christ God, how I hated it." He's also written to Mr. Barrett informing him that Miss Caroline Berniers will not return to work and to Anna's coat department that she's going on an extended European tour. He's not forgotten Lily. For her he has a new diamond ring to replace the wedding ring he bought at a pawnshop for twenty dollars. There's still more. In the envelope he's waving there's $150,000 in cash, half for him, half for his partner. And to celebrate the festivities he's bought champagne and caviar, which he takes to the kitchen. He's the successful Julian they've always wanted: "I like things this way; making bargains, talking big—I don't take my hat off in elevators anymore."

The three pathetic souls are alone surrounded by their gaudy gifts. Lily doesn't know where he got the money. She only knows about the lady on the train who calls him every night at six. Carrie is sure he's gone crazy; she wouldn't be seen in these "whore's clothes." But when she discovers that the mortgage is indeed paid off, she admits that she's always hated the house; she pretended to like it for Julian's sake. Lily wants her old ring back, and as she goes to retrieve it the telephone rings. She races to the phone before it can ring again: "No, he isn't. This is his wife. What is *your* name?" She stares at the phone, hangs up, and throws her diamond against the window as Julian returns with the champagne and caviar.

At first Anna insists that the phone didn't ring, then Lily confesses. She knows it wasn't nice to tell the lady he wasn't here. Julian has a better word, "respectful." And it's not "respectful" of Carrie not to play the new piano. Carrie tries a waltz while Julian dances around the room, first with his "infant bride," then with Anna, tangling her long evening coat in her legs, and not to slight Carrie, takes her a glass of champagne and forces a spoon of caviar into her mouth. Carrie, near the breaking point, shouts, "You're laughing at me. You've never laughed at me before." Anna's head is drooping; Lily is almost in tears. Julian cannot understand. He bolts another glass of champagne and stares at them: "What's the matter with everybody? We're not having a very nice party." And the curtain closes on their pathetic dream world. We must wait to know where Julian got the money, wait for the explosion that must come.

It's morning when the curtain rises again. The spinet and refrigerator are still in the middle of the room, the clothes are draped everywhere. Anna is polishing Julian's shoes. Carrie is bringing coffee. Julian is still asleep, having spent most of the night in the garden drinking. Carrie had hoped that everything would be gone; she must get to work before Mr. Barrett opens Julian's letter. (In an early version more was made of Sam Barrett. Julian had had an affair with his wife. Carrie was in love with him, and Barrett wanted to take her to Europe.) Although Anna is equally worried, she wants to risk the new life and go to Europe. Why is Carrie so sure that trouble will come? Simply because "it always has." Lily enters, a nightgown

Toys in the Attic WERNER J. KUHN

over her dress, staring at them as if seeing them for the first time. Julian has not slept with her; she doesn't know if he wants breakfast. Carrie, no longer able to cope with this madness, hurries to work.

As she crosses the porch, Albertine and Henry appear. Hearing her mother, Lily runs out, then back for her shoes, gives up and races to kiss her mother, apologizing for having been mean to Henry on the telephone. Albertine has prepared the garden wing for them, or she'll give them the lake house and Mr. Warkins can draw up the papers. She's also giving them a check for $5000. That's not the help Lily needs. She wants to know about Mrs. Warkins. Does she have a low voice, is she in love with Mr. Warkins? Albertine doesn't remember her. Lily tries desperately to explain what's happened. Julian lost the factory, yet they're rich. He's been talking to some woman. She's afraid Julian will leave her. Last night she walked the streets until she heard a "noise way up, and I went in. There were people, and a woman stood before them on a box. The people talked about themselves right out loud. One woman had lost a leg but she said it was growing back and she proved it." The lady on the box was waving a knife which she kept kissing. After everyone had gone Lily tried to buy the knife; she wanted it more than anything. "The lady said the knife of truth would dress me as in a jacket of iron flowers and though I would do battle, I would march from the battle cleansed. Then I fell asleep—" It was after that, at two in the morning, she called Henry. He came and brought her back to the Berniers.

Lily is still pursuing the truth. She must know if her mother sold her to Julian, if he married her for her money. Their life has been changed by that woman who helped to make him rich. Last night Julian wanted to sleep alone; it's been that way ever since the lady came to Chicago. Albertine assures her there are times when a man wants to sleep alone. If there's another woman, she'd better be sure. She should be happy that Julian has money and doesn't have to come crawling to her: "He would have come to hate your money." That's the only thing Albertine feared.

Again the phone rings. Albertine restrains Lily on the porch as Anna answers and awakens Julian who appears in his robe. He's sorry he wasn't able to return her call. Everything worked fine; he's got the "nice clean bills" in his pocket. He'll meet her where they agreed at eleven o'clock. "Don't worry about me. He just beats women. I'll be there. Goodbye, my dear." We now know that Lily's suspicions are real, that Julian may face another threat.

Julian is undisturbed, ready for breakfast, and taking the juice Anna has brought him, goes out to greet Albertine and Henry. He has a present for her, a flame-red lace mantilla and a gigantic comb. He doesn't know when she'll wear them and neither does she, but she's delighted. "Who wants a roast of beef?" Pointing to the gaudy display of presents inside, Julian explains: "For years they tell me about what's going to be, what I'm going to do, you know, get rich and big time. The more I fail, the louder they cheer me with what we're all going to have. . . . Well, when it came, I guess it was hard to believe, maybe even frightened them. . . . They thought I'd come home broke—God knows I always had—You don't know about that, but *they* do, and they got ready to give me all they had and tell all the same nice lies about how the next time. And then there I come, strutting like a kid—Rich. Rich. Rich." Julian understands himself. If Mrs. Prine may be bored by talk of money, he isn't.

This has been the happiest week of his life. He has gone right into the office of a man he hated, hated since he was a child, told him straight that he had something the man wanted, and he'd take $150,000 for it. The man ordered him out; he could get his money from women, "your sisters or your wife. You married her for it." Is that what people thought? Albertine doesn't know about other people; she never thought that. If she doesn't want to hear about his business adventure, she has no choice. The man could not understand how he had managed to acquire two acres of swamp land before he did, and Julian wouldn't tell him. His decision had to come fast; Julian would come back on Tuesday to collect: "And I walked out the happiest man in town. I paid back my life some way or other—" He shows her the bills to prove his success.

Before Julian has finished, Gus again arrives with the ice. Julian is delighted to display the refrigerator; he bought it for him more than for his sisters. Gus does not miss his moment: "In Chicago they keep it in the parlor?" When Julian peels off more bills for Gus, down payment on the farm he's always wanted, Gus refuses to take the money. He doesn't want "that kind of trouble again"; what's more, he doesn't really want a farm. Albertine understands; people make up things they think they want.

Real trouble has now begun. Carrie, returning slowly through the garden, must talk with Julian alone. Mr. Barrett had read the letter before she arrived; Julian must apologize. As she goes into the house to wait, Julian refuses to follow. Lily must show her mother her new ring. It must be around somewhere. He races into the house shouting, "Seen a large diamond ring?" He takes the breakfast tray Anna is carrying, asks her to iron a shirt for him, and goes with her to the kitchen, still ignoring Carrie's pleas.

Carrie is at the porch window listening as Lily explains to her mother that she exchanged the ring for the lady's knife. She's going to tell Julian the truth. Albertine knows this is not the moment for truth. She must go in and dress and say nothing; Henry will try to retrieve the ring. Albertine and Henry are alone on the porch with Carrie at the window. They know more than they've had a chance to speak. There is another woman. Julian is not sleeping with her, though Henry knows that he once did. Albertine is sure that Warkins bought the two acres. He "owns fifty percent of the interstate agreement to take the railroad route along the docks." He must have been astounded that "Julian knew about the best secret in years." Mrs. Warkins must have told Julian about the land. Henry knows more about Mrs. Warkins; she's his cousin. Her husband doesn't know that she's colored; Julian did and didn't care. "She's a foolish woman and grateful for such things." This, "God knows," Albertine can understand. She touches his hand; Henry smiles and puts her hand to his face. As they start to leave and Albertine discovers Carrie at the window, she does not lose her composure: "Are you writing a book, Miss Carrie?" Carrie can match her coolness: "This is our house, Mrs. Prine."

As Albertine and Henry depart through the garden, Lily runs into the parlor screaming for Julian and her mother. She's cut her hand. When Julian appears and kisses her hand, she clings to him desperately: "And last night I fell in here and hit my leg. You could cure that, too. Please. Make me cured, Julian. Let's go to bed and maybe you'll be pleased with me—maybe. (*She puts his hand on her breast.* Anna *turns away*; Carrie *stands staring at them.*)" As he picks her up and starts to leave, Carrie cannot restrain herself: "I read in a French book that there was nothing so abandoned as a respectable young girl." Julian agrees: "Otherwise nobody could stand them."

Carrie cannot endure the thought of them in bed. Julian doesn't know that Lily went out last night, that she gave her ring away. Carrie says, "I think she's a crazy girl. . . . I think there's a crazy girl in there." Anna wouldn't go that far, though she did see her deliberately cut herself and say a kind of prayer over a knife. Lily is Julian's problem, not theirs. But it's their business, Carrie insists, when "our brother sells something to Mr. Cyrus Warkins for a fortune. Warkins is a powerful and dangerous man in this town, and Julian would be a baby in the hands of such a man." Anna knows about the Warkins; Julian slept with Mrs. Warkins ten years ago. He told her. That Carrie will not believe. If he had, he would have told her and not Anna. Carrie's hysteria cannot be controlled: "He's married to a crazy little whore who cuts her hand to try and get him into bed. The daughter of a woman who keeps a nigger fancy man. I'll bet she paid Julian to take that crazy girl away from—" They must ask Julian pointblank. Anna knows better; when you truly love, "you take your chances on being hated by speaking out the truth." Anna takes that chance with Carrie. She's been driven to a truth she's never expressed: "You want to sleep with him and always have. Years ago I used to be frightened that you would try and I would watch you and suffer for you." The accusing words can't be retracted. Carrie desperately wishes she'd never heard them: "You were all I ever had. I don't love you any more." As the curtain falls, Anna accepts the consequences; that was the chance she took. The unspoken truce in their battle for Julian has been broken irrevocably.

As the third act begins, Anna is fussing with her suitcases, preparing to depart. Carrie is picking out a tune on the spinet. Julian is still flying on top of the world as he enters singing, matching his lyrics to Carrie's tune: "This is the big day, this is the great day. Oh, it's money day, the end of trouble day." He was planning to leave today, but if they wish he'll wait until tomorrow. He doesn't know where he's going, or for how long, but they needn't worry. He'll come back, and before he leaves he'll deposit $20,000 in their savings account. Before he goes he'll walk down Sailor's Lane and share his wealth with another good lady and tell her to "have a good life, baby, and then I'll walk her down to the depot and put her on the train."

Lily has joined them. She'll go anywhere with him as long as they can be alone in a room together, "the not happening" of last night will not happen again. In her excitement she drops the knife. It's the sacred knife of truth. She wants him to swear on it. Julian cannot fathom her nonsense: "For Christ's sake, Lily. What the hell's the matter with you? Stop talking foolish. Maybe kiddies should marry kiddies." She only wants to be sure that they'll go away together forever, that he'll come back for her. Julian cannot understand everyone's gloom. On this best day of his life, can't "somebody please look happy"? Lily follows him to the porch, kissing him goodbye as he runs out through the garden.

Anna is sure that when Julian comes back for Lily, they'll be gone forever. She had wanted to be around with his children, "something nice to grow old for." She's sure that Julian saw Carrie's lust. He may not have known what he saw, but he will later, just as she did. Carrie realizes now, more than ever, that she hates Anna, that they must learn to live with hate.

Anna goes to the porch, urging Lily to dress and pack. With Julian gone, Lily's old worry has returned: did her mother pay Julian to take her? She once heard her mother tell Henry how she longed for the day they'd be alone together, that she'd pay anything for that time. If Julian loves someone else, she wants to go away. Anna refuses to listen to her and walks around the house into the garden.

Lily turns to Carrie for comfort. Last night Julian was thinking in bed, "and thinking isn't the way to make love." Carrie doesn't know much about gentlemen in bed and doesn't want to learn from her. Lily won't be stopped. She wonders if Carrie has never slept with a man. Carrie is in no mood for slumber-party confessions: "Shall we have a pillow fight or make fudge? I don't like these girlish confidences." Still Lily continues. Carrie might like to know that Julian was thinking of her. Lily is irritating the new wound. She had wanted to like Carrie and now she's frightened of her. The word is not her exclusive property. Carrie too is frightened, about not being pretty any longer, about not having a job, about an old maid's candied oranges, "as a right proper treat each Saturday night." Lily persists. Did Julian ever tell her that Mama paid him? She's gone too far. Julian only told them that he had fallen in love and was going to be married. It was the day before Anna went to the hospital for an eye operation. He also told them that Anna was to have the best room in the hospital and that the great Dr. Kranz was coming from Philadelphia to perform the operation. Julian said he'd won money in a poker game. If Lily has more questions, she should ask Mrs. Cyrus Warkins: "She'll be in New York. You can have many a cozy evening." Henry and her mother know about Mrs. Warkins. Albertine was probably greatly amused that the great lawyer had married a part nigger and didn't know it: "They said Julian and the woman were together years ago. And my sister confirms the alliance." Lily giggles at Carrie's euphemism. Julian once told her that Carrie talked like an old maid when she was twelve, that "Gus used to say you kept your vagina in the icebox, that he'd seen it there and shut the door fast." Carrie is shocked; she's never heard such filthy talk. Lily did not mean to hurt her. It's just the way she and Julian talk in bed, saying things they'd never say any other time.

Somehow Lily must talk to Mrs. Warkins. Will Carrie help her tell the lady she wants just one more year alone with Julian? Carrie refuses. In one day she's lost her brother, her sister, and her job. Lily has been the "baby-rich girl, teething on other people," for too long. She'll have to start doing something for herself. Mrs. Warkins is part "nigger," Henry's cousin; Warkins is a "tough and tricky man with plenty of riffraff friends to do his dirty work, not a man to joke with." This news does not restrain Lily; she goes to the telephone and calls Warkins. He must tell his wife that she wants one more year with Julian. She knows that Julian had been kind to his wife years ago, that she's now trying to help him. She doesn't know where she is now, but Carrie prompts her. They're together in Sailor's Lane.

(Using this telephone call to precipitate the catastrophe came late in the play's development. In the early versions of the third act, the mysterious lady, then called Poppy [Mrs. Scarlotti], came to warn Julian about her husband. And later Dion Scarlotti appeared at the house to wait for Julian. Lily had been calling him, asking for his wife. When Julian arrives, Dino tells him the deal is off. He knows about Julian's affair with his wife. And when Poppy comes in again, Dino is enraged. She hated him so much she had to cheat him before she deserted him. She'd better leave town before he kills her. After he's gone, Julian pleads with Poppy to go away with him; they'll manage even without the money. Before Miss Hellman reached the final version, she knew that the Scarlottis' domestic strife had to be kept offstage, that giving them Italian names aroused irrelevant reactions, that the climactic moment must be centered on Julian, his wife, and his sisters.)

After her telephone call, Lily goes to dress as Anna appears, ready for traveling. She intends to use the boat ticket, though she and Carrie certainly can't go together. Julian doesn't need her, or them, any longer. Carrie thinks he does, that they'll have to find a new way of living together. As Anna moves to the porch, carrying a plant, she meets Albertine and Henry. She's not lost her sense of humor. She wonders if she'll look foolish carrying a camellia plant to Europe. Albertine assures her it's becoming, "soft around the face." Anna goes around the house, and Lily, finally dressed for the day, comes to say goodbye to her mother. Albertine has retrieved the ring. She's had enough of Lily's childish adventures. Never again will she "spend time in what you call an upstairs room with a morphine addict who holds seances to cover up what she sells." Lily refuses to believe her mother; that must be Henry's story. "As you lie in bed with him, Henry makes the plans and tells you what to do." The cut goes deep. Bed is "where I forget the mistakes I made with you." Still Albertine wants to help if she's needed. Lily must not punish her forever. We share Lily's perplexity when she asks, "Is something the matter with me, Mama?" Henry restrains Albertine's answer. For a fleeting moment we wonder if he could be her father. That secret, if that is the secret, remains concealed in the attic. In spite of her call to Warkins, Lily is still afraid Julian will desert her, that she'll have no place to go. Albertine assures her that she can come home, and Henry says he won't be there when she comes. That prospect seems to comfort Lily, though she has no chance to say more.

Julian is stumbling toward the house, his face and hands cut and bruised. He's been badly beaten. As he slips on the steps, Anna and Carrie move to help and then back away. If they don't understand Julian, at least they respect his pride. He doesn't want a doctor. He's taken Charlotte Warkins to her brother's house; Henry had better warn her not to stay in town. Two thugs sent by Cyrus Warkins dragged them into an alley, took all his money, and beat him. He swears he never told anyone who put up the money for the land. Henry must tell her that. He went to the police, but who would believe that he ever had more than fifty dollars in his pocket? As he collapses on the floor and then lifts himself to a chair, Lily escapes to the porch, followed by her mother. She did it. Albertine calms her. If she really loves Julian, she must comfort him and have enough pity "not to kill him with the truth." She accepts her mother's advice and returns to Julian.

As Lily sponges his face, Carrie assures him that things will be all right, bad things simply happen to people sometimes. Julian understands Carrie; she likes him this way; it's been like that all his life. He's less worried by his loss than by "assing it up, all my God-damned life, all my life it's been the same." Carrie has gone to the porch to get Anna's luggage; she's glad that nothing worse happened. "We're together, the three of us, that's all that matters." Albertine reminds her that there are four. If some day Carrie reduces it to three by telling Julian about Lily, she wants to know so that Lily can come to her. Carrie is only concerned with the present, with returning the gifts, paying their debts, and finding a job.

Julian tries desperately to recapture his pride. There's an "old saying, money is a real pure lady and when the world began she swore herself an oath never to belong to a man who didn't love her. I never loved her and she guessed it." Lily is helping him into the bedroom as Carrie goes out through the garden. She's going to buy something to make a good soup: "You always liked a good soup when you didn't feel well." Henry puts his hand on Albertine's shoulder and says goodbye; presumably he'll warn Mrs. Warkins. As the curtain comes down, Albertine is starting to leave and Anna is picking up her large valise.

Calm has returned to the Berniers household, though their

dream worlds have been shattered. With all they now know, with their lives scarred beyond forgetting, chances for happiness appear slim. But they have not fully sensed the destructive power of their love; they'll probably find another dream world, however fragile, in their love for Julian.

Toys in the Attic is one of Miss Hellman's best plays; some declared it her most mature play. Almost as if she knew that her first original drama in nine years was also to be her last, she marshaled the dramatic powers that had served her in the past, tempered the melodramatic excesses, enriched her characters with a luminous, if neurotic, humanity, and bound them tightly and irrevocably to their destructive course. She enfolded them in the decaying atmosphere of the South that she knew by instinct, though the locale served only to give the ring of truth. Home for Julian and his child bride could have been anywhere.

The Berniers, like the Hubbards, hanker for worldly comforts, but they're driven by love, not by avarice and greed. "In *Toys*," one critic remarked, "it isn't vixen teeth that bite, but human lips denied a kiss." Like the sad dreamers in *Autumn Garden*, they are bound in a web of self-deception. Success for Julian is not the rainbow's end it seemed to be. Love can harbor devastating winds. Dreams fulfilled lose their magic when they cease to be dreams.

The play achieves the magnitude and human revelation that have always been the mark of serious drama, that "arduous, immemorial job," as Kenneth Tynan put it (*New Yorker*, March 5, 1960), "of showing us how and why we suffer." It is the work of a dedicated professional who knows her powers and uses them. The language is honed to a sharp edge. Incidents evolve with a cold and clear serpentine grace and become so tightly intertwined that they cannot be sprung apart. As Robert Brustein noted (*New Republic* March 14, 1960), "her work is constructed with all the rigidity and tensile strength of a steel girder." Every dramatic hair is in place; nothing is superfluous, every dramatic gesture contributes to the central action. Her characters are original creations. They may not be lovable;

they are believable and brutally alive. We may not find comfort in their company; we are fascinated by their pathetic, neurotic lives. We may never stake a full emotional investment in them; yet we can never turn our eyes away. Sorry as we are to see Julian's toys shattered, our moral sensibilities are not really shocked: we never believed that this boy-man, this blowhard weakling, had the capacity for becoming a whole man.

Some critics again thought they detected Chekhov close by, as if sad souls trapped by dreams and frustrations were his exclusive property. One writer labored the comparison out of hand, insisting that Miss Hellman had really adapted the essence of *Three Sisters,* an idea that had never crossed her mind. Chekhov could have had a hand with some lines, a Chekhovian haze did, at moments, linger over the Berniers household, but the presence of Freud was much more evident.

Although Miss Hellman had in her youth lived through the period of the Americanization of Freud, had heard the watered-down Freudian talk common to literary parties, and had had her own experience with analysis, she had not, except in *Another Part of the Forest*, sought his help with the lives of her characters. And now when she did probe the destructive powers of sexual compulsions, particularly as manifested in New Orleans, some critics were certain she had come under the spell of Tennessee Williams, forgetting that she had dealt with the Southern scene while he was still "a California chicken-plucker," as one critic remarked. Unlike Williams', her Freudian explorations never make you feel that "they are part of a private exorcism shared in public." Nor does she tolerate exotic diversions or toy with verbal music as Williams does.

If the play misses being her best, it barely misses. The flaws are not distracting to the naked eye in the theatre. Some critics thought she loitered too long with Anna and Carrie at the beginning before setting her dramatic trap. Others were disturbed when she seemed to shift from her inquiry into the moral consequences of Julian's adventure to a treatise on abnormal psychology. She should not attempt to write on two levels.

If she wished to draw on Freud, she should have gone further. Julian could have discovered the true nature of Carrie's love for him, reviled himself for his own weakness, and then attempted to purge himself of this hidden evil and failed. This was not, of course, Miss Hellman's way. She was less concerned with stirring our human sympathies than in exposing the quality of life as she saw it, in showing us the destructive powers of love, showing us that well-meaning souls can often inflict more harm than those possessed with evil.

All seven of the daily newspaper reviewers praised the play; five were ecstatic in welcoming Miss Hellman's return with an original play. And at award time, the Critics' Circle quickly selected *Toys in the Attic* as the best American drama of the season. As usual Miss Hellman had been supported by superb performances from her actors: Maureen Stapleton (Carrie), Anne Revere (Anna), Irene Worth (Albertine), and particularly Jason Robards, Jr. His portrait of Julian was described as "powerful" and "memorable." But he did not deserve all the credit, as Brooks Atkinson noted (New York *Times*, March 6, 1960): "When performances are vivid, it follows that the play must have a core of vitality that enkindles the actors. Miss Hellman is accordingly the author of the performances as well as the play." Some critics thought that Arthur Penn's direction could have developed more naturalness and ease, that it was "too tightly tidy." He could have made more of "those Chekhovian stillnesses in which everything is sensed but nothing is comprehended."

It was a remarkably successful return for Miss Hellman. Only *The Children's Hour* outdistanced the 464 New York performances of *Toys in the Attic*. With her name again blazing on Broadway, Random House quickly printed the play, dedicated to Richard Wilbur, and brought out a Modern Library edition of six plays, adding *Another Part of the Forest* and *The Autumn Garden* to the collection of four already in print. She elected not to include *The Searching Wind* among her collected original works. When Random House invited her to supply a new preface, she refused. In the introduction to *Four Plays*, "I said that I wanted to live to be a better writer. I still want just that. No need to write about it again."

While *Toys* was still running in New York and before it began its extensive tour of the country, Miss Hellman went to England to supervise the London production, which opened in early November, 1960. Unfortunately the success story was not repeated, largely, it appears, because the British actors did not capture the compelling intensity the play demanded.

In London, Miss Hellman talked with a reporter about the theatre and about her writing (London *Times*, November 9, 1960). She dreaded the high pressure of New York production with so much money riding on big success or quick failure. When she had begun in the theatre, you could say, This will never be a smash, but some people will like it. Now, "if you suggest that a flop might still be a good play, you are treated rather as though you've committed blasphemy." She abhorred the modish critics who dictated what type of play would be accepted, and in spite of her recent success, the new breed seemed not to like the neat and convincing construction that she favored, preferring the looseness of a *Waiting for Godot*. She also told the reporter that she was working on a new film adaptation of *The Children's Hour* for William Wyler: "Despite many disillusions I still cling obstinately to the belief that writing can be done with your left hand while your right is busy with something else."

When she returned to New York, she could not continue her writing, even with her left hand. Before she had gone to England, Hammett had been complaining again of a self-diagnosed rheumatism in his gun shoulder, a pain that probably resulted from the emphysema he had had for many years. She insisted on a thorough examination, and when the report was in, she and the doctor did not share the news with Hammett. Rheumatism would be more endurable for him than knowing he was suffering from nonoperable lung cancer. He accepted the extra attentions of a nightly martini, of attractive trays of food, of extra books, of having his shoulder rubbed. If his pain ever became unbearable, he never spoke of it. Eight years later she recalled these trying days, commenting how impossible it is for anyone to put himself in the place of the sick. She had always wanted to be with people who were younger and not physically sick. "I was insensitive to the real problems of the sick—how to stand up, how to walk down stairs. It was a terrible thing to watch, since the last days of emphysema deprive the brain of oxygen, to see a man who had such respect for thinking and intelligence not able to think, and for him to know it."

On New Year's Eve she returned early from a party with neighborhood friends to find him at his desk staring at a book of Japanese prints, the book upside down. Even when the practical nurse told her that he had been talking irrationally and they took him to the Lenox Hill Hospital the next morning, she refused to believe the end was near. She took a flying trip to Cambridge to find a nursing home for him. They had made plans to move to Cambridge together, where she was to teach a seminar at Harvard during the spring term, and she assured Hammett that those plans would not be abandoned. That hope seemed to sustain him until he dropped into a coma, and on January 10, 1961, at the age of sixty-six, he died.

Two days later 300 friends, including Quentin Reynolds, Bennett Cerf, Dorothy Parker, Leonard Bernstein, Arthur Kober, and Lionel Trilling, gathered for a memorial service. In her eulogy Miss Hellman praised him as "a man of simple honor and great bravery. He didn't always think very well of the society we live in and yet when it punished him he made no complaint against it and had no anger about the punishment." The next day Kermit Bloomgarden, Howard Bay, and Miss Hellman went to Washington for the interment. Whatever some of his countrymen thought of him, Hammett loved his country and wanted to be buried in Arlington National Cemetery. As they rode in the limousine from the superintendent's building to the grave site, Howard Bay noticed that a lone figure in a Volkswagen was following them. The young man was one of his soldier friends from the Aleutians who had somehow learned of his death.

She did not recover quickly, nor ever completely, from the loss of her closest and "most beloved friend." She has never written more movingly than she did of Hammett in the introduction to the collection of his stories, *The Big Knockover*,* and again in *An Unfinished Woman*: "I know as little about the nature of romantic love as I knew when I was eighteen, but I do know about the deep pleasure of continuing interest, the excitement of wanting to know what somebody else thinks, will do, will not do, the tricks played and unplayed, the short cord that the years make into rope and, in my case, is there, hanging loose, long after death."

* Edited by her and published in the United States in 1966 and also in England under the title *The Dashiell Hammett Story Omnibus.*

XVII

My Mother, My Father and Me

Although Miss Hellman had completed a preliminary outline of *The Children's Hour* before Hammett's death, John Michael Hayes now took over the task, deviating markedly from her outline. He underlined the Lesbianism with a vengeance, with furtive kisses and embraces. Mary's incriminating gossip was whispered to her grandmother while they were riding in a limousine. A fleet of Cadillacs rescued the children from the school. Martha hung herself after the confession, and in the final scene, Karen, weeping beside the grave, insisted that Martha "was a clean and honorable woman." Miss Hellman's copy of this script, dated April 18, 1961 (then titled *Infamous*), is generously dotted with her notations, "Awful—L.H."

When it reached the screen in February, 1962, under the original title, directed by William Wyler, who had done the first film version, and with Shirley MacLaine (Martha), Audrey Hepburn (Karen), Fay Bainter (the grandmother), and Miriam Hopkins (the aunt), the critics found it embarrassing, heavy-handed, dated, and unbelievable. If the story had seemed too daring in 1936, it was too tame for 1962.

Toys in the Attic was Miss Hellman's last original play. She may never have thought that she was rounding out her playwriting career, but she was honored as if she had reached the climax of her twenty-five years' service to the American theatre. In May, 1960, she was elected to membership in the American Academy of Arts and Science, along with Brooks Atkinson and Jacques Lipchitz. In April, 1961, the women's division of Albert Einstein College of Medicine of Yeshiva University gave her their Achievement Award. At a dinner in her honor in June of the same year, Leonard Bernstein presented her with the Brandeis University Creative Arts Award, a medal and $1500, and, also in June, Wheaton College conferred a Doctor of Literature degree. The following February the National Institute of Arts and Letters elected her vice-president, and in May, 1963, the American Academy of Arts and Letters, the parent organization of the National Institute, elected her to membership, along with Thomas Hart Benton and Bruce Catton. The next month she received another Litt.D. from Douglass College (the women's division of Rutgers). In January, 1964, she and Ben Shahn were given the gold medals awarded every five years by the National Institute of Arts and Letters for extraordinary distinction in the arts. In April, 1968, Tufts honored her again—they had conferred an M.A. in 1941—with the "Award of Distinction" of Jackson College (the women's division of Tufts).

If the eulogies to her achievements indicated to some that she had concluded her career as a playwright, she did not share that view. While she was at Harvard during the spring of 1961, she became fascinated with the satirical riches of Burt Blechman's novel, *How Much?* She was intrigued by the notion of trying her hand at an unconventional play. Her excitement was strong enough to dispel her former resolves never to attempt another adaptation and to keep her working at the new play for the next year and a half.

She did not devote herself exclusively to the play. During the summer of 1962, she was busy building a new and smaller house on Martha's Vineyard which Howard Bay had designed for her. Situated at the bottom of a sandbank on an acre of land she had retained when she sold the old house, its large windows and wooden deck gave a magnificent view of the harbor and the ferry dock a half-mile away.

When she delivered her new script to Bloomgarden in the fall of 1962, her enthusiasm had not dimmed, though she was not convinced that she'd found a new niche for herself or that the American theatre could any longer tolerate a serious dramatist. She found the theatre of the sixties depressingly bleak. In an interview with Thomas Meehan (*Esquire*, December, 1962), she spoke fully and frankly about the Broadway scene. For the most part the theatre was a bore; all the fun had disappeared. No longer could one delight in a good play as one might enjoy a good book, not a great book, just a good book. In the twenties the theatre had been extraordinarily alive with talented writers—O'Neill, Kelly, Howard, Kaufman, Rice—who had something to say, who were breaking new ground and going new ways. Now we are surfeited with homey little comedies in which "everybody talks as if they'd gone through four years of college and read the latest best-seller," or pseudo-dramas, tickling us with "a little glimpse of homosexuality, a mite of dopesters," trading on "ten-cent-store Freud," with cheap and shallow explorations of love and aloneness. Writing must be more than "throwing things about and being adventurous"; the aim had to be higher.

Among the absurdists, Beckett was the "only man who should be taken seriously. He's good." Ionesco was a charming writer, and that would be enough if the "pretend-depth wasn't in the way." Brecht was, of course, in the big league. *Three Penny Opera* and *Mother Courage* were the great plays of our time. Although there was a great deal of nonsense about him and by him, his was the "truest talent of the last forty to fifty years." Williams and Miller were the strong American voices.

Williams is a "natural dramatist who knows what he's doing by instinct." Sometimes he knew too much, and through no fault of his own he'd been forced to worry about success and failure. "It takes a long time for all of us to learn that the theatre is a world of fashion, and fashions turn, and I guess you just pray you'll live long enough to see them turn back again." *Streetcar* was certainly his best play. She admired Miller's "force and spirit." Although she didn't like *The Crucible* because she didn't like theme plays, *Death of a Salesman* was a remarkable drama. She thought Miller wrote too much newspaper stuff, too much writing about writing, but that was his business. He was good and, she thought, would be better. The public should not complain because he'd not written a play recently; competitiveness was an easy disease to catch. A writer should write when he was ready to write. Inge's plays were not "up her alley." Albee showed remarkable promise.

Generally, Broadway acting was at a high level, though she missed such vivid star personalities as W. C. Fields, Fanny Brice, and Laurette Taylor. Our only eccentrics seem to have "invented themselves and that's no good." Everyone in the theatre worked so hard at being charming, to be loved by everybody else. "We're all so smooth to the touch." The strong influence of the Actors' Studio had been good for some, bad for others.

Government subsidy might help, if they would put up the money and then go mind their own business, but she feared the bureaucrats. She was glad that Off Broadway was thriving, even if most of the productions were bad. Two facts of Broadway life disturbed her: The theatre was no longer attractive to the young, and no one had discovered the means to make it better fun and more interesting than a movie. The pressures on the playwright had become intolerable, when it now took a run of six months to pay back the investment on a serious play.

Miss Hellman was not bubbling with optimism as she approached the production of *My Mother, My Father and Me*. In turning with the fashion, she knew she was climbing out on a limb that might not support her. "Maybe overboard" appears as a frequent marginal notation in the early manuscripts.

That she had entered a new world of mad confusion and clutter was clear immediately the curtain opened on the Halpern's New York apartment: A living room crowded with pillows, boxes, lamps, candlesticks; ornaments on ornaments, draperies over draperies. Berney's tiny bedroom at the side is stacked with photography and jewelry equipment, an exercise machine, two typewriters, clay and a half-finished torso, an Indian headdress, bows and arrows, a canoe in which a dog is sleeping, and a tape recorder. A skylight closet room upstage is crammed with cleaning equipment, an ironing board, and a cot. In 1963, it looked like a setting for a new version of *You Can't Take It with You.* Now it would appear suitable for Mrozek's *Tango.*

Berney is squeezed into his room painfully experimenting with a folk song on his guitar. Herman Halpern is facing the TV reading a newspaper. Rona Halpern, in front of the mirror, is fumbling with a new mink hat. She's heard something in Berney's song our ears have missed. It's lovely. It's made her cry. Herman must tell the boy it's made him cry too. Herman looks up and screams. If the hats have been reduced, they should have been. He doesn't understand female economy. He should know that it's wise to buy fur in the spring. People who can pay don't have to walk their feet off as she does. He suggests she walk the hat back to the store.

With her usual quick strokes Miss Hellman has introduced the principals. When Hannah, a good-looking Negro servant, enters with the coffee tray, we're prepared for Rona's instructions. The coffee must be served in the drawing-room part of the living room. Hannah is a liberated Black. If Rona wants the tray somewhere else, she can move it herself; Mrs. Halpern has picked up too many fancy notions since she "met the goys in that flea walk-up down the block."

When Herman sees the coffee service, he screams again. The price tags are still on it. It was reduced because the pot had a dent. If they keep the tags clean, she'll take it back tomorrow. Berney refuses to join them; she should know that he never eats before his folk-song festival. Rona understands; she's delighted that he's finding himself. Herman does not share her enthusiasm: "Finding himself at twenty-six? With a ukelele?" At his age Herman was supporting his two sisters, his aunt, and his mother.

Mention of mother was an unfortunate slip. Rona's mother may come to stay with them. If she does, Herman says he'll move to a suite in the Waldorf-Astoria, with six rooms so that when he blows his "head off, it can flop around in a little comfort." Black comedy comes easily to Herman. His torments have not concluded. He spies another acquisition, a new ring on Rona's finger. She assures him it's only semiprecious and was on special sale for charge customers.

While he's adjusting to the newest treasure and to the prospect of Rona's mother, the lights come up on Berney reciting chapter twenty-two of his life story into the tape recorder. He doesn't make it through the first sentence before he begins another song. Berney's attention span is short. As Hannah comes to his room, he's singing, "The life of a nigger ain't no good." He means no offense; he's trying to tell the world about the enforced degradation of the Negro people. Hannah has no truck with such nonsense: "Take nigger right out of your Jew-boy mouth." Berney understands her abuse: "The rescuing of a minority has many a dangerous dung hole for the liberal."

As Hannah departs and Berney goes back to dictating, the doorbell rings and a tall thin girl, Filene, walks across into Berney's room, ignoring Rona's attempt to introduce her. Herman is struck by the name. Even if she's Greek, she must be connected with the Boston store with the bargain basement. Perhaps Berney is getting some sense.

Another visitor arrives offstage, through the kitchen door, much to Hannah's annoyance. It's Rona's mother, Jenny. She too crosses immediately to Berney's door with a caged bird for him. Berney is allergic to birds, even if it is named after her dead husband. She's also brought an outlandish necktie for Herman and a shaggy fur piece for Rona. She got the money from her candlesticks. Rona is appalled that her only heritage has been sold; she'll buy them back. Overcome with daughterly remorse, she urges Jenny to come and live with them. Her pleas become more insistent as Jenny picks up her bird and starts to leave. At the door she slips, steadies herself, agrees to stay, and goes out.

Frantic at the prospect, Rona starts emptying the contents of the ironing room, preparing a place for her "own flesh and blood." Hannah should be pleased to have someone to help with the work. Hannah knows better; she's not going to take care of "no old lady." Rona assures Herman that she'll reform: do the shopping herself, not buy anything extra, and return all the newest acquisitions. As Rona races in and out, piling up her bundles, Filene exits and Berney announces to his tape recorder that he's abandoning the guitar for medicine. He's always wanted to be a doctor.

The lights fade on this madness and come up on a small inset scene in a restaurant. Rona, with new packages, joins Mrs. Parker at a table. Mrs. Parker quickly orders two double martinis, though her tongue is already well loosened. She's sure that the man across the way is staring at her; she buys her clothes in Paris; her analyst is working on her drinking and wants her to have a child. Rona is astonished at the analyst's price, $40 per session, the same as a Miami Beach hotel: "But then that's for two in a room. I guess in analysis they don't allow two on a couch." After a second drink, their disjointed chatter pours out faster and louder. Rona must honor her mother. Mrs. Parker knows there's nothing to be learned that can't be learned in the arms of a man. Rona discovers new horizons. She has not known the pleasures of martinis at noon or that analysts charged so much. Her consumer instinct has been aroused. Miss Hellman is at her sardonic best in this brief vignette of New York ladies at their high-noon ritual.

As the lights fade on the restaurant, Jenny is moving into the apartment, loaded with a fishing rod, the bird, a man's overcoat, and large valises. No one greets her, except Hannah, who catches her sneaking in. Hannah is not surprised that Mr. Halpern has sold her furniture. He'll sell anything; Rona will buy anything. Hannah and Jenny are off on the wrong foot immediately. Jenny finds dirt on the table; she's an expert on dirt: "We live in so many poor places, and always everybody says Mrs. Stern's apartment is the only apartment fit for white people." Hannah won't tolerate such talk; she's quitting. The Halperns can find themselves "a Jew-type nigger."

Berney comes in utterly dejected. When he tried to enroll in medical school and told them he wanted to cure cancer, the common cold, and insanity, they ignored him. Rona, returning with a new set of packages, is delighted that her mother has arrived. She's prepared the ironing room for her. Herman does not share her enthusiasm until Jenny offers to be their colored girl and wash the dishes. He's sure that will make her feel less like a charity case.

There is mass confusion as they gather for dinner. Hannah weaves in and out with the food; Rona chatters about Mrs. Parker and her analysis; Berney tries to take a picture of Grandma at her first meal with them, but they've forgotten to get a chair for her. Hannah has prepared beef Bourguignon; the lobsters Rona expected have been thrown in the garbage because Hannah refused to handle them. Jenny finds the food too rich, spits it out, and starts for the kitchen to get some bread. Only two slices can be found. Tomorrow Rona will buy plenty, and Herman suggests she get ten loaves and throw out eight. Jenny has a better idea; she'll bake bread and also wash the walls. As a warm-up she goes to the kitchen to help with the dishes. When we hear a crash, Rona knows the sound: "The Meissen. Belongs to Altman's." Jenny has concluded the dinner with a flourish.

Herman must go to Manhasset, Long Island, instead of to the Italian movie with Rona. Florentine Footwear is floundering, almost bankrupt; his rich cousin might bail him out. The lights fade and come up on the fireplace of an elegant mansion; dance music can be heard in the background. The butler will inquire if Mr. Heim is available. Left alone, Herman pretends to dance with Moe's wife as he practices his plea for a $25,000 loan, just for sixty days. He's told everyone in the shoe business that he's Moe Heim's cousin. Contemplating the trophies on the mantel, his optimism begins to fade. Who did Moe bribe to get these silver cups? And where does he get M. Heim and Sons? He's got no sons. Still he's defended him. "When they say that's crooked, I say it's not. What's crooked one generation, is a foundation the next." If he can't manage $25,000, how about ten? Herman is muttering under his breath when the butler returns. Mr. Heim is in a board meeting; he'll call Herman later.

Back in the apartment, Jenny is scrubbing the walls and Berney is busy at his easel, Filene posing for him in the nude. Miss Hellman took a giant step toward the new freedom in the theatre, even if she restricted the audience to a rear view. As Filene tumbles back on the bed, Berney giggles in embarrassment and tries to cover her with a raincoat. He wants to take her home. She'd rather stay and have him read a poem.

When Rona returns from her movie, the stage is set for a mad moment. Just as Rona discovers that Berney's door is locked, she also smells smoke. Jenny pulls down the drapes as she races to the kitchen to rescue her bread. Filene comes out in her raincoat, not yet buttoned. Rona breaks into tears as she sees her bare flesh and screams at Berney, "You have besmirched your mother's house. Besmirched. Your mother." She doesn't know how she can sleep after this, and she's not forgotten Jenny's blob on the wall and the burning bread. She needs a hospital and nurses. She doesn't get them, but she does get a doctor.

The lights fade and come up on Rona on a couch with Dr. O'Hare, an attractive man in his late thirties, sitting behind her and patiently listening to her confessions. She's talking mostly about Mrs. Parker and desperately encouraging him to make a pass at her. When he pats her shoulder, she quickly grabs his hand and pulls it to her breast. When he doesn't respond, she's insulted. She can "find better things to do with forty an hour than be hurt every minute," and as the couch begins to roll off for the scene change, she insists his watch is wrong. She's paying for three minutes more and she wants her full hour.

Jenny is now with Berney in his room. She wants him to play the guitar, but he's given up music. He's testing his bow and arrow, off on his Indian kick. The Indians have no place in our modern world: "We took their lands, killed their animals, cut down their mountains, put filth in their rivers. They are charity patients now, like you and me." Jenny doesn't know about the Indians. She knows that Berney should find something that's alive, like a girl. She didn't object to Filene. He'd better take a bus and get away.

As the lights come up on the Parkers and Halperns at bridge, they're unable to hear their bids against Berney's shouting and drumming. Mrs. Parker is amazed that a twenty-six-year-old would be beating a tom-tom; no doubt some kind of therapy. The men make a futile stab at business talk. Herman doesn't invest in the Street; he's too tied up in shoes and "shoes stink." Mr. Parker is stroking Rona's arm and talking of the Kennedys; American women struggle through the menopause dreaming of John Kennedy or Rock Hudson. Sex should be taken out of public life, be reserved for a motel room. Rona is shocked; certainly no one thought of the Eisenhowers that way. Their bridge-table nonsense is interrupted by Filene and two new weirdoes, Mrs. Lamb, a strange woman of forty, and Binkie-Pie, a small and emaciated young man. As they file across and crowd into Berney's room, Filene stops to introduce herself: "Evening, folks. My name's Susannah-Dear Bunchlet from Camolia, Alabama, University of Mississippi graduate. My father was living off an old nigger lady and raping me in the afternoon, so I shot him and left home." As she enters Berney's room, Binkie-Pie pulls the manuscript of a novel from his brief case and begins to read. Both rings of the Halpern circus are lit up simultaneously. When Rona apologizes for allowing girls in Berney's room, Mrs. Parker understands why the psychiatrist gave up on her; that sort of thing is hard to cure. Parker doesn't share his wife's enthusiasm for the analyst after five years and $35,000. Herman is astounded that so much could be invested in somebody's head: "I'm in the wrong end of the business." And if Parker thinks that Jewish people don't have neuroses, he's wrong: "We got everything. What other people got, we got more."

As Berney's phonograph starts playing and Binkie-Pie continues reading, a third ring lights up. Jenny has discovered Hannah in her room, in bed with a man. As the man scrambles out and disappears, Rona tries to subdue Jenny's screams. She must stop that crazy sex talk, and Hannah must bring in the lobster salad. Mrs. Parker is disappointed. She had hoped for something Jewish, like hot pastrami. Relative calm returns for a moment, as Mr. Parker turns his lustful eye on Hannah and gives Herman the Wall Street view of the business world. Conditions will not improve without a war and the "small investors got no confidence there'll be a war."

Suddenly Hannah smells smoke. Jenny has locked herself in and is brewing tea over her sterno stove. They all race to the ironing room and Mr. Parker finally breaks down the door. Jenny tips over the sterno can and battles the intruders with a butcher knife. Rona is screaming, "You hit your daughter! You hit your own daughter!" Hannah is shouting for a strait jacket. It's like a Harrigan and Hart slam-bang finale. As the curtain is coming down, Jenny is desperately calling for Berney, and when Berney tells Binkie-Pie to scrap his novel—dope, drink, and homosexuality are not enough—Binkie-Pie conks him on the head with the manuscript. Miss Hellman had never brought down a curtain on such farcical madness. We can only wonder where we go from here in the weird and absurd world of the Halperns? What will happen to Jenny?

The answer comes immediately the curtain is up on Act II. The Halperns are assembled in the waiting room of the Golden

Age Nursing Home. Herman is in the phone booth trying to placate an Internal Revenue man: yesterday he was sick, today he's taking care of his dying mother. Herman's in trouble and has to go to the office. Rona must "get it as cheap as she can" and make up her own mind. She refuses to do any more bargaining; nothing is too good for her mother, and she's already humiliated herself trying to find the cheapest place.

The lights dim on the waiting room and come up on another doctor's office. A new set of shifting scenes have been prepared for Act II. As Rona enters, the doctor is speaking French into the phone. According to the nurse, he's just as adept in Turkish and in German. The doctor is clearly a phony. He's more interested in Rona than in her mother. His name is Zachary Katz, but she must call him Zatz: "Say to yourself, from this minute of my life Zatz is my friend, my confessor, my staff, and my aid. Say it, dear, and you will feel lighter." Rona does and moves toward him as the lights shift back to the waiting room. While Berney has been dozing, Mrs. Compton, one of the inmates, has dismantled his Leica camera and now dumps the pieces in his lap. The nurse wheels Jenny away to lunch and to her little nook. She's protesting and calling for Berney and Rona, and Berney is shouting after Mrs. Compton; he wants her name and address for his lawyer; she's ruined his Leica.

The lights fade and come up on Herman and Tonio in the office of the Florentine Shoe Corporation. Herman is carrying an odd-looking shoe, unfit for human foot: Macy's will never take them, particularly since the last ones melted. The new shoe is not their most desperate worry. Mr. Kelly, the Internal Revenue man, wants to know about the payments to Frank James. The partners insist that James is dead, until Herman thinks of a better explanation. James is really his son; he changed his name so he could be a poet at night. Who would believe a poet named Bernard Halpern? Kelly demands to see the bookkeeper, Blanche Knopf. (An "in" joke? Blanche is the wife of the publisher Alfred A. Knopf.) Blanche knows nothing about

James; she just follows instructions. She's been listening to big news on the radio, prospects for a new war: "We can't allow a foreign power to intrude into Biannina. It's in Africa, or Asia, or someplace." Herman is elated; the war can save them from bankruptcy. He's on the phone immediately to Walter Copside. Copside won't want to be caught without a full stock of shoes for the army the way he was last time.

The lights shift to Berney's room. Hannah, her friend Styron, and Berney are listening to the radio report about the Negro student who is trying to enter the University of Alabama. Berney wants to help the downtrodden people; he wishes he had been born a Negro. Styron suggests that if he's not having enough trouble being a Jew, he could pretend he's black: "Lots of people do now."

Again the lights fade and return to Dr. Katz's office. Rona is standing by the desk sobbing; the doctor is stretched out on the couch. She's never done such things before, terrible things. Does he "do our things" with his wife? He doesn't. As he's trying to ease her conscience, the phone rings. It's Herman reporting his good news about the war. Rona quickly buttons her blouse; she must hurry to lay in supplies for the siege. As Katz assures her that Jenny will be safe in his hands at eighty per week and Rona argues that the price was seventy, they are left in darkness.

The lights are now on three old crones: Mrs. Lazar, Mrs. Compton, and Mrs. Kaufman, settled into their beds at the nursing home. Jenny is being wheeled in by the nurse. The ladies quickly explain the Golden Age system. All the rules about diet and smoking are devised to keep them alive longer. If she's got any money, she must hide the deposit boxes and put her savings accounts under false names. Before they're bedded down, Mr. Lazar wanders in, untieing his pajamas because he's got something to show the new lady. When the nurse restrains him, he assures her that she mustn't be jealous, there's "plenty for everybody."

While the ladies are slumbering, Berney is at a small bar

listening to a jazz band with his radio tuned to the war news. He's angry with the couple next to him, "waiting liked doped pigeons for the bomb." He turns up the radio, forcing them to hear the message: "The right to attack and the right to defend. The God-given right, never to be surrendered by free men. . . . For our children's rights and their children's rights, across unknown seas and uncharted deserts—" Berney is also unhappy because he's not black and will never be able to play the saxophone: "This ain't the age for white boys." He's finally in tears, shouting, "The last night of the world, and this is the way it ends, not with a bang but a whimper," as he's hustled out and the lights return to the Home.

Mrs. Lazar is reading the Bible; Mr. Lazar is holding her hand. He's "applicated" for the room of a couple he's sure is dying. She isn't interested. She's saving her money for Abraham, though she doesn't like what she reads about him. When she meets him in heaven, she's going to tell him, "Abraham, you tricked Pharaoh, you old shit." Lazar is shocked; he never knew she knew the word. We didn't know Miss Hellman knew it; she's sampling the theatre's new free speech.

As Jenny comes in to use the waiting-room phone, Mrs. Compton stops her. She wants to keep the phone free for a call from her broker. Jenny will make it short. She's calling the Shamus Benevolent Association to ask them to send her her $500 funeral money; she's decided to forego a funeral. Perhaps Mrs. Compton will make a deal with her. She'll give her $50 of the $500 if she'll advance her the money. Mrs. Compton agrees to let her have $370, or $420 if she dies within ten days. They're signing the papers as the lights return to Rona and Dr. Katz.

Rona is now on the couch, tormented with guilt, though distracted by Dr. Katz's visionary dreams. He's going to develop a chain of nursing homes across the country, tied in with chain grocers and chain drugstores. He also has a scheme in which Herman can participate, an "honor shoe" for the dead to sell for $2. It's ridiculous to bury the dead in expensive shoes. When Katz refuses to stop talking business long enough to give her another kiss, Rona says she's not going to tell Herman about the shoe: she'll tell him "that you tried to rape me in your office in order to reach into his factory."

Now, for the first time in Act II, the action returns to the Halpern apartment. Berney is on the bed in his darkened room. Rona comes in, more loaded than ever, and when Herman returns desperate for a drink after his battle with Internal Revenue, she tries to tell him about the "man who," but she's too busy unloading her new treasures: a side of beef which Posito didn't want to charge, long underwear, a bomb hood, a mink coat with a vicuna lining, sterno cans, a massage table that can double as an outdoor bed, two fresh salmon, a picnic kit, a set of Thomas Hardy. Herman wants to know what she used for money. She's too occupied with her oxygen tank and the self-inflatable rubber boat (it does!) to worry about money. Herman is screaming, as Berney enters with a valise, his head wrapped in a bandage. He wants $50; he's going to enlist. Herman wants to know on which side; he might make a little dough by laying a bet. Rona is searching frantically for her sleeping pills so she can kill herself. Herman hopes she's got enough for him. When Berney reduces his request to $25 and then to $20, Herman tells him the war is over, in fact it never began. He'd better go back and lie down while the bed's still there.

The lights fade on the Halperns and come up on Jenny. Berney is beside her, explaining his last frustration and how "Mama said they were dirty little cowards for not having a war." He's not given up: "It takes a little time to find yourself in this stinking world." Jenny insists that he take her $370 and not worry about her or about Mama and Papa going to jail.

The final transformation takes us cross-country. Berney, sitting in a small tent, surrounded by Indian trinkets, is reciting chapter forty-four of his autobiography into his tape recorder: Grandma disappeared from the Home and finally turned up at the Belmont Free Hospital, where she died. The Halperns did not go to jail, and Herman is now making something called an "Honor Shoe." He wrote once, offering $100 if Berney would publish his book under the name of Frank James. When a train is heard in the distance, Berney stops recording and joins the Indians, who are laying out their blankets and jewelry. One of the Indian women invites Berney to share her dinner, "roast beef and spaghetti." He's revolted by the suggestion. "Mama Suni," he tells her, "you would do better to make a batch of the maize cakes and boil the sorrel and wild carrot. I cannot say often enough that little will be accomplished until we return to the ways of our ancestors—" Berney is beating his tom-tom, the Indians are squatting by their wares, and the trainload of "suckers" is approaching as the curtain falls.

If Miss Hellman's comedy seemed dark and grotesque, it was not so brutally sardonic as the novel. Although she adopted the main line of action and the principal characters from *How Much?*, her satiric thrusts ranged more widely, and she was not so preoccupied as Blechman with the Golden Age Society (G.A.S.) Nursing Home. Blechman's inmates were repeatedly having to "pish," complained endlessly about their sleazy accommodations and about their purses and deposit boxes being systematically pilfered by Dr. Katz.

To make a full transformation from novel to play and to make a play that was her own, she added characters and incidents that could expose other corruptions in American middle-class society. To give the Halperns' perverse passions a more solid dramatic credibility, she invented the Parkers and Berney's beatnik companions. She also added Berney's fumbling attempt to paint the naked Filene, his enchantment with the Indians, the alliance between Berney and Jenny, the new war which could save Herman from bankruptcy, the jibes at the Negrophiles, and the ridiculous animosities between Negro and Jew. The theatrical effects of crashing china, fire in the bedroom, Hannah in bed with her boyfriend, and Jenny hysterically flailing the air with her knife are also Hellman additions. At one point she contemplated two scenes that were later abandoned: Rona buying a burial plot and Berney being interviewed for admission to a medical school. One grotesquely comic scene in the novel she apparently thought too gruesome for the theatre. Jenny has been repeatedly moved from smaller to smaller rooms until finally she is occupying the morgue. One day an inspector appears without warning, and Katz persuades Jenny to pretend she's dead.

The dialogue, neat and sharp as usual, belongs almost exclusively to Hellman, as do the savage verbal assaults on the corruptions in family life, at the insane tribal rites of the restless beatniks, at psychiatrists, at the hyperbolic consumer instinct, and at the slick shysters who operate homes for the aged. Unfortunately the massive mixture of angry and sardonic truths becomes too oppressive. She has pursued the pretensions and frauds of our world so fiercely, jumping from target to target, that we feel no compassion for the objects of her scorn, there is no mirth in our laughter. As one critic remarked, the play lacks the moral suasion of satire that comes from being half in love with what one loathes, cherishing the sinner while hating the sin. Her cartoon monsters are caught in a middle world somewhere between the plausible nonsense of *You Can't Take It with You* and the exotic insanities of the absurdists. When Miss Hellman abandoned her customary discipline and craftsmanship, she loosened the reins with a vengeance. If she had a larger purpose, to say that these frauds and pretensions were the inevitable corruptions of affluence, that message was lost.

Normally Miss Hellman approached opening night with a degree of confidence, knowing that she'd done her best with the script, that Bloomgarden would give her the best possible production. This time was different. She had suggested that they hedge their risk and try it first Off Broadway. Bloomgarden could not be persuaded. Hellman was a Broadway name and that's where she belonged. He had hired Gower Champion, the "hot" young director who had given *Carnival* such a brilliant unified tone. He could do the same for her play. Unfortunately Bloomgarden's confidence was misplaced. Champion not only lacked the abandon and ferocity of imagination that was required, he seemed incapable of controlling the actors. Two weeks prior to the opening, Arthur Penn was brought in, but his suggestions came too late. If he thought Ruth Gordon (Rona) played the first scene as if she were in an insane asylum, she was not disposed to change. She depended more on the sideline coaching of her husband, Garson Kanin. She and the other strong-minded actors—Walter Matthau (Halpern) and Lili Darvas (Jenny)—had outmaneuvered Champion and they stuck with their own solo performances.

If the cards seemed stacked against the play during rehearsals and the Boston tryout, the ace of spades was flipped for opening night at the Plymouth Theatre on March 21, 1963. The critics took their usual seats, but their morning-after reviews did not appear. The newspaper employees were on strike. The reviews would not have helped, except to alert the public to a new Hellman play. When they were printed later, they did not support her excursion into sardonic domestic comedy. Although they grimly suffered her thrusts at contemporary society and shared her abhorrence for such vulgarities, they could not approve her massive and disjointed mixture. She had scattered her shots too hysterically. Their slim praise was reserved for the beatnik scenes and for Howard Bay's ingenious settings. When the play closed after seventeen performances, Miss Hellman was more discouraged than she'd ever been. She wished she had stuck to her guns and insisted on Off Broadway. She may not have thought that this would be her final play; she did know that she'd require a long convalescence before she could return to the Broadway battleground.

XVIII

Past and Present

Although she had had the tentative beginnings of a new play in her typewriter before she turned to Blechman's novel, she did not return to it. Only twice during the sixties did her name appear on the theatre broadsides: with the motion picture *The Chase* in the spring of 1966 and with the revival of *The Little Foxes* at Lincoln Center's Vivian Beaumont Theatre in the fall of 1967.

She had always maintained a second life outside the theatre, and now this became her whole life. She traveled, taught again at Harvard and at Yale, wrote magazine articles, attended conferences, and, for the first time, looked back at what she'd seen and what she'd done, not in the theatre but in her other life. These brilliant and absorbing memory pieces appeared in 1969 in *An Unfinished Woman.*

In the summer of 1963, she attended the Edinburgh Festival and the concurrent sessions of the International Drama Conference. Her impressions were recorded in an unpublished piece, "The Beautiful City of Edinburgh." The English participants in the conference—Joan Littlewood, Harold Pinter, Laurence Olivier, and Alec Guinness—and the representatives from France, Germany, Russia, and the United States all seemed to have been infected with the fashionable disease of the well-established: they delighted in flailing the establishment. Only squares questioned the avant-garde. Common sense seemed to have evaporated. They had all forgotten that even the wise society lady never buys her clothes at the beginning of the season. But if they all sang the same tune, each sang his own nationalistic variation. The Americans made jokes and looked unhappy; the Russians were prim; the French raced into generalities; the English spoke very good English; and the Germans made impractical practical suggestions.

Later in the year she went to Israel to cover the Pope's visit. In her article for the *Ladies' Home Journal* (April, 1964), "Land That Holds the Legend of Our Lives," she recounted her difficulties in getting into Jordan. The authorities at first barred her because "they said I was a well known Zionist, which will amuse Zionists who used to say that I should be and were angry that I wasn't." Although she diligently followed the Pope's path, visiting such shrines as the site of the Last Supper, her reporter's eye focused on the little people on the fringes of the processional: the Dominican scholars who seemed unhappy to be away from their books, the nuns who sang in Hebrew. She wrote of her own first-remembered religious experience, when as a child of six or seven she had become so distraught in a New Orleans church that she had run out crying. Since that day and throughout her life she had been "stirred and comforted and discomfited by people of strong belief." Undoubtedly this memory had helped her to write about Lily's religious fanaticism in *Toys in the Attic*.

Bound as any writer is to his own life experience, she always thought it dishonored the profession to exploit autobiography and drop the fictional shield. When she returned to New York, she found that her compatriot Arthur Miller had done just that.

No one who read the newspapers could fail to identify Miller and Marilyn Monroe in *After the Fall.* Although Miss Hellman had scrupulously avoided public criticism of her colleagues, she could not now restrain herself. The press had devoted inordinate columns of copy to the Miller play. In January, *Show* ran a pre-opening piece, "Arthur Miller Ad-Libs on Elia Kazan," and in April, a long and favorable review. *Show* seemed the proper platform from which to speak.

In May, 1964, *Show* carried her parody of Miller under the heading, "Lillian Hellman Asks a Little Respect for Her Agony, An eminent playwright hallucinates after a fall brought on by a current dramatic hit." It began, "As all the civilized world knows, 'Buy My Guilt' was written by Lillian Hellman and is now being performed in the converted tiger cages of the Bronx Zoo on a most advanced thrust-retreat stage." Miss Hellman had claimed that the play was not autobiographical. The editors knew better. The events followed too closely on her life. Everyone knew that she was adored by five men, and in the play she was adored by five men—her father; Phil, dressed in kilts and sneaking around the stage "trying to cut off his arm as a proof of love"; Rudy Valentino ("Miss Hellman was once married to Rudolph Valentino"); Sam, a youthful adventurer; and Helmut Schneider, a German flower expert. The public, of course, knew that she was now married to Max Schneider, who owned a greenhouse.

The play also documented the insensitivity of middle-class parents toward their child, "and more importantly, with Miss Hellman's appearance before the House UnAmerican Activities Committee, her inner struggles, her unselfish concern with weaker and less fortunate friends, her final admirable admission that all of us must stand trial for the rest of us." Her play, as expected, had stirred many individual guilts, and she had received many admiring letters, plus "a few downright angry complaints." The editors were honored to print a sampling of her replies. She assured Sam he was not in the play and that she had changed his name to Samson. He should certainly remember the scene when he "got drunk at the prom and cried to me about that awful incident with your mother, the sexual one, I mean? Well, I have changed it to your aunt and nobody will ever guess because the actor wears a blond wig. You were an albino." She thanked Phil for saying that she wrote like a dentist: "I know how much you admired dentists." He must remember that he once offered to have his arm shortened to match hers, "but I liked your arm as it was, and could only cry out, 'I am a stranger to my life.' (That line is in Arthur Miller's new play. Nothing that a great writer hears or sees is ever wasted.)" To dear Papa she wrote that she could not forgive him: "Everybody knows that I am filled with compassion and pity, and the poetry of it, but forgiveness is something else." He should remember the day when she was six and woke from her nap hungry for the love of her mother. In the kitchen Fanny said "you had taken my mother for a walk. I ran through the house, not believing, tricked, crying, broken, knowing that never again could there be trust, never again in all the years to come." It was that day that Fanny said, " 'Shut up, you stinker,' and completed the act of breaking a child's heart. I never told you about Fanny because I love Negroes, although I did tell the House UnAmerican Activities Committee of this ugliness in order to explain to them why so many people were able to mislead me and to use my lust for the right for Russian purposes." Even if she could not forgive him, still he would find a ticket at the box office on Monday, at no charge.

For anyone who had seen Miller's play, her parody was devastating. She had never indulged in such a scathing personal attack, but she could not forgive Miller for his brazen disregard for the rules of the game, as she told the interviewers from the *Paris Review* (Winter-Spring, 1965): "So you put on a stage your ex-wife who is dead from suicide and you dress her up so nobody can mistake her. Her name is Marilyn Monroe, good at any box office, so you can cash in on her and cash in on yourself, which is maybe even worse."

Another magazine article that spring offered a strong contrast. "Sophronia's Grandson Goes to Washington" (*Ladies' Home Journal*, March, 1964) covered the March on Washington. She wrote about the early morning on the steps of the Lincoln Memorial, when she mingled with the crowd watching the buses unload their bewildered cargo. She twisted through the Alabama delegation trying to spot Sophronia's grandson to whom she had sent money for the trip. Apparently he had found a better use for the money. She talked with Bayard Rustin, who had organized the march in a small office in Harlem. And although her ears became numbed by the perpetual "We Shall Overcome," she was moved by the results of Rustin's engineering. By one o'clock over 210,000 were gathered to hear Dr. King. Never before had she heard anyone stir a crowd so eloquently. Weary as they were, their hearts were heated to their cause when the march began. A young man from Gadsden assured her that this was the only way to make a revolution: "Get the kids on the road so they can see for themselves." The boy with him, he told her, had "seen so much meanness, he's willing to die like a man. When you're willing to die, you've won." Miss Hellman had a sharp eye for the vivid human details that make an event, that give life to a headline. She could have carved another career for herself as a reporter.

For sixteen years Hollywood had been off-limits, but apparently the blacklist was now graying with age. Sam Spiegel, who had had such success with *Lawrence of Arabia* and *Bridge on the River Kwai*, invited her to adapt Horton Foote's *The Chase*. Spiegel owned the rights and for six years had kept the novel on his desk.* Now the blood-thirsty violence of Foote's story had blazed into the headlines: Kennedy had been struck down by a sniper's bullet. And though the country mourned, in some reactionary strongholds there were more cheers than

* A dramatization of the novel had failed on Broadway in 1952.

tears. Enraged by the events in Texas, Miss Hellman welcomed the chance to dissect a Texas town and explore the undercurrents of brutality.

For a year she struggled to temper the melodrama and to give believable force to the story of the escaped convict who returns to his hometown and is senselessly murdered. He is shot down because the tensions between blacks and whites, between the starkly poor and the absurdly rich, have so cultivated the appetites for violence that everyone thirsts for blood and wants to be in on the kill. Unfortunately her script did not hold up under Hollywood pressure.

With the improvements devised by the producer, the director, and Horton Foote, brought in to adapt her adaptation, everything became overheated, lurid, and phony. The Texas town—one critic said it should have been called Gomorrah—was boiling over with adultery, alcoholism, intolerance, and greed. It was as if Hollywood had imported carloads of stereotyped Southern decadence. In the final, climactic scene, when the prisoner is being led up the steps of the town hall at dawn, through the crowd of blood-thirsty citizens, one of them steps forward with a gun and kills him. Arthur Penn staged the moment as if he were restaging the Oswald-Ruby horror. Even the expert performances of Marlon Brando, E. G. Marshall, Janice Rule, and Jane Fonda could not save it from being a "phony, tasteless movie." One critic said it was not even a good "bad picture." After Miss Hellman saw the film in February, 1966, she told a *Times* reporter (February 27, 1966): "Decision by democratic majority vote is a fine form of government, but it's a stinking way to create. So two other writers were called in, and that made four with Mr. Spiegel and Mr. Penn, and what was intended as a modest picture about some aimless people on an aimless Saturday night got hot and large and all the younger ladies in it have three breasts and— Well, it is far more painful to have your work mauled about and slicked up than to see it go in a wastebasket." Hollywood had not changed during her absence.

She had not before, nor now, staked her life on Hollywood. While she was occupied with *The Chase*, she was also assembling the stories for the Hammett volume and for the first time trying to find words for her loving memories of him. Writing of him, she also wrote of herself, and finding autobiographical indulgence less unpleasant than she had anticipated, she began toying with the idea of a collection of "remembrance pieces." The spring of 1965 provided a good time to experiment with remembering. She had accepted the invitation of John Hersey, the novelist and Master of Pierson College, to conduct a seminar in literature and writing for a selected group of Yale freshmen.

Once a week she met with the eight students enrolled in English 24. The sessions were easy and informal. She talked with them about Gertrude Stein's Oxford lecture on "How Writing Is Written," Conrad's *Heart of Darkness*, and Blitzstein's adaptation of Brecht's *Three Penny Opera*. She did not propose to instruct them in playwriting. "Playwriting is a peculiar form, either you've got the feeling for it or you haven't." At one time she had held to the theory that a good writer could write anything; now she knew better. She had tried to turn novelists into playwrights without success. In attempting to reduce *The Last Analysis* from the eight hours of playing time it would have originally required to a normal length, Saul Bellow lost a good novel without making a good play.

As much of her life as she had lived in the theatre, she often found herself "thinking I know as little about the mechanics of it, how do they do this, how do they do that, as the most uninitiated member of the audience. And then, I think: 'You must be loony, kid, you ought to be locked up.' " Most of what she saw now was either just plain bad or dull. She had liked Rodgers and Hart's *Pal Joey*, back in the season of 1940-41, but since then she had found little genuine excitement in an American play. She felt like a stranger in the theatre, asking, "What am I doing here? I don't understand the people sitting next to me. Everyone seems to me old and square and rich. If the play is serious, they are so glum they look as if they were in another ward of the hospital. . . . I have a sense of sadness about my not understanding the theatre anymore. I don't know where it is, not the commercial theatre, or the noncommercial theatre either. I think the same thing has become true of the theatre as in painting—the avant-garde has met and embraced the establishment. Now it's all just fashions. The only time I've felt happy and excited about the theatre in many years is when I've seen or read something of Beckett, then, I've been at home." Her students must not accept the fabulous-invalid theory: "We forget that invalids can stay invalids, they don't always die and they don't always recover." Above all, she advised them to ignore writers who talked about themselves and their writings. For the most part they were "fancy talkers" who could not speak the truth about their own writing.

She did not tell them that with all her skepticism she had been conferring with Mike Nichols about a revival of *The Little Foxes* and had given him permission to proceed. As an end-of-the-term wind-up for her chosen eight, each submitted a scenario of a story enriched with an idea and then developed a scene or short story based on it. In this and whatever writing they might attempt later, they must remember that writing was not easy. It was playing into a neurosis to make out that anything worth doing was simple. Meeting with her young Yale men had been an exhilarating experience, and she was sure she had learned more from them than they from her.

During the summer at Vineyard Haven and in the fall when she went to Russia, London, Paris, Budapest, and back to Russia, she continued with her memoirs, and the trip abroad not only sparked her recollections but also provided new observations, mixed with the old, that would find their way into *An Unfinished Woman.*

She arrived in Moscow in October, just twenty-two years after her wartime visit. Somehow the city had become drearier than she had remembered, like Los Angeles with the addition of biting cold winds. With all the drabness, she delighted in morning walks across Red Square to study the strange wonders of St. Basil's. With all the gloominess of the National Hotel—a proper setting for nightmares—she found herself dreaming of her days with Hammett at Hardscrabble Farm. She had a warm reunion with Raya, who had been her translator and companion on her earlier visit, and with Captain K., who had been writing a thesis on American writers. He wanted to know all about Faulkner and *Sanctuary* in a few quick sentences, and about Norman Mailer. She obliged with her recollections of Faulkner when she had known him in the early thirties. Mailer, she thought, was "a wonderful writer, a natural, the best kind, who wasted time being famous, but maybe he won't waste it anymore. I don't know. You can't know about actors and Norman is an actor." She went with Frieda Lurie, an official of the Writer's Union, to collect her royalties for the publication of her plays. (The Russians did not acknowledge any financial obligation for performances of the plays.) When she stuffed the ten bundles of rubles into the paper sack with the toys and the jar of caviar she had bought, the lady in charge was annoyed that she refused to count the money before signing the receipt. Miss Lurie explained that Miss Hellman was like a Russian; she didn't care about money. That seemed to satisfy her. The Russian people were as warm and friendly as she remembered them from her previous visit. The United States might be their enemy, but an admired enemy who had found the good life to which they aspired.

After the dark winter days of Moscow and then of London—a close second in shivering, sunless days—Paris in April and then Budapest provided a welcome rejuvenation. In Paris, like every visitor, she walked everywhere, invariably discovering new vistas that somehow seemed not to have been there earlier. Paris may not have recaptured the full bloom of its prewar charm, but it was still a match for any city in the world. She searched out new restaurants for lunches or dinners with old friends and in the high-ceilinged dining room of a country hotel, opening onto a spring-fresh garden, she enjoyed the incomparable delight of a Loire salmon.

Budapest was a handsome and countrylike city; it seemed the "ideal city for people who like people." She could not discover why Ernst Lubitsch had once told her, "If you have a Hungarian for a friend, you will never need an enemy." She had an elegant dinner with a handsome and gracious blue-stockinged couple, friends of Edmund Wilson. Her taxi driver and his two little girls took her for a day-long picnic in the hills above the town. And in no city she had ever visited, even Paris, did she feel such an irrepressible urge to discover the sights by walking. Her impressions of Budapest were reported in "Interlude in Budapest" (*Holiday*, November, 1967) as well as in her memoirs.

Back in Moscow in early May to attend the Fourth National Congress of the Union of Writers as their guest, she was housed in the Pekin Hotel. Although built in the fifties, it was already shabby and must never have been comfortable for foreigners, except perhaps for the Chinese visitors for whom it was built. She was taken to a Richter concert where old ladies simpered and bowed and sent flowers to the platform after each number. One evening Captain K. escorted her on a long subway ride to his secluded room in a small pink house in the outskirts of the city, where they spent most of the night talking about literature, about Hammett, and about the theatre. She tried to make him understand that she didn't like the theatre anymore, though writing plays was what she did best: "I have cut myself away from it, don't go much, don't learn, don't even want to. And I am getting old and I can't understand how that happened to me." She made a quick excursion to Leningrad with Raya, where she saw an awful production of a five-hour Gorki play and visited the apartments of Pushkin and Dostoevski. When the Writer's Congress began on May 22, she found she could endure only one day. The conservative faction had taken control of the sessions. No protests about past or present censorship would be permitted; all thoughts must be centered on how "to free men from the dirt and filth of Western society." She skipped the remaining meetings and returned to New York to help Mike Nichols with the casting of *The Little Foxes.*

The happy homecoming she had anticipated after her long absence lasted for only a few days. On June 7, 1967, Dorothy Parker died at the age of seventy-three. In quick succession, she had now lost her two closest friends. The Parker-Hellman friendship had survived many fallow periods and overcome many obstacles. Miss Hellman had never liked Dottie's husband, Alan Campbell, and Hammett rebelled at Dorothy Parker's "embrace-denounce" way with her friends. Through the years she had been constantly on and off the wagon, in the last years mostly off, and Miss Hellman had found it increasingly difficult to ignore her heavy drinking and her shabby living, as if she were destitute. The quick tongue that had produced the incredible catalogue of Parker witticisms had become dull and repetitive. In an emergency Miss Hellman always rushed to help but stayed only until the immediate crisis had passed. On one occasion she sold a Utrillo landscape and endorsed the check to her; later she sold a Picasso gouache. Both paintings had been "gifts" from Mrs. Parker, "her charming way of paying off a debt." There was no acknowledgement of the first check, and the $10,000 for the Picasso, along with three other checks, was found in a bureau drawer after her death. Apparently she wanted to forget that she had any money. In the early years of their friendship, Miss Hellman assumed that like the others she had served as target for the Parker wit when her back was turned, but when so many people told her that she was the one friend of whom "Dottie consistently spoke with respect, affection, and admiration," she finally believed it, out of character though it seemed.

On June 9, 1967, a hundred and fifty literary and theatre friends gathered at Frank Campbell's chapel at 81st and Madison for the funeral. The service was short and simple. Zero Mostel explained in his opening tribute that it had been

"Dorothy Parker's express wish that there be no formal ceremonies at all. If she had had her way, I suspect she would not be here at all." Lillian Hellman spoke of her strong individuality: "She was part of nothing and nobody except herself; it was this independence of mind and spirit that was her true distinction, and it stayed with her until the end, young and sparkling." She recalled their many late-at-night conversations, when "gulping what we called a watered extract of Scotch, Dottie would put aside the gentle manner and let fly. Then I would roar with laughter that always ended in sober recognition that the joke had a brilliant diagnosis of people or places, or customs, or life. She never spoke of old glories, never repeated old defeats, never rested on times long gone. She was always brave in deprivation, in the chivying she took during the McCarthy days, in the isolation of the last, bad sick years. The remarkable quality of her wit was that it stayed in no place, and was of no time."

Her will, dated February 6, 1965, named Lillian Hellman as executrix and assigned her entire estate to Martin Luther King. Future earnings from her copyrights were to be put in trust with the income to go to King. Although she had always held strong feelings about civil liberty and Negro rights, she had never met King.

With her dearest friends gone, Miss Hellman could not escape a deep sense of loss, but she refused to live in the past even when she was writing about the past. And fortunately the new production of *Foxes*, scheduled for a fall opening, kept her mind on the future.

Although she had great confidence in Mike Nichols and Howard Bay, she had not discovered any fresh hope for the American theatre, or for her place in it. And she had already registered her skepticism about such cultural enterprises as Lincoln Center, where the play was to be performed. How unfortunate it was that such overpowering and earnest institutions were in the hands of people who meant well but who had little understanding of what art was about and who seemed not to understand that culture must arise spontaneously; it could not be induced by constructing buildings.

Whatever myopia may have afflicted the boards of directors of New York's new cultural complex, it did not affect her production. Saint-Subber, the Broadway producer who held the initial rights, and Jules Irving, the producing director of the Vivian Beaumont Theatre, gave the play a first-class production with New York's best actors: Anne Bancroft (Regina), George C. Scott (Ben), Margaret Leighton (Birdie), E. G. Marshall (Oscar), and Maria Tucci (Alexandra). The critics found it "an indelible theatrical experience." Here was a distinctively American play from the American repertoire that rated a strong place beside the works of Ibsen and Strindberg. It was a virtually perfect play of its kind; it had the commanding strength of a documentary combined with the suspense of a melodrama, "lean and candid, muscular and mettlesome in the bold black-and-white strokes it makes against a money-gilded world." Never had the Vivian Beaumont stage held such dazzling and "luminous performances," and Howard Bay's elegant square room set on the thrust stage with a grand staircase up-center used the facilities of the theatre to their best advantage. For the first time, one critic remarked, the Beaumont open stage did not seem to be "sprawling off into infinity." Walter Kerr and Clive Barnes, who manned the powerful critical guns at the *Times*, found in the play and in the performances, that "literally made you hold your breath" (Kerr), the real hope for an American National Theatre. Barnes wrote, "For the first time at the Vivian Beaumont I have seen something that looks, moves and behaves like a national theatre."

Some critics were disturbed by the inconsistencies in Southern accents. Anne Bancroft retained too much of the Bronx and Margaret Leighton too much of England. One thought that Mike Nichols did not supply "enough lubrication to still the clanking of the plot." For some the cast was too strong. The subtleties in the play were buried under the weight of their actor personalities. The play was, of course, viewed differently in 1967 than it had been in 1939. Then it was regarded as an attack on predatory capitalist morality; now it was an indictment of greed, hate, and the lust for power at any time, in any place. Jack Kroll (*Newsweek*, November 6, 1967) thought it extremely difficult "to stage a play like this in a day that has lost the self-confidence of Miss Hellman's classic liberalism and the faith in the well-made play as a carrier of ideas and feelings."

The audience ignored the skeptics and packed the Vivian Beaumont for the scheduled limited run of sixty performances from October 26 to December 16. As the closing neared, the demand for tickets was so great that the production was moved to the Ethel Barrymore Theatre for forty additional performances, December 19 to January 20, 1968, even though the extension required a number of cast changes. Margaret Leighton shifted to Regina, E. G. Marshall to Ben and Charlie Chaplin's daughter, Geraldine, played Alexandra. After concluding its New York stand the production took to the road for a national tour and in the summer covered the straw-hat circuit with Geraldine Page playing Regina. Few plays from the American repertoire have been revived with such spectacular success.

There were other revivals of *The Little Foxes* in the sixties. In 1963, a Paris production survived unfavorable notices because of the presence of Simone Signoret as Regina. Capitalizing on the attention generated by the announcement of the production at Lincoln Center, CBS carried the old Goldwyn film on television on September 23, 1967. Miss Hellman immediately filed a $500,000 suit against Samuel Goldwyn and the Columbia Broadcasting System contending that her contract prohibited the motion picture on TV and that they had "wilfully and knowingly" ignored this stipulation. The suit was not finally settled until February 26, 1970, when Judge Scileppi of the Court of Appeals sustained the rulings of the lower courts in favor of Goldwyn and CBS. In his opinion the contract only prevented the live broadcast of her play, not the broadcasting of the movie; that right had been assigned to Mr. Goldwyn, who had sold it to CBS.

To have the Hubbards brought back to life and the play enshrined in a kind of unofficial theatre Hall of Fame as an American classic was, of course, a rare honor. The new attention did not, however, impel her to begin Act I of a new play. She was more intrigued by the invitation of Professor Reuben Brower, Master of Adams House, to conduct another seminar at Harvard, and when she arrived in Cambridge, she also agreed to share her time with a group of students at the Massachusetts Institute of Technology. And she did not limit her conversations to the theatre or to writing but talked about politics and about art. As she once said, "I don't think you can teach writing. The most you can do is stimulate somebody who might be a writer." Even if she repeatedly insisted that hers was a learning nature rather than a teaching one, according to Howard Bay, she had a remarkable talent as a teacher. She could guide the pen of a would-be writer without damaging or dishonoring his own ideas.

She was fascinated and exhilarated by her contact with the new generation. She found them warm-hearted and "deeply good-mannered." "They offer you what they have, they take what you can give." A year later, after the Harvard students had disrupted the campus and broken into buildings, she tried to understand them and speak for them. In an interview with the New York *Times* (July 1, 1969) she said, "Who likes to see anything destroyed. But who likes what we did. My parents didn't like it when I got drunk or left home." The older generation did not help matters, going about "with flags pinned on them saying 'moral dinner-party attitude.'" She wondered how many parents would stand behind their children, how many of them in denouncing students meant to be denouncing their own sons. She was sure that "these kids are not going to be frightened as we were. They're not old enough to fear betrayal." She did not approve of putting the blame on Nixon. "I'm not sure it belongs on him, or even on his friend Billy Graham, with whom he's confused. It's the temper of the time."

For some years Miss Hellman had avoided the platform; her name had not appeared on the lists of sponsors of political and social causes. Now with shrill bitterness in the voices of the young generation, hate in the voices of the Blacks, violence spreading unpredictably across the country, she feared that a frantic government would invent repressions and oppressions that would outmatch McCarthy's most vicious machinations. If much of the violence seemed senseless—the assassinations of Kennedy, King, and Kennedy—or perhaps the painful eruptions of a sickness in the society, there was also sickness in the government that might be even more dangerous.

She did not enlist with any group or speak as often and vigorously as she had in the forties. She did give her name, her presence, and her voice when she thought they would help. She appeared on the platform with Eugene McCarthy at his climactic Madison Square Garden rally. In December, 1968, she joined "100 notables," including John Kenneth Galbraith, Andreas Papandreou, Arthur Schlesinger, Jr., Jean-Jacques Servan-Schreiber, and Henry Kissinger for a seminar at Princeton. Sponsored by the Institute for Advanced Study and the Paris-based International Association for Cultural Freedom, intellectuals from both sides of the Atlantic assembled to share their views on the troubles facing contemporary American society. The best brains could evolve no panacean solutions, and at the end of the week one delegate expressed the futility most of them felt: "If my colleagues and I all drop dead today, there'd be big obituaries tomorrow, but no social effect."

When Anatoly V. Kuznetsov, the Soviet novelist, defected and sought asylum in England, Miss Hellman deplored the self-righteous welcome he was given. In an editorial-page article, "The Baggage of a Political Exile," in the New York *Times* (August 23, 1969), she protested against our easy acceptance of any political refugee. Unlike Solzhenitsyn and

Yevtushenko, Kuznetsov had never raised his voice against the bureaucracy, against the political censorship of the artist, as long as he was on Russian soil. As he himself confessed, "I signed no protest then or later. I saved my own skin." Didn't one have a right "to boggle when Kuznetsov, in his efforts to escape to England, tells himself that informers are what they like most of all"? Were we still suckers for the old ploy: " 'I admit to cowardice and quite rightly trust that most men will not judge me harshly because I have made them recognize themselves.' (I heard those words of forgiveness about informers so often during the time of Joe McCarthy that I asked myself if Christian charity had not deprived us of heroes.)" She was sure the American dinner-party lists for Kuznetsov were already drawn up, that after dinner, "in a chair by the fireside—the favorite position of Whittaker Chambers, once upon a time—he will speak to the guests of freedom, but somebody should tell Kuznetsov that freedom earned by betraying innocent friends is a contradiction in terms." Miss Hellman feared that too many Americans, supported by their government, were ready to turn the clock back twenty years.

In April, 1970, she appeared on a panel with Professor John Fairbank of Harvard at the meetings of the Association for Asian Studies in San Francisco to protest the government's senseless intimidation of Asian students. If she was not in the center of the arena, as she had been twenty years earlier, she had not lost her passion for individual freedom, and she feared the Bill of Rights was again about to be buried under a new madness.

When she finished her 1968 spring term at Harvard, she had also finished her book of memoirs. Although the publisher thought the book was ready for the press, she insisted on taking the manuscript with her to Martha's Vineyard for the summer. With three months of undisturbed rewriting, even if altering no more than a phrase or a word—changing "shivering" to "shaking," "twenty-two years later" to "many years later"—

she knew she could deliver a better book. Her early habits were deeply ingrained. She would share her words with the public only when they were right and rightly in order.

Delay and patience were well rewarded. When *An Unfinished Woman* appeared late in the spring of 1969, the publishers, proud of their prize, launched it with a gala dinner at the Four Seasons.* The standard cocktail party was not enough. Newspaper and magazine editors relaxed their space restrictions to give their critics the extra inches they needed to trumpet their praise. And with the public supporting their enthusiasm in the bookstores, the National Book Award in the spring of 1970 provided an appropriate climax.

An Unfinished Woman is not a conventional autobiography, yet, as one reader remarked in a letter to the editor, "It's just like her which is, I suppose, the best thing one dare say about an autobiographical work." Or as Stanley Young said in his New York *Times* review (June 29, 1969): "We must as onlookers remind ourselves that a *persona,* as Jung used the term, is only the private conception a human being has of himself, his idea of what motivates his action and of how he wants others to judge him. . . . Miss Hellman's self-portrait may puzzle her public but not herself and friends."

Only in the first third of the book does she allow chronology to govern her narrative. After that she swings freely among her remembrances of places, times, and people—all intimately observed, all colored with some special personal involvement. As one critic commented, it was "a technique that would be pure quicksand in the hands of a writer less sure of her mind." With her sure mind and her firm literary hand, the technique gave a simultaneity to her daydreaming. It was as if the reader had been invited to share a few hours with her, hours of private remembering.

Frank and honest as she is in juxtaposing the odd pieces of

* Arthur Kober, her former husband, noting the extraordinary festivities, suggested that he should probably write a companion book to be called "The Finished Man."

her life, never self-caressing, never attempting to charm or ingratiate herself, and strongly as one senses her aversion to sham and pretense, she often stops short of a full revelation. We may learn that she has a low tolerance for phonies and phoniness, that she disdains the so-called sophisticated life, that she admires "people who refuse to speak until they are ready to speak," but large stretches of her remembered landscape are shielded from view. When she approaches them, she frequently turns aside with an enigmatic, "We were never to speak of that again." If at times we wish she would say more, she somehow makes us understand that she's sketching a reluctant subject who cannot yet tolerate a definitive portrait. As she said once, she has no enthusiasm for being a bookkeeper of her life. Nor does she encourage biographers who would like to keep books on Hammett and Parker, whose literary papers she keeps safely out of sight.*

Although she almost completely ignores her professional life in the theatre, as if she were leaving the way open for this present endeavor or as if she cherished the art of living more dearly, she does, in a way, provide a cultural history of her generation. Her vignettes of many leading figures—Fitzgerald, Hemingway, Gershwin, Goldwyn, Faulkner—whose paths crossed hers are sharp and vivid. Her longer memoirs of Dashiell Hammett and Dorothy Parker glow splendidly with the human warmth that is so much a part of Miss Hellman's nature, a part too infrequently recognized. (The leading ladies in her plays are not the key to Miss Hellman!) And her chronicle of personal victories, defeats, and encounters with the shattering events of her time are so mirror-clear that anyone of her generation can catch glimpses of himself.

She has never written better prose. Throughout it has a spare and muscular, often tough, rationality, warmed by a loving hand. Many anecdotes and episodes are dramatized as if for a play, with the same pithy dialogue she had mastered for

* Among the mass of questions I've put to her, however, she "preferred" not to answer only one.

the theatre. The final paragraph might well have substituted for the speech in *The Autumn Garden* that Hammett rewrote. It could have been the final revelation for General Griggs, as it was here for her:

> But I am not yet old enough to like the past better than the present, although there are nights when I have a passing sadness for the unnecessary pains, the self-made foolishness that was, is, and will be. I do regret that I have spent too much of my life trying to find what I called "truth," trying to find what I called "sense." I never knew what I meant by truth, never made the sense I hoped for. All I mean is that I left too much of me unfinished because I wasted too much time. However.

When she was presented with the citation and $1000 check for the best book of the year in arts and letters at the National Book Awards celebration at Philharmonic Hall on March 4, 1970, after graciously acknowledging the honor, she spoke briefly of the new terror that troubled her. She was dismayed at the growing acceptance of "guile and pretense" as a way of life in Washington. She asked herself and the fifteen hundred guests, "Why aren't we worried that in a democracy our Vice-President is forced to mask his fear of dissent with words like effete, when, in fact, he means that those who disagree with him are abnormal or homosexual or outside the circle of respectability?"

In the new chaos of violence and uncertainty, she had also worried about finding peace and relative safety for herself. Her Martha's Vineyard house had been broken into twice. At a dinner party early in 1968, just five blocks from her house in the "safest section" of New York, three men had insisted that she must be protected on her walk home. For years she had walked these streets without fear. That spring Howard Bay searched Boston for a house that might please her, but she found she needed more time to adjust to the thought of moving. Finally, in the spring of 1970, she sold her house on 82nd Street and in the fall moved into a Park Avenue apartment.

She now has no plans for the future, except to get busy on a new book and to teach for a month at Berkeley and a month at M.I.T. in the spring of 1971. Irrevocable long-range plans have always frightened her. As she said recently, "I have never had any personal goals. I never thought about the future. I think you must play out your nature. I never had any plan. It might have been better if I did. I do think people have to be very daring to have a plan in this world." If she never tries to gypsy-eye the future, neither does she torment herself with sentimental dreams of refurbishing the past. She lives in the present with her uncertain thoughts of tomorrow. She worries about the sad state of the world, as she always has. She worries about not writing—her chief preoccupation. Writing has not become easier or more difficult; she discovered that with the memoirs. It is simply troubling when it's not being done.

The added years, the scars from the hurts that have never been completely exorcised, may have left their marks, her friends may detect momentary signs of weariness, of a new mellowness, yet these signs signal no reduction in physical vigor nor any dulling of her razor-sharp mind. Her step is still firm and graceful, her lithe figure seems always comfortably drawn up to its full five feet four inches, her voice is warm and clear. Her neatly chiseled features may carry the unavoidable insinuations of age, but they still form an easy smile as she speaks. Studying her, as one inescapably does in talking with her, one wonders why she seems always to have been conscious of her appearance. Once recently, when she had been enticed into appearing on a TV talk show, she asked Mrs. Leonard Bernstein if she didn't think her head was too big for her body. Her concern for how she looks has dictated her major extravagance, a passion for expensive and well-designed dresses. And she has always favored the most feminine costumes. The manly muscularity of mind in her writing is not reflected in her dress.

The reporter who wrote, "She is a tough-minded lady who can take the tops off bottles with her teeth," may have known her plays; he did not know her. In the plays she may appear brutally intolerant of human frailties. In life she could not knowingly hurt another human being, whatever his faults. She might ignore him; she would not hurt him. Perhaps at times she has ignored too many. One of her friends once chided her for restricting herself to those who achieved success, thus missing an awful lot of interesting people. Another perversity has caused her embarrassments, usually more amusing than damaging. She has an unfailing memory for names of people she met casually years ago and cannot retain the name of her dinner partner long enough to carry her through the evening.

If Miss Hellman were not to write another line of dialogue, she would still hold her top billing in the record of the American playwrights of the Roosevelt and postwar years. But in a theatre intolerant of the repertory system and suspicious of revivals, only a new Hellman play could return her name to the Broadway lights where it belongs. As uninviting as she may find that prospect, one hopes that she might somehow discover again the excitement she once found in working up a play. "There are just two happy moments in writing a play," she once said. "The first is when you get the idea. It's glorious. This play is going to be the best ever written. There's nothing on paper to disillusion you. The other happy moment is when you write 'curtain' at the end of your script. The rest is mostly misery." A new generation would be enriched if she could again endure the misery. The theatre needs her tough mind, her stout heart, a heart that never turns spongy-soft, her stinging indignation, her passion for uncovering evil, her troubled and troubling characters, her infallible command of authentic dialogue, her sure instinct for theatrical excitement, her clear eye for scenes and characters that can find their only true life on the stage. Above all, in a theatre overrun with rash and careless amateurs, the voice of the professional desperately needs to be heard.

From the beginning, in all her writing, and above all else, Miss Hellman has been a committed professional. Her words were released to the public only after she had lived with them long enough to know that they were, at that moment, her best. No Hippocratic oath could have bound her more tightly to the demands of her chosen profession, and although her enduring reputation will rest with her original plays, magazine editors, book publishers, and motion-picture producers were always assured of a solid professional job whenever her services were engaged.

Her best-remembered plays may be overlaid with the decaying atmosphere of the old South, yet their dramatic vigor does not depend on their Southern essence. She has simply chosen, as any wise writer does, the idiom and atmosphere ingrained in her own life. If most of her plays depict the scenes and lives of the upper middle class, she has chosen the life mirror in which most of her Broadway audience could see their reflections. Her moral indignation has ranged widely over the sick anxieties of humanity, with her sharpest barbs aimed not at the eaters of the earth but at those who "stand and watch them do it." And whatever her immediate point of attack, at a Hellman play "you always knew you'd been in a fight."

Her moral and political convictions were deeply rooted in her thinking, in her naked view of the world's malaise, in her own torture by the witch-hunters, yet, just as she refused to run wild with the radical political packs, in her plays she avoided bare-faced propaganda. As she once said, "I don't like generalizations about the world, or 'large' subjects. You may get to them through the play you do, but you start out with people." Man was at the center of her world, in her life and in her plays.

Acknowledgments

My major debt is to Miss Hellman. Although this is in no sense an authorized biography which Miss Hellman wanted written or on which she collaborated, she graciously jogged her memory to supply answers to my most trivial questions and provided many essential corrections on the manuscript. Without her help and without her memoirs, *An Unfinished Woman*, this book could not have been written.

Many details were supplied by Howard Bay, Kermit Bloomgarden, Harold Clurman, Arthur Kober, Louis Kronenberger, and Herman Shumlin, all of whom talked and wrote of her eagerly and affectionately.

Dr. F. W. Roberts and his staff at the Humanities Research Center at the University of Texas made my stay in Austin pleasant and productive. The Office of Research and Advanced Studies at Indiana University eased the burden of travel and typing. I am especially grateful to Professor Richard M. Ludwig for his wise suggestions and to William H. Y. Hackett, Jr., and Edward G. McLeroy, who smoothed the path from manuscript to book.

For permission to reprint I am indebted to the following:

From the manuscripts in the Lillian Hellman Collection at the University of Texas. Reprinted by permission of Lillian Hellman and the Manuscript Committee, University of Texas.

Acknowledgments

From *Another Part of the Forest* by Lillian Hellman. Copyright 1947. Reprinted by permission of the Viking Press, Inc.

From *The Autumn Garden* by Lillian Hellman. Copyright 1951. *An Unfinished Woman* by Lillian Hellman. Copyright 1969. Reprinted by permission of Lillian Hellman and Little Brown and Company.

From *Candide* by Lillian Hellman and Leonard Bernstein. Copyright © 1957 by Lillian Hellman. Copyright © 1955, 1957 by Leonard Bernstein. *The Children's Hour* by Lillian Hellman. Copyright 1934 and renewed 1962 by Lillian Hellman. *Days to Come* by Lillian Hellman. Copyright 1937 and renewed 1965 by Lillian Hellman. From the introduction to *Four Plays* by Lillian Hellman. Copyright 1942 and renewed 1970 by Lillian Hellman. *The Lark* by Jean Anouilh, translated and adapted by Lillian Hellman. Copyright © 1955, 1956 by Lillian Hellman. *The Little Foxes* by Lillian Hellman. Copyright 1939 and renewed 1967 by Lillian Hellman. *My Mother, My Father and Me* by Lillian Hellman. Copyright © 1963 by Lillian Hellman. *Toys in the Attic* by Lillian Hellman. Copyright ©1959, 1960 by Lillian Hellman. *Watch on the Rhine* by Lillian Hellman. Copyright 1941 and renewed 1969 by Lillian Hellman. Reprinted by permission of Random House, Inc.

From *The Lark* by Jean Anouilh, translated by Christopher Fry. Copyright 1956. Reprinted by permission of Oxford University Press.

From the New York *Times*. Copyright 1946/47/49/51/52/55/66/67/69. Reprinted by permission of the New York *Times*.

From *The Searching Wind* by Lillian Hellman. Copyright 1944. Reprinted by permission of Robert Lantz–Candida Donadio Literary Agency.

From *The Selected Letters of Anton Chekhov*. Edited and with an Introduction by Lillian Hellman. Translated by Sidonie Lederer. Copyright 1955. Reprinted by permission of Farrar, Straus and Giroux, Inc.

Notes on Sources

Only those sources are indicated which might be of special interest. For full bibliographic details and for a more complete listing of the books and articles on which I have depended, the reader should consult the Selected Bibliography.

Chapter III

Page

29. Hammett letters, quoted here and later, are in the Lillian Hellman Collection, University of Texas.

Chapter IV

37. Shumlin reading *Children's Hour:* Interview with Shumlin, and Margaret Case Harriman, "Miss Lily of New Orleans."

55. Brooks Atkinson, New York *Times*, Nov. 21, 1934. Joseph Wood Krutch, *Nation*, Dec. 5, 1934.

Chapter V

69. Krutch, *Nation*, Dec. 26, 1936.

Chapter VII

81. Hammett on *Foxes:* Harriman, "Miss Lily of New

Orleans," and Clarke Robinson, "Silhouettes of Celebrities."

82. About *Foxes:* Hellman, "Time of the 'Foxes,'" and Tallulah Bankhead, Letter to the Editor, New York *Times,* Oct. 29, 1967.
85. Krutch, *Nation,* Feb. 25, 1939.

Chapter VIII

111. Warning on door at Hardscrabble: Harriman, "Miss Lily of New Orleans."
130. Hellman on *Watch:* Thomas Meehan, "Miss Hellman, What's Wrong with Broadway?"
132. Atkinson, New York *Times,* Aug. 24, 1941.

Chapter X

180. George Jean Nathan, *Theatre Book of the Year, 1946.* Wolcott Gibbs, *New Yorker,* Nov. 30, 1946.
179. Atkinson, New York *Times,* Nov. 21, 1946. Hellman, "Author Jabs the Critic."
183. Hellman on writing: Interview, New York *Sun,* Dec. 16, 1949: Phillips and Hollander, "The Art of the Theatre"; Alden Whitman, "Lillian Hellman Gives her Harvard Seminar Lesson in Writing for the Screen"; Introduction to *Four Plays.*
184. Interview with Stern: Tape in Modern Poetry Collection, University of Chicago Library. A portion was printed in *Contact,* No. 3, 1959.

Chapter XI

201. Letter to Blitzstein: Hellman Collection, University of Texas.

Chapter XII

226. Hellman on *Autumn Garden:* Gilroy, "Lillian Hellman Drama Foregoes a Villain."

Chapter XIII

234. H.U.A.C.: Hearings, 82nd Congress, Second Session, "Communist Infiltration of the Hollywood Motion-Picture Industry," Part VIII, May 19-21, 1952, pp. 3541-3549.
240. McCarthy committee: Reports of Permanent Subcommittee on Investigations of the Committee on Government Operations, U.S. Senate, 82nd Congress, Part I, March 26, 1953, pp. 83–88.
242. Quoted passages: Hellman, *The Selected Letters of Anton Chekhov.*

Chapter XIV

245. Van Loewen letter: Hellman Collection, University of Texas.
268. Hellman on *The Lark:* Schumach, "Shaping a New Joan."

Chapter XV

283. Leonard Bernstein, "Colloquy in Boston."

Chapter XVI

285. Seymour Peck, "Lillian Hellman Talks of Love and 'Toys.' "

Chapter XVIII

335. Irving Drutman, "Hellman: A Stranger in the Theatre."

Selected Bibliography

A large quantity of reviews and news items, from the 1930s to the present, is not included in this bibliography.

THE PLAYS

Another Part of the Forest. New York, 1947.
The Autumn Garden. Boston, 1951.
Candide. New York, 1957.
The Children's Hour. New York, 1934.
[William Roughead, "Closed Doors; or, The Great Drumsheugh Case," in *Bad Companions*. New York, 1931.]
Days to Come. New York, 1936.
The Dear Queen. With Louis Kronenberger. Unpublished. Copyright, December 30, 1932.
Four Plays. Introduction by Lillian Hellman. New York, 1942.
The Lark. New York, 1956.
[Jean Anouilh, *L'Alouette*. Paris, 1953.]
[Christopher Fry, *The Lark*. New York, 1956.]
The Little Foxes. New York, 1939.
Montserrat. New York, 1950.
[Emmanuel Roblès, *Montserrat*. Paris, 1954.]
My Mother, My Father and Me. New York, 1963.
[Burt Blechman, *How Much?* New York, 1961.]

The North Star. Introduction by Louis Kronenberger. New York, 1943.

The Searching Wind. New York, 1944.

Six Plays. Introduction by Lillian Hellman. New York, 1960.

Toys in the Attic. New York, 1960.

Watch on the Rhine. New York, 1941.

BY LILLIAN HELLMAN

An Unfinished Woman. Boston, 1969.

"Author Jabs the Critic," New York *Times* (Dec. 15, 1946), II, 3:4.

"Back of Those Foxes," New York *Times* (Feb. 26, 1939), X, 1:4.

"The Baggage of a Political Exile," New York *Times* (Aug. 23, 1969), 26:3.

"The Beautiful City of Edinburgh," unpublished manuscript in the University of Texas collection.

The Big Knockover. Introduction by Lillian Hellman. New York, 1966. Published in England as *The Dashiell Hammett Story Omnibus*. London, 1966.

Book reviews, New York *Herald Tribune Books:* Sept. 26, 1926, 21:1, 26:2; Oct. 24, 1926, 22:1; Nov. 28, 1926, 14:2; Oct. 23, 1927, 22:2; Dec. 4, 1927, 40:3; Dec. 11, 1927, 16:2; Feb. 24, 1929, 27:3; June 2, 1929, 12:1.

"A Day in Spain," *New Republic*, 94 (Apr. 13, 1938), 297-98.

"I Call Her Mama Now," *American Spectator, I*, 11 (Sept., 1933), 2.

"I Meet the Front Line Russians," *Collier's*, 115 (Mar. 31, 1945), 11, 68-71.

"Interlude in Budapest," *Holiday*, 42 (Nov., 1967), 60-61.

"Land that Holds the Legend of Our Lives," *Ladies' Home Journal*, 81 (Apr., 1964), 56-57.

"Lillian Hellman Asks a Little Respect for her Agony," *Show*, IV (May, 1964), 12-13.

"The Little Men in Philadelphia," *PM* (June 25, 1940), 6:4.

"Perberty in Los Angeles," *American Spectator*, II, 15 (Jan., 1934), 4.

"Reports on Yugoslavia," New York *Star* (Nov. 4 ,13:1; 5, 9:1; 7, 8:1; 8, 9:1; 9, 6:1; 10, 11:1; 1948).

"Richard Harding Davis, 1938," unpublished manuscript in the University of Texas collection.

The Selected Letters of Anton Chekhov. Edited and with an introduction by Lillian Hellman. Translated by Sidonie Lederer. New York, 1955.

"Sophronia's Grandson Goes to Washington," *Ladies' Home Journal*, 80 (Mar., 1964), 78-80, 82.

"The Time of the '*Foxes*,'" New York *Times* (Oct. 22, 1967), II, 1:7.

ABOUT LILLIAN HELLMAN

Adler, Jacob, H. *Lillian Hellman*. Austin, Texas, 1969.

———. "Miss Hellman's Two Sisters," *Educational Theatre Journal*, 15 (May, 1963), 112-17.

———. "The Rose and the Fox: Notes on the Southern Drama," *South: Modern Southern Literature in its Cultural Setting*, Louis D. Rubin Jr. and Robert D. Jacobs, eds. New York, 1961, 349-375.

Bankhead, Tallulah. *Tallulah*. New York, 1952.

Bernstein, Leonard. "Colloquy in Boston," New York *Times*, (Nov. 18, 1956), II, 1:6.

Brown, John Mason. "A New Miss Hellman," *Saturday Review of Literature*, 34 (Mar. 31, 1951), 27-29.

Clark, Barrett H. "Lillian Hellman," *College English*, VI, 3 (Dec., 1944), 127-33.

Collinge, Patricia. "Another Part of the Hubbards," *New Yorker*, 23 (March 15, 1947), 29-30.

Downer, Alan S. *Fifty Years of American Drama*. Chicago, 1951.

———, ed. *The American Theater Today*. New York, 1967.

Drutman, Irving. "Hellman: A Stranger in the Theater," New York *Times* (Feb. 27, 1966), II, 1:1.

Dusenbury, Winifred L. *The Theme of Loneliness in Modern American Drama.* Gainesville, Florida, 1960.

Felheim, Marvin. "*The Autumn Garden:* Mechanics and Dialectics," *Modern Drama*, 3 (Sept., 1960), 191-95.

Fleischman, Earl. "*The Searching Wind* in the Making," *Quarterly Journal of Speech*, 31 (Feb., 1945), 22-28.

Gassner, John. *Theatre at the Crossroads.* New York, 1960.

Gilroy, Harry. "Lillian Hellman Drama Foregoes a Villain," New York *Times* (Feb. 25, 1951), II, 1:2.

Gould, Jean. *Modern American Playwrights.* New York, 1966.

Harriman, Margaret Case. "Miss Lily of New Orleans," *New Yorker*, 17 (Nov. 8, 1941), 22-26, 74, 76-81. Reprinted in Harriman, Margaret Case. *Take Them Up Tenderly.* New York, 1944, 94-109.

Hughes, Charlotte. "Women Playmakers," New York *Times Magazine* (May 4, 1941), 10-11.

Isaacs, Edith J. R. "Lillian Hellman, a Playwright on the March," *Theatre Arts*, 28 (Jan., 1944), 19-24.

Knepler, Henry. "Translation and Adaptation in the Contemporary Drama," *Modern Drama*, 4 (May, 1961), 31-41.

Krutch, Joseph Wood. *The American Drama since 1918.* New York, 1939.

Lehmann-Haupt, Christopher. "The Incompleat Lillian Hellman," New York *Times* (June 30, 1969), 37:2.

Lewis, Allan. *American Plays and Playwrights of the Contemporary Theatre.* New York, 1965.

Mantle, Burns. *Best Plays of 1934–35.* New York, 1935. [The annual *Best Plays* volumes provide helpful facts: cast lists, opening dates, lengths of run, etc.]

Meehan, Thomas. "Miss Hellman, What's Wrong with Broad-Way?" *Esquire*, 58 (Dec., 1962), 140–42, 235–36.

Nathan, George Jean. "Playwrights in Petticoats," *American Mercury*, 52 (June, 1941), 750-52.

———. *Theatre Book of the Year.* New York, 1946.

Peck, Seymour. "Lillian Hellman Talks of Love and 'Toys,'" New York *Times* (Feb. 21, 1960), II, 3:4.

Phillips, John, and Anne Hollander. "The Art of the Theater: Lillian Hellman; An Interview," *Paris Review*, 33 (Winter-Spring, 1965), 64–95.

Robinson, Clarke. "Silhouettes of Celebrities," *World Digest*, XV, 2 (Jan., 1942), 78-83.

Schumach, Murray. "Miss Hellman Discusses Directors," New York *Times* (Oct. 23, 1949), II, 1:2.

———. "Shaping a New Joan," New York *Times* (Nov. 13, 1955), II, 1:7.

Stern, Richard G. "Interview with Lillian Hellman," tape in the Modern Poetry Collection, University of Chicago Library.

———. "Lillian Hellman on her Plays," *Contact*, 3 (1959), 113-19.

Triesch, Manfred. *The Lillian Hellman Collection at the University of Texas*. Austin, Texas, 1966.

Van Gelder, Robert. "Of Lillian Hellman," New York *Times* (April 20, 1941), IX, 1:4.

Weales, Gerald. *American Drama Since World War II*. New York, 1962.

Whitman, Alden. "Lillian Hellman Gives her Harvard Seminar Lesson in Writing for the Screen," New York *Times* (May 10, 1968), 54:1.

Index